Praise for *Four V*

"This brilliant book is packed full accounts and using that information to identify shares with real potential to outperform. Algy's knowledge and wisdom, built from years of experience constructing and developing stock screens and examining company accounts, shine through on every page. If you want to learn about stock screening, you will be richly rewarded. Even if you don't use screens, reading it will arm you with insights and skills to make you a more perceptive and wiser investor.

The section on understanding company accounts alone is worth the cover price and should give you an edge on spotting high (and low) quality companies. If there were such a thing as a screen for quality books that help stock pickers outperform, this one would come top of the list. Read it and you'll be itching to put the strategies into practice to help improve your returns."

—*Rosie Carr, Editor,* Investors' Chronicle

"This is an essential book for every private investor, with winning formulas that anyone can execute. Algy not only explains his screens but the rationale for his screening criteria – he even goes through his clean-up formulae in Excel. Meanwhile, the book is cleverly structured so that more expert investors can focus on the key areas of value add."

—*Stephen Clapham, founder of investor training consultancy Behind the Balance Sheet and ex-hedge fund partner*

"This excellent book enables, inspires and supports the investor to focus on what truly matters to consistently beat the market. At times it felt like this book was personally written for me, the private investor. The beauty of psychology is wonderfully interwoven throughout, educating and reiterating its importance, enabling the reader to reflect and grow."

—*Peter Higgins, private investor, interviewer, podcaster, charity ambassador*

FOUR WAYS TO BEAT THE MARKET

Every owner of a physical copy of this edition of

FOUR WAYS TO
BEAT THE MARKET

can download the eBook for free direct from us at
Harriman House, in a DRM-free format that can be read on any
eReader, tablet or smartphone.

Simply head to:

ebooks.harriman-house.com/fourwaystobeathemarket

to get your copy now.

FOUR WAYS TO BEAT THE MARKET

A practical guide to
stock-screening strategies
to help you pick winning shares

ALGY HALL

HARRIMAN HOUSE LTD
3 Viceroy Court
Bedford Road
Petersfield
Hampshire
GU32 3LJ
GREAT BRITAIN
Tel: +44 (0)1730 233870

Email: enquiries@harriman-house.com
Website: harriman.house

First published in 2023.

Paperback ISBN: 978-0-85719-941-6
eBook ISBN: 978-0-85719-942-3

British Library Cataloguing in Publication Data

A CIP catalogue record for this book can be obtained from the British Library.

Mum & Dad

CONTENTS

INTRODUCTION

THIS BOOK IS about four market-beating equity investment strategies and how stock screens can be used to better understand and implement them.

The strategies are all based on well-proven, common-sense ideas: buying into excellent businesses (Quality); backing companies that are primed to bounce back after disappointment (Contrarian Value); hunting out businesses that are overlooked because they are dull (Dividend Investing); and targeting companies that just keep on delivering positive surprises (Momentum).

Good stock screens can whittle down lists of hundreds or even thousands of stocks to focus on those that are most likely to meet a strategy's requirements, providing a manageable number of ideas for further research.

As well as helping readers to develop a deep understanding of the strategies, this book is intended to provide a deep understanding of what it takes to construct a good screen and take the next steps in researching individual stock ideas.

Is it all about numbers?

It's easy to think stock screens are all about numbers. But while they draw on numbers, stock screens are actually mostly about understanding how and why successful investment strategies work. Only a basic level of numeracy is required.

It is knowledge of the mechanics behind the most profitable and proven investment strategies that allows us to focus on the numbers that matter most when screening markets to find winning shares. The same knowledge helps us adapt screens to changing circumstances. It also helps us to comb through the ideas highlighted by screens to identify the real gems and avoid the duds.

Who is this book for?

While this book has not been written for total beginners, it does aim to provide all the essential building blocks needed to create and use screens and to sift the results.

Readers with some existing basic knowledge of investment and share dealing can expect to finish this book with an understanding of:

- Why screens provide an investment edge.

- How screens can be used as part of an investment process.

- The data needed to construct screens and how to interpret it.

- How to identify the best shares highlighted by screens and avoid duds.

- The ideas that underpin four powerful and well-recognised investment strategies, and four screens that have profited using these approaches over a decade.

How the book is structured

The book has three parts.

Part One looks at why stock screens provide investors with an edge, along with the role screens can play in the investment process.

Part Two explores five practical building blocks needed to create and interpret screens.

1. We'll develop a practical understanding of how company accounts work, which is vital to interpret fundamental data (Chapters 3 to 7).

2. We'll find out what fundamental data – including a gamut of ratios – investors need to have access to for building screens that mimic proven investment strategies (Chapters 7 to 10).

3. We'll run through some of the most useful red flag ratios to smoke out shares that look good on the surface (and often pass muster with stock screens as a result) but may hold hidden dangers (Chapter 10).

4. We'll examine how to research the ideas suggested by screens to get a deeper appreciation of whether a stock is worth buying (Chapter 11).

5. Finally, we'll look at the kind of screening functionality and data we need to have in order to construct screens, along with some of the data services available to UK investors (Chapter 12).

In Part Three, we take a deep dive into four strategies:

1. Quality
2. Contrarian value
3. Dividend investing
4. Momentum

We'll learn about the investment philosophies that sit behind these approaches and look at the evidence that explains why and how these approaches deliver superior long-term returns for investors.

We'll also review screens that have been built using knowledge of these strategies and have beaten the market by a country mile over a decade.

The performance figures in the book are all based on live monitoring of the strategies in the 10 years from when I first started to publish stories based on their output in the *Investors' Chronicle* magazine, a Financial Times Group publication.

At the start of Part Three I'll also explain how the performance of the screens has been calculated.

How this book came about

My journey leading up to writing this book is a 10-year one.

While I've been a financial journalist for almost a quarter of a century, it was only in 2011 that I started to devote a considerable amount of my working life to tracking and writing about a selection of screening strategies. This took the form of a weekly column in the *Investors' Chronicle* magazine. It's this column that all the performance data in this book is taken from.

The seeds of my interest in using fundamental data to identify market-beating investments were sown long before the column was born, though. The light bulb went on at the turn of the millennium, when I read Jim O'Shaughnessy's wonderful book *What Works on Wall Street*. It was a book recommended to me by my then mentor Lawrence Lever, the founder and executive chairman of financial publisher and information company Citywire (a company I now work for once again). I could not quite believe that an investing-by-numbers approach had historically produced the investment riches that O'Shaughnessy unearthed.

I had a similar experience of disbelief when I started rigorously tracking a selection of screens. I've watched in awe and wonder as so many of the strategies I followed clocked up spectacular returns.

As the years rolled by, I have read, researched and learned more about the ideas and thinking behind the strategies I've sought to replicate through stock screens. I confess to having experienced a little jealousy, too. My profession has prohibited me from buying the stocks I write about. This is standard practice for financial journalists in the UK to prevent conflicts of interest.

This book is really about passing on the lessons I've learned from my reading, writing and road-testing of screens, to those who want to apply them to their investing.

The choice to look at data from the first 10 years of monitoring the screens, which takes us up to the end of 2021 in the case of the last screen to hit the decade mark, not only reflects the fact that 10 is such a neat number. It also coincides with a job change for me, which meant I handed my stock screening column over to a very able colleague.

The periods the live performance studies referenced in this book cover take in one sharp sell-off associated with the Covid-19 pandemic. However, they miss out on more recent market ructions created by rising inflation and interest rates, the war in Ukraine and uncertainties caused by a move towards de-globalisation. While it feels a shame not to be bang up to date when we have experienced such consequential events in 2022, the longevity of the phenomena that underpin the strategies we'll explore means all the important lessons we'll learn very much stand.

The studies are all focused on UK stocks which reflects the fact the *Investors' Chronicle* magazine is written for a UK audience. However, the big pieces of data-driven research into the ideas behind the screens have been conducted on international, and especially US, stocks. So, what we will explore has relevance well beyond British shores. These investment strategies are very much international.

We begin with Part One: Why Screen Stocks?

PART ONE

WHY SCREEN STOCKS?

CHAPTER 1

MEET THE STRATEGIES

L ET'S START OUT by meeting the strategies and screens we will get to know a lot better later in this book. For each, we'll briefly look at:

1. *How it's done:* how the screen has performed over 10 years of study.

2. *How it works:* what kind of companies and shares we'll be seeking to identify.

3. *Why it works:* the common-sense explanation for why the strategy works.

4. *When it works:* when the strategy has been most effective historically.

5. *Academic studies:* some evidence from research by academia and the finance industry that shows the approach has long-standing merit.

This is just a taster, though. Something to whet our appetite before we explore practical considerations and the tools we need in order to construct great stock screens in the rest of Part One and Part Two of this book.

In Part Three we'll come back to the strategies again with the aim of building a really deep understanding of their workings. This is not only important in helping us construct screens; it should also help us identify stocks that offer something special regardless of the context in which we come across them. After all, if we really know and understand what we are looking for, we put ourselves in a far better position to find it.

A clarity of purpose also helps us better understand our own successes and mistakes. And it allows each of us to form an appreciation of what investment approaches gel most with our own personality and risk appetite. These are vital factors in helping us improve what we do as investors, while also building resilience.

Resilience is very important when investing. We all feel pressure to give up on good strategies and investments during periods of disappointing performance. Such periods are an inevitable and regular feature of investing. Really understanding what we're doing allows us to take a step back and better decide whether what we are experiencing is something to be endured, or whether there is a genuine problem with our investment process.

The four strategies

1. Quality

How it's done

The total return in the first 10 years since the inception of this strategy in August 2011 was 508%, or 422% assuming annual costs of 1.5%, versus 120% from the FTSE All-Share Index.

How it works

We will hunt for companies that:

1. make consistently high returns on the money they invest in their own businesses and;

2. have an opportunity to grow by reinvesting their profits at a similarly high rate of return.

Why it works

While human psychology causes us all to overestimate the number of companies that can produce high-quality growth, we tend to underestimate the value that will be created by those companies that actually do deliver. That means many excellent investment opportunities are often undervalued and hidden in plain sight. By backing superior companies, we can achieve superior returns.

When it works

This style of investing is prized for the fact that in the past quality stocks have tended to hold up well in downturns. The flipside of this is that they tend to underperform when markets are in their initial red-hot recovery phase following a downturn. We might say this is because high-quality companies tend not to have so much to recover from.

But there is something else investors need to keep in mind with quality strategies at the present time. Quality investing grew incredibly popular over the decade the screen performance data covers. It became what investment pros call a 'crowded trade'. This means the valuations of many high-quality stocks got very rich, introducing valuation risk for the shares of otherwise dependable companies. As a result, small disappointments can cause substantial share price falls even when the underlying performance of a company still looks impressive. Interest rate rises around the globe in 2022 punctured the valuations of many otherwise dependable stocks.

Broad changes in sentiment are also a clear and present danger, especially given rising interest rates are generally seen as negative for highly valued stocks. Meanwhile, when prices are already high, there is less potential for rising valuations to drive returns.

Academic studies

Many studies by academics and investment professionals have found that focusing on company quality produces outperformance.

One landmark 2010 study by Robert Novy-Marx looked at the 500 largest US non-financial stocks from 1963 to 2010.[1] It tracked a long-short portfolio which bought the fifth of stocks with the most attractive gross profit-to-asset ratio (a popular measure of quality) and shorted (bet on a price fall) the least profitable fifth. The study found investors using this strategy would have produced a monthly, value-weighted average return of 0.31%.

This study gained particular attention not just because of the impressive monthly returns. It was of added interest because the quality strategy performed well when a value strategy performed badly and vice versa. This made quality a great hedge with value.

At the time of Novy-Marx's research, the long-short value strategy he tested boasted superior historical returns to his quality strategy (0.41% monthly value-weighted average return). However, quality investing has gone on to shoot the lights out over the decade that followed the first publication of the paper, while value strategies have done very poorly. Just to show how cyclical these things are though, in 2022 it looks like the tide may be turning value's way once again.

2. Contrarian value

How it's done

The total return in the first 10 years since the inception of the strategy in July 2011 was 330%, or 270% assuming annual costs of 1.5%, versus 88% from FTSE All-Share.

How it works

We will hunt for companies that:

1. appear cheap compared with their potential to generate profit and;

2. have achieved higher levels of profitability in the past that could be recaptured.

Why it works

When companies perform poorly, it is our natural inclination to believe it will always be so. Meanwhile, the pain of holding poorly performing shares ultimately creates an irrationality in owners that causes selling at almost any price. Such periods of capitulation are often preludes to a recovery and substantial share price gains. The darkest hour comes before the dawn.

When it works

Value investing is in its element during the early stages of a market recovery. The flipside is that the strategy is normally at its worst when markets are selling off. This is because the dynamics of value investing are exaggerated by periods of deep pessimism.

Often it is the weakest companies that outperform most when markets recover. This feature of the value phenomenon is often labelled a 'dash to trash'. However, a good value strategy will look to invest in decent and resilient companies to give it the best chance of doing well across the market cycle and avoiding irrecoverable losses.

Over the 15 years to the end of 2021, traditional value investing strategies have performed very poorly, only doing well when shares recovered strongly from the Covid-19-related slump in late 2020. However, as we will see later, there are strong grounds to think the increased importance of intangible investments and associated accounting rules have caused many traditional measures of value to become misleading.

The screen we will look at avoids some of the key issues associated with intangibles and has done very well.

Academic studies

While value investment strategies were among the first to formally be presented to investors back in the 1930s, courtesy of Benjamin Graham and David Dodd, the evidence of the strategy's effectiveness based on hard data is more recent.

The data-driven reputation of value investing was built on a hugely influential 1992 study by Nobel laureates Eugene Fama and Kenneth French.[2] The academics identified value as one of three influences on future share price performance. They later went on to increase their three factors to five.

Fama and French tested a long-short strategy based on buying the cheapest fifth stocks based on price-to-book value and shorting (betting for a share price fall) the most expensive fifth.

A more recent study by the investment firm Research Affiliates,[3] which we will find out about later in the book, put the average outperformance of this long-short strategy at 3% a year from 1963 to mid-2020. This included the ghastly period of underperformance from 2007, when the strategy produced average negative annual returns of –5.4%.

3. Dividend investing

How it's done

The total return in the first 10 years since inception of the strategy in March 2011 was 346%, or 284% assuming annual costs of 1.5%, versus 79% from FTSE All-Share.

How it works

We will hunt for companies that:

1. advertise their dullness by showing a preference for paying dividends over investing in growth, but;

2. offer underappreciated quality based on their resilience and reliability.

Why it works

Dull companies have historically tended to outperform over time by doing less badly when markets fall but trailing during strong bull markets. This is an unappetising sales pitch for professional investors to make to would-be clients, which leaves this opportunity well-known but underexploited. The strategy should not be confused with the often-perilous practice of simply chasing high-yield stocks.

When it works

In most circumstances, a good dividend investment strategy will probably never wow anyone. It usually does less badly, sometimes a lot less badly, when markets fall, while not doing quite as well when markets rise. However, its charm is that it clocks up gains steadily over time and ultimately produces strong outperformance.

One of the key attractions is that this style of investing has traditionally allowed its followers to get a decent night's sleep, even when markets are volatile. Ideally, it will generate outperformance in a way that is as dull as the companies it targets.

Academic studies

Pim van Vliet and David Blitz, two proponents of dividend investing at investment firm Robeco, found a strategy targeting low-risk, higher-yielding US large cap shares produced annual returns of 15.1% from 1929 to 2016 compared with 9.3% from the market.

In addition, van Vliet and Blitz found their strategy reduced downside risk and showed a positive return over every decade they tested it. Their approach also performed well in European, Japanese and emerging stock markets, where there was less extensive data to test.

4. Momentum

How it's done

The total return in the first 10 years since the inception of the strategy in December 2011 was 371%, or 305% assuming a 1.5% annual cost, versus 109% from the FTSE 350.

How it works

We will be looking for companies that:

1. are trading so strongly that analysts are having to materially upgrade their profit forecasts and;

2. are experiencing strong share price gains.

Why it works

The future is unpredictable, so analysts' profit forecasts are normally wrong. Nevertheless, their forecasts tend to represent a decent best guess at what the future may hold at any given point. As such, they influence investors' decisions. Persistent upgrade cycles can develop due to trends that are hard to factor into forecasts. These upgrade cycles can drive share prices higher over lengthy periods.

When it works

What a momentum strategy really likes is a well-established and long-running investment trend. Dominant trends tend to be most pronounced when market and economic conditions are strong and potentially overheating. However, momentum will latch onto any strong trend in any business cycle and can be surprisingly agile in switching allegiance to the new hot thing even when the wider market is struggling.

What momentum investors should fear most is a whipsaw in performance. This is what happens when there is a sudden reversal in a prevailing market trend that the momentum strategy has been riding. Trends can reverse at almost any time, but it is most likely to happen when markets peak then pull back. During such periods, stock market heroes can quickly become zeros.

That means momentum strategies are most at risk during bear markets, especially if a bubble has developed during the preceding bull market and the pullback is swift. The more narrowly focused a market's winners become, the more risk momentum strategies are likely to face.

Academic studies

One of the most exhaustive studies produced on momentum was released in 2008 by Elroy Dimson, Paul Marsh and Mike Staunton, of London Business School. It covered total returns since 1900 for stocks, bonds, cash, foreign exchange and inflation in 17 major markets, including North America, Asia, Europe and Africa.[4]

The authors identified momentum as a prevalent predictor of returns everywhere.

The problem academics have had when it comes to taking momentum from their studies to the real world is reconciling the costs associated with the portfolio turnover needed to exploit the phenomenon with the outperformance measured. Generally, the costs are perceived to cancel out most of the advantage, although it is now possible to buy many momentum-focused ETF products.

None of the four strategies we've briefly met require investors to use stock screens in order to pursue them. Indeed, a lot of individual judgement is needed to assess whether a stock truly captures the spirit of a given investment approach, which screens are ill-suited to provide on their own. However, there are very good reasons for us to use screens to focus our efforts, which is what we'll explore in Chapter 2.

CHAPTER 2

WHY STOCK SCREENING WORKS

THERE'S A LARGE and consistent body of evidence that suggests stocks with certain financial characteristics outperform. With this knowledge, we should be able to improve our chances of identifying promising investments.

But why should we use stock screens to help us?

In this chapter we'll explore some of the intellectual and psychological underpinnings of stock screening.

For readers who want to focus purely on the practical elements of stock screening, this could be an opportune time to skip ahead to the next chapter. But for a deeper understanding of the value of screening and screen building, the insights from some great psychologists are illuminating.

Before we dive in, there are two important things to understand:

1. The first is that the process of constructing stock screens forces us to unpack our ideas in order to formulate criteria. This is an extremely valuable exercise. It makes us focus on deciding what factors we think are most influential on achieving our goal – identifying stocks that are more likely than others to perform well. This process helps us see the wood from the trees. We are far less likely to be seduced by attention-grabbing details of an investment case that feel more important than they really are. Screens help us consider the whole investment case.

2. The other important thing to understand is the value in not trying to be too clever. With stock screens it is usually best to keep things simple. If we get too complex, we are likely to end up with too narrow a focus. Stocks that fit an overly tight criteria will often do so by chance rather than because they embody exactly what we are looking for.

More expert than the experts

Imagine having built a career on your ability to form judgements on which important decisions are based. Maybe you have or have had such a career?

Making judgements is central to some of society's most high-status and important jobs, from doctor, to judge, to politician. It is also the central task of investors. Generally, these professionals achieve their standing due to huge amounts of education, experience, effort, and raw talent.

Now imagine occupying one of these illustrious roles and being told that your judgements were worse than those based on a simple checklist, algorithm, or equation. That's basically what stock screens are.

Such news would be devastating. In fact, the only reasonable response may well be to reject such silly findings.

And that's just what assorted professionals have been doing ever since 1954, when psychologist Paul Meehl presented evidence that simple, formulaic judgements almost always do as well as or better than judgements by professionals – or 'clinicians', to borrow the term from Meehl's ground-breaking book, *Clinical Versus Statistical Prediction*.[5]

The study, which Meehl later called his "disturbing little book", reviewed existing research to try to find out whether 'mechanical' methods of prediction using formal processes, such as checklists and algorithms, outperformed subjective and informal 'clinical' predictions.

The research he reviewed spanned many fields from medicine to the military. His central conclusion was pretty categorical:

"In spite of the defects and ambiguities present, let me emphasize the brute fact that we have here, depending upon one's standards for admission as relevant, from 16 to 20 studies involving a comparison of clinical and actuarial methods, in all but one of which the predictions made actuarially were either approximately equal or superior to those made by a clinician."

Studies since the publication of the "disturbing little book" have consistently confirmed Meehl's finding. This includes the counterintuitive discovery that models built on factors identified as important by experts normally produce better judgements than the experts themselves.[6]

Meanwhile, the many people who have doggedly tried to disprove Meehl's conclusion have never got far. In other words, we can be fairly sure his observation has merit.

Screens complement skill

Meehl was someone who should have had an axe to grind against subjective judgement and decision-making. As a teenager he lost his mother after she had a tumour misdiagnosed by a doctor. He later described this as a case of "gross medical bungling [which] permanently immunized me from the childlike faith in physicians' omniscience that one finds among most persons". The use of checklists in hospitals, which only started to gain widespread acceptance around the time of Meehl's death in 2003, is now credited with having saved hundreds of thousands of lives.

However, Meehl's views towards expert judgements were actually more nuanced and less challenging than many perceived them to be at the time his book was published. For one thing, he felt that mechanical judgements should be overruled if there was information that fell outside the process's remit. He gave the example of an algorithm that predicted a man would go to the cinema but failed to account for the fact he'd just broken his leg. The red-flag indicators we will explore at the end of Chapter 10 will help us identify 'broken leg' results from stock screens.

Beyond this, Meehl's general view was that mechanical processes could provide great support to professional judgements rather than simply replace them. As investors we should look to screens to improve what we do rather than to replace our role as decision-makers.

The value of this combination of human and mechanical judgements is something a young psychologist named Daniel Kahneman was to realise when he tried to apply Meehl's ideas during military service in 1955 as a 21-year-old lieutenant in the Israeli Defense Forces.

Kahneman would go on to win a Nobel prize and recast the way the world thinks about finance and economics. But even for such a great mind, the Israeli army had trusted someone very young with a lot of responsibility. As Kahneman explained it in his bestselling book *Thinking, Fast and Slow*, "Odd as it sounds today, my bachelor's degree in psychology probably qualified me as the best-trained psychologist in the army."[7]

One of the key tasks given to the young lieutenant was to overhaul the system used to evaluate new recruits. Kahneman regarded himself at the time as "no more qualified for the task than building a bridge across the Amazon." Fortunately, Meehl's "disturbing little book", which he had read the previous year, gave him an idea.

The existing system for assessing new army recruits was clearly failing to add value. Assessors, mainly young women, were tasked with making 'holistic' recommendations on recruits based on a 20-minute interview.

Kahneman introduced a new, checklist-style evaluation system for recruits. The system was based on scoring individuals for six key attributes, which included things like 'responsibility' and 'masculine pride'. The checklist was carefully designed to try to identify what was really important in determining a recruit's future success. The questions the assessors were required to ask were formulaic and factual. This was done to reduce the often-incorrect influence of first impressions. Once scores had been given, they were fed into a simple algorithm which made a recommendation. It's all sounding very stock screen-ish.

The Meehl-inspired evaluation system proved far more effective than the old assessment method. In Kahneman's words the system had gone from "completely useless" to "moderately useful".

There was one problem with the new system though. The assessors hated it. They were close to mutiny. They didn't like being turned into robots, and they still believed in their intuition.

Kahneman made a concession. He introduced a final assessment into his process. He empowered the assessors again by asking them to close their eyes and come up with a 'holistic' score once all the other scoring was complete. This, of course, was the very judgement that had proved such an unreliable basis for the old system. Expectations were very low for predictions from this final score. But something remarkable happened.

As a result of considering objectively and individually the key attributes relating to candidates' likely success before making their judgement, the assessors' holistic score went from being demonstrably useless to the most valuable predictive indicator in the new system. The assessors turned out to be right; they did have predictive skill. However, they were only able to harness this predictive skill by using an intelligent checklist that forced them to systematically consider all the important factors on which their judgements should be based.

"I learned from this finding a lesson I've never forgotten," wrote Kahneman. "Intuition adds value even in the justly derided selection interview, but only after a disciplined collection of objective information and disciplined scoring of separate traits."

The lesson for investors is that to make the best possible judgements and decisions, it is vital to have a well-designed, systematic process. That is something stock screens can give us when hunting for investment ideas. This is a key reason why stock screens give investors an edge.

Keep screens simple

The other great lesson from statistics and psychology is the value in keeping the number of data inputs into our screens small and making criteria as simple as possible.

It feels like the more information we have to base our judgements on, the better decisions we should be able to make. But what we feel about things is often very different to how they really are.

One of the first of many experiments illustrating this common folly was conducted in 1973 by a trail-blazing psychologist called Paul Slovic.[8]

Slovic's experiment involved a group of horse handicappers. These were professionals who made their living from their ability to predict race outcomes. Slovic was keen not just to test their predictive powers, but also to see how they perceived their own abilities.

The experiment started with the handicappers being asked to predict the outcome of a race with no information. This was done to gauge what a random result looked like. The handicappers were then given five pieces of information about the horses in the race and were once again asked to make predictions. The process went on with an additional five bits of information being given to the handicappers each time until they ultimately had 40 bits of information.

How the handicappers felt about their own predictions changed a lot with their increased access to data. They became ever more confident. But the rub was that while the experiment showed access to information did give them predictive power, their predictions were just as good with five pieces of information as with 40. The predictions made with 40 bits of information were worse than those made with five in one very important way, though. The handicappers became drunk on the amount of data they were provided. They became way overconfident.

With five pieces of information, the handicappers' confidence in their own accuracy was a fairly good match for their actual accuracy, at 19% versus 17%. However, with 40 bits of information the handicappers thought themselves likely to be 34% accurate, when in actual fact their predictions remained correct only 17% of the time.

Overconfidence is a trait we all naturally display. Tempering it is extremely important for investors because it can cause very costly mistakes. That's because an investor who thinks they're more likely to be right than they really are will take on too much risk.

Simplicity trumps sophistication

Information does not only make us overconfident in our judgements. The judgements themselves can suffer. A study from 2007 demonstrated this by asking participants to pick between four different cars.[9] One car was clearly better than all the rest, and by a good margin. When given information on four attributes of each of the four cars, most people – about 60% – picked the best one. But when confronted with 12 different attributes, in their confusion, only about a fifth of participants chose the superior vehicle.

When it comes to stock screens, focusing on too many criteria means fewer or no positive results. The results that are positive are also far more likely to be flukes rather than the type of stock we're after.

Screens are also generally at their best when equal weight is given to all criteria. This may seem odd. After all, surely some criteria are more important than others when judging an investment case. But while this will almost inevitably be true, it is likely to be very hard to know what the most important influence on an investment outcome is at the time a judgement is being made.

A remarkable study from 1979 by a psychologist called Robyn Dawes was one of the first demonstrations of the mistake of trying to be too exacting when weighting criteria.[10] Dawes conducted an extensive study that discovered models that gave an equal weight to every factor they considered were at least as accurate as models that gave different weighting to inputs based on their historical importance. Dawes' findings were considered so shocking at the time that he struggled to even get his work published.

The insight from Dawes should not only give encouragement to those who embrace what he called the "robust beauty" of equal-weighted models – a category into which most stock screens fall. It also serves as a warning for those who try to draw overly precise lessons from history. Dawes' findings suggest that while we can learn what factors influence outcomes from past events, the exact way things played out is likely to have a lot to do with chance and will be different next time. Consequently, there is little value in being overly precise. Indeed, doing so could cause one to draw false conclusions based on the observation of chance occurrences.

Separating factors from fiction

In the field of investing, researchers have identified an almost impossible number of so-called 'factors' that they believe explain superior stock performance based on historical data.[11] Many of these factors are flimsy. Under further scrutiny they often prove to be a product of selective use of data or an elaborately forced fit. Trying to discover investment strategies by back testing data can all too easily become a case of putting the cart before the horse.

Ideally, a numbers-based investment approach is founded first and foremost on a common-sense idea. Preferably one that real-world investors already appear to be exploiting. The idea would then be broadly tested using historical data to see if it stands up. A screening system would then be built based principally on the common-sense idea that originally set the process in motion.

The four strategies we'll explore in Part Three of this book are backed up by many industry and academic studies. Most importantly though, as we'll find out, there are common-sense reasons to think the approaches should work. It's these common-sense reasons the criteria of the screens focus on.

Screening sense from a complex world

The decisions investors make on whether the value of an investment will go up or down are not black and white. It is also fiendishly difficult to determine whether both good or bad outcomes are the product of luck or skill. And much information investors come across is complex and contradictory. Balancing out the pros and cons of an investment is extremely hard, but stock screens help us to do this. They also help us to keep things simple by focusing on what matters most.

That's not to suggest we want to avoid embracing the complexities and uncertainties of the real world. But as a starting point, keeping things as simple as possible by identifying and focusing on the few things that really matter can greatly improve our chances of seeing the wood from the trees.

Table 1: Performance summary

	Quality	Value	Dividends	Momentum
10-year cumulative total return	508%	330%	346%	371%
10-year index total return	120%	88%	79%	109%
10-year outperformance of index	388%	242%	267%	262%
Screen compound annual growth rate (CAGR)	20.0%	15.7%	16.1%	16.7%
Index compound annual growth rate (CAGR)	8.2%	6.5%	6.0%	7.7%
10-year cumulative total return with 1.5% annual charge	422%	270%	284%	305%

Source: Thomson Datastream.

As Albert Einstein is credited with saying, "Everything should be made as simple as possible, but no simpler."

But to make things simple, we need to have a thorough understanding not only of the strategies we are pursuing but also the tools at our disposal. If this sounds daunting, just take a look at Table 1, which shows the potential gains to be made by using these screens. The results are worth it.

Next, in Part Two, we're going to find out about these tools, starting with a whistle-stop tour of company accounts.

PART TWO

THE BUILDING BLOCKS NEEDED TO CREATE AND INTERPRET SCREENS

We're now going to get a bit technical.

There is no way around this. Stock screens require an understanding of company accounts, ratios, fundamentals, and methods for analysing and researching stocks. These are the tools we need to employ if we are going to build screens that mimic successful investment strategies and exploit them.

For readers who know it all already, you could always skip Part Two. But we're going to explore ideas that are of value even to experienced investors. And recapping knowledge is rarely a bad thing.

CHAPTER 3

A LITTLE BIT ABOUT COMPANY ACCOUNTS

BOOKS ABOUT UNDERSTANDING and interpreting company accounts are long and boring.*

There are lots of fiddly and tedious rules to explain and tortuous examples to work though.

Relax. This is not one of those books.

However, it is impossible to understand stock screens without knowing a bit about accounts. The numbers in company accounts are the key source of raw material for screens, both in their unblemished form and converted into financial ratios.

The good news is that, as with many fields in which professionals are required to accumulate byzantine, subject-specific knowledge, the most important considerations about accounts for an outsider are in fact refreshingly simple and straightforward. Knowing what a company's accounts are actually trying to achieve is what really matters. This is the knowledge that makes everything else fall into place.

And guess what? The vital concept non-accountants need to know is actually so simple it can be expressed in a single word: matching.

---

* It is worth reading at least one nitty-gritty book on accounts. The book on the subject I cut my teeth on was *Interpreting Company Reports & Accounts* by Geoffrey Holmes and Alan Sugden (1999). If you're in the market for such a book, make sure you get an up-to-date edition. Accounting rules change all the time.

Strike a match

The point of company accounts is to appropriately match a company's costs against its sales.

Pretty simple, right?

So why does it take three separate statements (profit and loss, balance sheet and cash flow) and interminable pages of notes and written explanations to get this information across to shareholders?

There are two key complications in the matching exercise from which all the protractedness stems.

Two complications with matching

1. Spending does not align with sales

Firstly, the spending that ultimately results in a company making sales often happens years before the sales themselves occur.

For example, a company may build a factory that will be churning out products for decades to come. That means the initial cost to build the factory needs to be spread over those decades to match it to its contribution to sales. How to spread such costs is a complicated thing to figure out. And spending on acquiring another business, which could potentially contribute to sales throughout the rest of the buyer's trading life, can be especially complicated and confusing to account for.

Companies also have spending which has less of a lead time but still does not directly align with sales.

For example, there are raw materials that need to be bought before a product can be made. And most companies need to keep some stock on hand to satisfy demand. Some costs are also settled after the sales are made. A company may hold off paying its suppliers, for example, hanging onto the cash and using it for other purposes for as long as seems reasonable. Warranties granted to customers on future product faults may not be realised for years.

2. Sales are recorded before or after money is received

The second complication is that sales are often recorded when the necessary work is judged to have been done but before any money actually comes in. And some sales are recognised after money has been received.

This can simply be because customers do not pay invoices immediately or they pay for things in advance. But it can also be altogether more complicated. For example, companies operating long-term contracts may need to estimate the value of work done to give shareholders an idea of their sales, even though an invoice has not even yet been sent to the customer, let alone approved.

Lots of matching to do

With accounting there is a lot of matching up to do. Especially with big companies, it can get really complicated. Often items have to be matched on a best-guess (estimated) basis.

Ideally, the accounts give shareholders as easy and as fair an interpretation as possible about what has been going on over the course of a year. But naturally, when things are very complex, there is plenty of scope for jiggery pokery. We'll look at some red flags to watch for later. There is also the potential for companies with the best intentions and most thorough processes to simply get things wrong.

So now we know what we're talking about, let's have a quick run through the type of stuff found in the three main numbers-based statements in company accounts and how they relate to the matching exercise.

In the next three chapters, we will look in turn at the profit and loss, balance sheet and cash flow statements. We'll look at UK reporting conventions and terms, but with a few minor (mainly cosmetic) differences, this all applies to companies listed in other geographies.

CHAPTER 4

THE PROFIT AND LOSS

Table 2: Simplified profit and loss/income statement

	This year	Last year
Sales	£110m	£100m
Cost of goods sold (COGS)	−£66m	−£60m
Gross profit	£44m	£40m
Operating costs	−£22m	−£20m
EBIT/operating profit	£22m	£20m
Interest expense	−£5.5m	−£5.0m
Profit before tax	£17m	£15m
Tax	−£3.3m	−£3.0m
Profit after tax	£13m	£12m
Minorities	£1.1m	£1.0m
Shareholders profit	£12m	£11m
Shares outstanding	100m	100m
EPS	£0.12	£0.11

THE PROFIT AND loss (P&L) account, which is also known as the income statement, is the matching exercise from the last chapter in action.

Let's quickly whizz through the highlights of the statement.

Sales – COGS = Gross profit

First off, the P&L tells us the value of work done (during the year it covers) that the company has decided it should record as sales.

Next we're told the cost of goods sold (COGS) that relate to those reported sales. There is no precise definition of what COGS should include. Generally speaking, though, it consists of things directly associated with actual production of goods or services sold.

Sales minus COGS gives us a company's gross profit.

Gross profit – operating costs = EBIT/operating profit

We then have the company's operating costs, or to use an Americanism with superior descriptive powers, selling, general & administrative (SG&A) expenses. These are running costs not included in COGS, such as IT, human resources and marketing.

Once these costs are accounted for we get to a company's earnings before interest and taxes (EBIT), which is usually the same or similar to what is referred to as operating profits, although companies can sometimes have other operating items that only get factored in after calculating EBIT.

This line in the accounts can be used to create some very useful ratios, as we'll shortly see.

EBITDA

Usually, so-called 'depreciation' and 'amortisation' charges will be included as part of a company's operating costs, although these items can sometimes end up in COGS.

Depreciation and amortisation are the names accountants give to costs associated with long-life assets that need to be spread over several years in order to match them with sales. For example, the original cost of building the factory that makes the stuff the company has sold.

Depreciation is the name of the charge related to past investments in tangible assets, such as buildings or machinery, while amortisation relates to past investment in intangibles, such as software. Investors often add depreciation and amortisation back to EBIT to create the very popular profit measure known as earnings before interest, taxes, depreciation and amortisation (EBITDA). This can be considered a crude approximation for the underlying level of cash generated by a business. For companies that need high levels of ongoing investment, it can be very dangerous to pay too much attention to a profit figure like EBITDA that ignores depreciation and amortisation (DA), given that these cost items relate directly to a company's investment needs.

EBIT – interest = profit before tax

Next in the P&L we have interest expenses. As well as debt-related expenses, this also includes certain payments made towards pensions and an element of a company's rent bill.

The reason accountants treat rent in a similar way to debt interest payments is because as far as shareholders are concerned it is very debt-like. That's because a commitment to pay rent effectively finances the right to use an asset, such as an office, over an agreed amount of time. It's an alternative to raising debt to buy a property, or any other asset, outright. What's more, obligations to landlords need to be met before shareholders can get their slice of profits. Investors can get into big trouble if they ignore this fact.

Once finance expenses have been accounted for, we arrive at profit before tax. This number gets a lot of attention, but I personally find little use for it in stock screens.

Post-tax profit to shareholders' profit and EPS

The next expense revealed by the company in its P&L statement is what it reckons the tax is on the reported profits. This is generally different to the actual cash paid out in tax for the year, but hopefully not by too much. Subtracting this gets us to post-tax profit.

We're finally getting close to the bit of the statement that shareholders are really interested in. The profit that is left over for them. But before we get there, we have an item to subtract that is easy to overlook.

Many companies do not own all their subsidiaries. Nevertheless, they report 100% of their subsidiaries' sales and profits up to this point in the P&L so long as they have over 50% ownership. We now must take out the portion of profit that belongs to the 'minority interests' (the sub-50% holders) which are also sometimes referred to as 'non-controlling interests'.

Once we've subtracted the minority interests we can divide the resulting number, which is known as shareholder profit in the UK and net income in the US, by shares in issue. This gets us to the figure from the accounts that is probably the most pawed over by investors: earnings per share (EPS). The slice of profit each share entitles us to.

When produced with integrity, the EPS number represents the best effort by a company to match the sales it believes it made in a year to the costs it believes it incurred to generate them.

To varying degrees and depending on the company and the nature of its business, this number will necessarily be a product of estimation and professional judgement. In some extreme cases it can be close to guess work. Profit should not be confused with cash, or even with fact. However, for good companies the reported profit will represent a very good guide to what is going on in the business.

So P&L represents an effort to match sales and costs. The other two main statements in company accounts tell us how the matching has been achieved. Crudely, we can think of the balance sheet as the historical record of what's gone on to build the company and the cash flow as what's happened this year to achieve the matching.

Let's move on to look at these other statements now, starting with the balance sheet.

CHAPTER 5

THE BALANCE SHEET

Table 3: Simplified balance sheet

	This year	Last year
Non-current assets		
Property, plant and equipment	£55m	£50m
Leased assets	£11m	£10m
Intangibles (including goodwill)	£50m	£50m
Total	£116m	£110m
Current assets		
Cash and short-term investments	£5.5m	£5.0m
Receivables	£17m	£15m
Inventories	£17m	£15m
Lease (right-of-use) assets	£1.1m	£1.0m
Total	£39m	£35m
Total assets	£155m	£145m
Non-current liabilities		
Long-term debt	£50m	£45m
Lease (right-of-use) liablities	£11m	£10m
Provisions	£3.0m	£4.0m
Total	£64m	£59m
Current liabilities		
Short-term debt	£5.5m	£5.0m
Lease (right-of-use) liablities	£1m	£1m
Payables	£17m	£15m
Provisions	£1.0m	£1.0m
Total	£24m	£22m
Total liabilities	£88m	£81m
Total equity	£67m	£64m
Minorities/non-controlling interests	£5.5m	£5.0m
Shareholder equity	£61m	£59m

WHAT IS THE balance sheet balancing?

The answer is a company's assets and its liabilities.

The difference between these two is what is known as shareholders' equity. At some point in a company's history, when it first tapped money from shareholders, this equity would be equivalent to the amount of cash it pocketed.

As a business grows, and retains and reinvests its profits, shareholder equity should grow. This doesn't always happen. Quite often bad investments are made and anticipated profits never materialise. This can lead to companies having negative shareholder equity. But there can also be positive reasons for negative equity. When a company has returned a lot of cash to shareholders over its lifetime, this can cause equity to become a negative number.

The balance-sheet balancing act can be written as:

Assets – liabilities = total equity

Total equity includes assets and liabilities relating to the minority owners of subsidiaries. We need to adjust for this to find out what belongs to shareholders and calculate shareholders' equity. Shareholders' equity is the basis for the price-to-book and return-on-equity ratios we will explore in the coming chapters. So:

Total equity – minority interests = shareholders' equity

It is important to keep in mind that the balance sheet only tells us what was happening on a single day in the year when the accounting date fell. That means there is scope to window dress the numbers reported. For example, a company can hold off paying bills until just after its period end while incentivising its customers to settle invoices before that date. This would mean it had more cash on the balance sheet on the accounting date, but the situation would quickly reverse.

Many companies also have highly seasonal investment requirements, such as retailers that finance high stock levels over the festive period in anticipation of strong demand. Rather than having mid-November financial year ends, when balance sheets would be around their most stretched in preparation for the seasonal shopping bonanza, retailers tend to report financial years that finish around the end of January. By that time, new year sales have hopefully converted most of the Christmas stock into cash.

The key role the balance sheet plays in the matching exercise is to offer a home to the money spent and received by a company that is yet to find its way through the P&L. The balance sheet also records amounts that are expected to be spent or received and have already appeared in the P&L. Unless the business is wound up and the bits sold off, for most companies there are also many items on the balance sheet that will never find their way through the P&L.

There are two parts to the balance sheet: assets and liabilities. Both assets and liabilities are split into current and non-current items.

Assets

Let's start with what's found in the assets part of the balance sheet. Here we see both what the company owns and what it believes it is owed.

As mentioned above, the assets are divided into non-current and current.

Non-current assets

Non-current assets are considered by a company to have value stretching beyond one year, maybe forever in the case of assets like freehold property and goodwill.

Some of the assets are tangible, and these will generally be labelled as 'property, plant and equipment' on the balance sheet. Less physical assets, such as software, get labelled as 'intangible items' and get their own balance sheet line.

Bizarrely, companies are required by accounting standards to treat many of their most important intangible investments as a day-to-day cost. More on that hugely problematic bit of accounting in Chapter 7.

The proportion of non-current assets that need to be matched against sales during a year is done using depreciation and amortisation charges. The value of assets on the balance sheet is reduced by the depreciation and amortisation charged for the year.

One issue with spreading out the cost of an asset over its useful life is that the annual charge that goes through the P&L may be thoroughly out of whack with the actual replacement cost of the asset. Sometimes the replacement cost will be less but usually it will be more, which means the profits a company reports will usually be flattered by this accounting practice.[12]

Normally most of a company's so-called 'right-of-use' assets are also recorded as non-current. These are assets that a company rents. They are matched against sales over time through both a depreciation charge relating to their use and an interest charge relating to assumptions about how the asset would need to be financed if it were owned.

This accounting method for rental agreements seems convoluted and is imperfect in some respects. However, it does reflect the important fact that shareholders need to view a company's rental commitments in a very similar manner to debt, as discussed in the last chapter on the P&L. To do this an asset has to be created to balance with a corresponding debt-like liability.

One of the biggest intangible assets normally found in this part of the balance sheet is 'goodwill'. This represents the amount that has been paid for the acquisition of another business above the value of its readily identifiable assets.

When acquired businesses underperform, the value of goodwill often has to be reduced. The matching exercise requires this reduction to be recorded as a cost in the P&L. Essentially, this represents the admission of a past mistake. Shareholders need to judge whether the mistake is really in the past and was unforeseeable or whether it reflects an ongoing problem and is symptomatic of poor management judgement.

Current assets

The section of the balance sheet labelled current assets deals with items the company expects it will be running through its P&L during the coming year, or assets it could access within a year, such as 'cash and short-term investments'. Investors often pay particular attention to this section of the balance sheet for signs of jiggery pokery. We'll look at this later when we explore a few simple but very useful red flags in Chapter 10.

Included in current assets are 'receivables'. As the name suggests, this is the value of things (mostly cash) the company expects to receive soon. This item is also sometimes referred to as a company's debtors. A large part of this number is normally made up of sales that have been recorded by the company in the P&L, but on which payment is yet to be received. The number also includes goods and services a company has paid for early, such as rent paid in advance. These prepayments are waiting to be matched as a cost against sales when the good or service purchased is used.

The other item in current assets that is often a big number is 'inventories', which is also sometimes known as stock. This includes raw materials, work in progress and finished goods. The number represents cash costs the company has incurred but which will not be put through the P&L until sales are made to match against. When a company has old and unwanted stock, it is effectively future losses sitting on the balance sheet.

Liabilities

Moving on to liabilities, these relate to the financing of a company that is not attributable to shareholders. These are obligations that need to be settled before shareholders get a look in.

We again have non-current and current parts of the statement.

Non-current liabilities

The big numbers in the non-current liabilities section tend to be 'long-term debt', 'pension obligations', and the non-current proportion of the company's contracted rental commitments – known as 'lease' or 'right-of-use' liabilities.

Contingent liabilities are also sometimes found in this section of the balance sheet. These often relate to money that will need to be paid on an acquisition if certain conditions are met.

There can also be provisions recorded in this part of the statement. These are future cash costs a company has identified but are seen as separate to the costs incurred in the normal course of business. Often provisions will be used and added to each year, such as those associated with stock becoming obsolete or pay-outs on warranties.

Provisions can also relate to some kind of nasty event. These provisions can sometimes be significant cash gobblers for many years. This would be the case, for example, if a company closed multiple loss-making offices or shops but was still on the hook to a landlord for rent for years to come. A provision would be taken to cover the rent to be paid on the empty properties. It's important to watch out for this kind of provision because while it will get recorded in the P&L as a one-off big item as soon as the company can put a number on its problems, it can carry on being an annual burden on cash flow for a long time after.

In cash terms, you could think of this as a mirror image to the goodwill write-down we looked at earlier. In the case of the goodwill write-down the cash has already been blown – with provisions, the cash flow pain is yet to come.

Current liabilities

Provisions are also often found among a company's current liabilities. Here we also find many of the more pressing debt and debt-like commitments of a company we encountered in the non-current section. The difference being, they are classed as current if they are due within a year.

In this section we also tend to find most of a company's 'payables'. This is stuff the company needs to pay for. This tends to be chiefly associated with costs that have already been matched against sales, but which the company has not yet stumped up cash for. It's like free borrowing, which is great as long as a company does not take too many liberties with its suppliers. Payables can also include something called 'deferred income'. This is money a company has been paid by customers in advance for goods or services which it now must provide.

Certain types of debt can also be hidden within payables. So-called inventory financing, such as the borrowings used by motor dealers to finance full forecourts, can often be found within this accounting item. So too can invoice financing, where a company borrows money on the strength of invoices that have yet to be paid by customers.

Working capital

Payables classed as current liabilities are one of a collection of balance sheet items many investors pay particular attention to. These items are lumped together and called working capital. The reason working capital is of such interest is that it captures a lot of the important moving parts in the annual matching exercise.

Working capital represents a company's inventories and receivables (cash can be included too) from current assets minus current payables. The resulting number represents the amount of money the company has tied up in the day-to-day running of its business.

Very crudely speaking, if working capital is rising as a proportion of sales a company is becoming less efficient at turning profits into cash, while the reverse is true when working capital to sales falls.

We'll see when we look at red flags that it can be much more telling to look at the individual components of working capital rather than working capital as a whole.

We will get a better understanding of how working capital movements work as we dive into the cash flow statement in the next chapter.

CHAPTER 6

CASH FLOW

Table 4: Simplified cash flow statement

	This year	Last year
Operating cash flow		
EBIT	£22m	£20m
Depreciation & amortisation	£5.0m	£4.5m
Use of provisions	−£1.0m	−£0.9m
Increase in receivables	−£1.5m	−£1.4m
Increase in inventories	−£1.5m	−£1.4m
Increase in payables	£1.5m	£1.4m
Cash from operations	£25m	£22m
Cash interest expense	−£6m	−£5m
Cash taxes paid	−£3m	−£3m
Net cash from operations	£16m	£14m
Investing activities		
Capital expenditure / purchase of property, plant and equipment	−£10m	−£9m
Acqusitions	–	–
Net cash outflows from investing	−£10m	−£9m
Financing activities		
Dividends paid	−£6.6m	−£6.0m
Net shares repurchased	−£3.1m	−£2.8m
Lease payment of principle (rent)	−£1.0m	−£0.9m
Increase in debt	£5.5m	£5.0m
Increase in cash	−£0.5m	−£0.5m
Net cash outflows from financing	−£5.7m	−£5.2m

Source: FactSet

WE'RE FINALLY ON to the third and final main statement in the accounts. The one that looks at cold, hard cash.

Don't infer anything about its importance from the position it is given in the order of the three financial statements in the UK. It is the place I personally choose to start reading companies' report and accounts.

It is worth keeping in mind, though, that while the tangible nature of cash can give comfort, there are actually quite a few ways inventive accountants can rig these numbers.

The cash flow statement unpicks the matching work that has been so laboriously achieved with the P&L. Cash flow is broken down into three sections. The first concerns itself with cash from a company's trading activities, known as cash from operations.

Cash from operations

Operating cash flow adds back the non-cash items that were matched up with sales to get to the operating profit figure. One of the largest numbers added back is usually the depreciation and amortisation charge, which relates to investments made in previous years. Charges relating to write-downs are reversed and the hidden use of provisions is factored in. Some elements of profit, such as gains made on asset disposals, are taken away.

The company also adjusts for changes in working capital here. If payables have increased (we'd expect them to if the company is growing) then this will show up as additional operating cash flow. An increase in payables is positive because it reflects a rise in bills the company has not yet paid.

In the same vein, if receivables have increased, this will have a negative impact on cash flows because the company is owed more than was the case at the start of the year. Rising inventories also mean less cash, as more money is tied up in goods on shelves, work in progress, and the like.

After the company has done all this, it can tell us what cash it generated from operations. Next a few more adjustments are made. Any income received from dividends from associates or subsidiaries is added back. Net interest is usually taken out here, although sometimes this happens in the financing section of the statement. Finally, actual cash taxes are subtracted.

That takes us to the end of the first section of the cash flow statement, giving us a number called 'net operating cash flows'.

Cash flows from investing activities

Having done so much work unmatching things, it is now time for the cash flow statement to start to substitute what it removed and replace it with the corresponding cash spent. The first run at this is done in the 'cash flows from investing' section of the statement.

This tells us how much the company invested in its businesses during the year (often referred to as capital expenditure or capex). We also now take account of how much was spent on any acquisitions and how much it received from any asset or business sales.

Cash flows from financing activities

Finally, we have the financing section of the cash flow statement. This tells us what borrowings the company paid off in the year and what new debt it raised. It also gives the figures for how much money was raised through the sale of new shares and how much was spent buying them back. We also find out how much was paid out to shareholders in the form of dividends.

A counterintuitive item in this section of the cash flow statement relates to a portion of the rent paid by the company during the year. Remember, rental obligations are treated like debt in the accounts. That means the financing section includes money handed over to landlords, which is treated as the equivalent of paying down debt (often called 'lease payment of principal'). This is separate to the portion of rent that is treated like an interest payment.

The rules that require companies to treat rent obligations as debt are fairly new. They only came into force at the start of 2019. Annoyingly, it seems many data suppliers have yet to cotton on to the fact that the 'lease payment of principal' item in the final section of the cash flow statement needs to be factored into free cash flow (FCF) calculations, which we're about to find out more about. The logic of the accounting rule is that this portion of the annual rent bill is effectively maintenance spending on the rented asset.

Free cash flow

FCF is one of the most useful cash flow numbers for investors. It tells us how much cash a company has generated in a year that it's free to do whatever it wants with. It could pay dividends, buy back shares, reduce debt, make acquisitions, or just sit on it. However, we must calculate it ourselves as it has no formal place in the cash flow statement. There is also no formal definition of how it should be calculated.

The good news is that it is not too hard to get a rough-and-ready figure for FCF. From net operating cash flow (the figure we get at the end of the first section of the cash flow statement) we subtract all the money invested in the business (the capex) and the portion of rent payments (repayment of principle) found in the final section of the statement. Done.

A better FCF number can be obtained by figuring out what portion of the capex represents spending needed to maintain operations as opposed to spending on growth. Money that a company has chosen to invest in growth is after all money the company is free to do what it wants with. Sometimes companies provide shareholders with a maintenance capex figure. If this is the case, it's always worth checking how the calculation has been done and what assumptions have been made. We'd then subtract just the maintenance capex to get our FCF rather than all capex.

We've now got a good feel for the three main financial statements. In annual reports, these statements come with copious notes to help investors understand the complexities of the work done in producing them. While these notes can be extremely illuminating, considering them goes beyond the scope of this book. Instead, we're going to look at how investors can take nuggets from the accounts and blend them with other financial data to create the incredibly insightful metrics which power stocks screens.

But before that, we will take a quick detour with Chapter 7 to understand a key issue that vexes accountants and blindsides investors who are not in the know.

CHAPTER 7

ACCOUNTING FOR INTANGIBLE INVESTMENT

GIVEN ACCOUNTING IS an exercise in matching costs to sales, it is odd that some of the most important spending decisions made by modern businesses are hopelessly mismatched. This mismatched spending relates to a company's intangible investment. Intangible investment includes spending on things like intellectual property, brand building, and software development. This kind of investment powers some of the world's most spectacularly successful companies, from Microsoft to Coca Cola.

There are some types of intangibles that are matched sensibly by being recorded as assets and then having their cost spread over their useful life, as is the case with tangibles. However, most intangibles are treated as day-to-day costs. The expense is all taken upfront, despite the benefit being felt over many years.

Intangibles have become ever more important for businesses. Work by research group ITAN-Invest and consultancy McKinsey estimates a 29% increase in the investment share of intangibles in the 25 years to 2019. What's more, the evidence points to higher investment in intangibles leading to faster growth for companies across all sectors.

The nature of intangible spending goes some way to explaining the weird way accountants treat it. Often a lot of money can be forked out on intangibles with no result. This is the case for drug companies, for example, that spend millions on developing a treatment that ultimately fails to pass regulatory tests. And if the drug is a success, it may be very hard to estimate how valuable the asset will prove to be over its life or over how many years its life will stretch.

But should the drug prove to be a multi-billion pound blockbuster, the balance sheet will offer few clues to the investment it took to get it there because the spending will already have been written off as a day-to-day cost. Indeed, the lightweight balance sheet will mean the company will look like it needed to invest very little to achieve vast profits, even though this will not have been the case.

This accounting regime also leads to the weird situation where a company investing heavily in intangibles to pursue a growth opportunity depresses reported earnings even if it's successful. This is because the cost of the investment in growth will be taken upfront, despite the benefit being expected over years. The company could appear to be making a loss. However, as soon as the company puts the brakes on growth by lowering its investment in intangibles, it will seem that earnings are taking off because costs will fall. The matching exercise fails to give investors a clear impression of what's going on.

The value to investors of many companies' profit numbers and balance sheets are greatly diminished because of how intangibles are treated in accounts. This is a major issue when considering how to construct stock screens. It is also a big issue when considering the ratios that we'll explore in the next chapter.

Fortunately, some key numbers for investors are unaffected by the mismatching of intangible investments. Two important ones are sales and FCF.

Acquired intangibles

One other bizarre accounting twist is that something funny happens when it comes to identifying intangible assets that are acquired when another business is bought. In this situation, certain intangibles which normally would be treated as a cost are required to be identified and put on the balance sheet. Having done this, the acquiring company has to start to amortise those assets (spread the cost out over the expected useful life). However, the ongoing maintenance spending on those acquired intangibles must be treated as a cost. This leads to a situation where there is effectively double counting of maintenance costs on certain acquired intangibles (actual maintenance investment plus the amortisation cost).

This very odd situation means companies often report 'adjusted' profit figures excluding amortisation of acquired intangibles. This is fair enough. At least it is if the amortisation being ignored only relates to intangible items that have been created due to acquisition accounting rules. Yes, the issue gets even more convoluted.

As already touched on, sometimes in the normal course of business companies are allowed to report some intangible investment as an asset. Such spending includes the purchase of certain types of software and development spending when there is a very clear expectation sales will result. Amortisation from this kind of intangible should not be excluded from profit calculations even when it is from an acquired business. After all, future spending of this type will be recorded as an asset not a cost, so it will not be double counted. But when making adjustments, there is the potential for companies to bundle all amortisation charges from acquired businesses together. Most don't, but if this is done, it boosts adjusted profits beyond what is easily justifiable.

It's all quite a mess. And unfortunately, it's a mess that investors are left to clear up. As for stock screens, the issue is too nuanced and requires too much judgement for most data providers to cope with. We need to be aware of these problems and aware there is no easy fix.

The good news is that by simply being aware of these accounting oddities we put ourselves ahead of many investors who are happy to gloss over such details or simply aren't aware of them.

It also helps us appreciate the advantage we can gain by focusing on financial ratios that are not affected by the way intangibles are accounted for. We'll meet a few such ratios in the coming chapters. They're going to come in very useful for the stock screens we'll explore in Part Three.

CHAPTER 8

FINANCIAL RATIOS AND FUNDAMENTALS

IN PART ONE we looked at the reasons why it makes a lot of sense to use simple checklists and scores to aid good judgements about complicated situations. I have my own scoring checklist for stocks. I try to score a stock on four factors that research suggests are key influences on share price performance.

The factors are quality, growth, momentum and value.

In this chapter we'll look at some of the ratios that can be used to assess how companies and their shares measure up in each of these areas. We'll also look at a few 'red-flag' ratios, too, at the end of Chapter 10.

We're starting with measures of company quality.

It is important to point out that for most ratios, there is no one fixed way to make the calculation. It is therefore more important to understand the concept and then investigate the exact formulas being employed by the data provider you use. We'll look at this issue more in Chapter 12 when we look at what we need from stock screening tools, with reference to the many ways to calculate the ubiquitous price-to-earnings (PE) ratio.

Quality ratios

There are four types of quality ratios we'll look at:

1. Returns a company makes on its investments.

2. Returns it makes on sales, which are also known as its 'margins'.

3. Metrics for measuring the health of the balance sheet and dividend.

4. A company's ability to convert profits into cash.

Quality is a key consideration for investors, so it's fortunate there are a lot of ratios that give us clues to how well a company is doing.

Quality #1: return on investments

The central idea behind many popular quality ratios is to measure how efficient a company is at producing profits and sales. This is often done by calculating the return made by a company on its investments. This generally offers the most complete view of company performance.

Something to keep in mind is that the record of what has historically been invested by a company can be skewed by several issues affecting the balance sheet. These include: the issues surrounding accounting standards for intangibles that we looked at in the last chapter; historical write-downs and impairments; and the historical return of money to shareholders, which reduces the size of the balance sheet.

Some find it helpful to think of return on investment ratios in a similar way to an interest rate on a bank account, not least as the convention is to present them as percentages.[13] It needs to be remembered, though, that the returns companies make from their investments are far less consistent than anything we'd get from cash on deposit at a bank and can go negative.

Probably the most widely used return-on-investment measures are return on capital employed (ROCE) and a similar ratio called return on invested capital (ROIC).

The reason these ratios are so popular is that they drill down to how well a company is doing at the operating level. They give us an idea of how efficient its core business is before we consider how the company itself is financed. It is performance at the operating level that is normally a key determinant of a company's long-term ability to make its shareholders rich.

ROCE

We'll start with ROCE. This ratio looks to EBIT from the P&L to gauge returns. EBIT is a measure of profit before payments to any of a companies' 'claimholders', including those that are not shareholders. That's a long-winded way of saying these are profits before interest. Remember, accounting conventions mean interest payments include money paid to pension schemes and landlords as well as lenders, so it covers the three big non-equity claimholders.

To calculate ROCE, EBIT is compared with something called capital employed. Capital employed gives us an idea of how much money the company's operations need to function. It is not quite as refined as the capital measure used by ROIC, as we'll see in a minute.

A key consideration when calculating what capital is employed by a company is differentiating between financing a company has to pay for and financing it gets for free. For most companies the most notable free source of finance is bills not yet paid to suppliers. These are included in the 'payables' figure in the current liabilities section of the balance sheet. This money is effectively like an interest-free loan.

The easiest method to adjust for a company's 'free money' is to subtract all current liabilities from total assets except short-term debt.

As an equation, capital employed looks like this:

Capital employed = total assets − current liabilities + short-term debt

A problem arises for stock screens when there are borrowings sitting within a company's payables. This would include things such as invoice and inventory financing. A standard treatment of payables from a data provider may not take this into account. It is often only possible to find out this kind of information by delving deep into the notes of a company's annual report.

If an adjustment is not made to the data, companies that have borrowings hidden in their payables will look like they require less investment to function (lower capital employed) than is really the case. This will make them look more attractive than they actually are based on ROCE. Investors should always try to stay vigilant.

ROCE expresses EBIT as a percentage of average capital employed.

ROCE = EBIT / average capital employed x 100

The average capital employed takes the level of capital at the start and the end of the year and averages them. This is done to try to get a better idea of what level of investment a company has relied on over the full 12-month period. One issue, which we touched on when looking at balance sheets, is that there can be a lot of window dressing by companies in their year-end balance-sheet snapshots.

ROIC

With the ROIC quality ratio, EBIT is adjusted to take account of the company's tax rate. The resulting number is given the not-so-catchy name of net operating profit after tax (NOPAT). In an equation NOPAT looks like this:

NOPAT = EBIT x (1 – tax rate)

ROIC compares NOPAT with invested capital. This is similar to capital employed but tinkered with to try to only reflect capital being actively used by the business to generate profit. So it would exclude, for example, investments in shares of other businesses. So invested capital is simply capital employed minus a company's non-operating assets.

The ROIC formula is:

ROIC = NOPAT / average invested capital x 100

RoE

A very shareholder-centric view of returns is provided by a ratio called return on equity (RoE). This compares earnings per share (EPS) with shareholder equity (NAV) per share.

I like to use this ratio for stock screens because it is relatively simple to calculate, which in my experience means there are reasonably clean numbers available from most databases.

Using RoE as my go-to quality screening metric is chiefly a needs-must choice. As a concept, I think it is generally an inferior ratio to either ROCE or ROIC. The reason for this is that the ratio is heavily influenced by how much debt a company has decided to use to finance its business. High levels of debt, as we'll explore in a minute, can seriously undermine a company's quality credentials. The problem for the ratio comes about because the higher a company's debt, all other things being equal, the lower shareholder equity becomes.

Thinking back to the balance sheet equation we met in Chapter 5, debt increases 'liabilities' which lowers 'shareholder equity'. We can see this in the balance sheet equation:

Assets – liabilities = equity

RoE compares EPS with shareholder equity per share, known more commonly as NAV, expressed as a percentage. So the smaller NAV is, the larger EPS will look in comparison to it.

RoE = EPS / NAV per share x 100

Higher debt does reduce EPS, too, because a company will have to pay more interest to lenders. However, the relatively fixed payments needed to service debt mean shareholders can benefit handsomely when times are good. That's because the same interest rate must be paid on borrowings regardless of how well a company is doing.

So, if shareholders have financed less of a company's operations, they will get to pocket proportionally more of the upside when times are good. But shareholders also face the risk of seeing the proportion of profits due to them disappear more swiftly should trading deteriorate.

In finance jargon this is known as 'financial gearing' or 'financial leverage'. What this means for the RoE ratio is that a high number can simply be a reflection of high balance sheet risk and a temporarily favourable trading backdrop.

High risk and high quality are not good bedfellows.

This conundrum means that when I devise stock screens that try to identify quality by looking for high RoE, I often include a test that suggests a company has an acceptable level of debt. I also often test for RoE consistency and run additional quality tests based on margins.

The performance over the last 10 years from my 'quality' focused screens suggests there is merit to the approach.

RoA

Another return-on-investment ratio that can be particularly useful when looking at banks is return on assets (RoA). This is calculated by comparing EPS with total tangible assets per share. We're only interested in tangible assets when it comes to banks because most of their intangibles are ephemeral to core lending operations. For banks, tangible RoA provides a measure of the profitability of their core lending activities before considering financing.

Normally, RoA is a very small number for banks, especially at times when interest rates are low. Faced with such low returns on their core activity, banks seek to boost shareholder returns (RoE) by lending out many multiples of shareholders' equity. The multiple of equity a bank lends out is known as its 'leverage ratio' and it represents tangible assets as a multiple of tangible equity.

Tangible RoA multiplied by the leverage ratio gives a bank's tangible RoE.

The more leveraged a bank is, the riskier it becomes. The run up to the Great Financial Crisis is infamous for having seen leverage ratios at US banks rise to over 30 times before it all came tumbling down.

The equations look like this.

Tangible RoA = EPS / tangible total assets per share

Leverage ratio = tangible total assets / tangible equity

Tangible RoE = tangible RoA x leverage ratio

Capital turn

Another useful quality ratio can be calculated by comparing sales with the gamut of measurements of a company's investments we've already explored: capital employed, invested capital, total assets, etc. Just as the ratios we previously looked at tell us how efficient a company is at generating profit, these ratios tell us how efficient it is at generating sales. These ratios are usually expressed as a whole number rather than a percentage. They are generally referred to as capital turn or asset turn. They can be very useful when analysing companies with low margins (we'll look at margins in more depth shortly). There are two reasons for this.

First, a company with high capital turn does not need to increase margins by very much to significantly boost its return on capital and thereby its ability to create value for shareholders.

Second, if a business operates in an industry where margins are persistently low, the most effective way to create shareholder value over the long-term can be to try to achieve higher sales from existing assets. In such circumstances it is worth paying extra attention to trends in capital turn.

So why is this the case?

We can explain the relationship between capital turn and return on capital through something known as Du Pont analysis. This method of understanding company profitability was invented at the eponymous Du Pont company in 1912 by a salesperson called Donaldson Brown. He created a formula that showed RoE was the product of a company's profit margin (profit as a percentage of sales) multiplied by capital turn.

Rather than using the per share figures used earlier to calculate RoE, we'll use the same numbers from the accounts but before dividing by shares in issue to more easily see how Du Pont works in the equations below. This means in place of EPS we'll be referring to shareholder profits. And we will use shareholder equity instead of NAV per share. So, our starting point is:

RoE = shareholder profits / shareholder equity

Now we can factor in sales:

RoE = (shareholder profits / sales) x (sales / shareholder equity)

We've met one of the items in the equation just a minute ago. Sales/shareholder equity is capital turn. The other item, shareholder profits/sales, is a measure of profit margin.

So that means:

RoE = profit margin x capital turn

Pretty neat!

By paying attention to the individual components of RoE, we can gain deeper insight into how a company is achieving its returns. This can give us clues to how it may be able to surprise the market either positively or negatively. Often less attention is paid to capital turn than to margin, which has a more intuitive appeal. Margin is what we will turn our attention to now.

By the way, the same Du Pont analysis can be performed with other 'return-on...' measures of quality, such as ROCE and ROIC, using the measures of profit and capital that are relevant to them.

Quality #2: margins (return on sales)

Margins are a great indicator of business quality. They are good at telling us whether the product or service a company sells is really special. But as we've seen, they are still just a component of the more holistic quality measures such as RoE and ROCE. That means they are a less complete indicator of a company's potential to create shareholder value. On the plus side, margins avoid the complexities, vagaries and history that can create issues when deriving ratios from the balance sheet.

There are three margin measures that are very useful for investors, and fortunately they are all very simple to calculate compared with the 'return-on...' formulas we've run through. Calculating margins simply requires us to express a chosen measure of profit or cash flow as a percentage of sales.

Gross margin

Gross margin compares a company's gross profit to sales. This is considered a very good measure of a company's ability to set prices. The trend in gross margins over several years can be particularly telling in whether a company is gaining, maintaining or losing power with its customers.

A key issue with this measure of profitability, though, is that there is no one definition of what constitutes gross profit. That's because there is no standard definition for 'cost of goods sold' (COGS) which is what's subtracted from sales to calculate gross profit. That means when comparing two similar companies, differing accounting policies may mean we are not comparing like with like.

Another major issue when looking at gross margins is so-called 'pass-through costs'. This represents money that passes through a company's profit and loss statement but is a cost entirely borne by the end client. For example, a company distributing fuel to petrol stations may have to record the cost of the petrol as sales even though it has an agreement with its customers that means this cost is passed directly on to them at zero margin. The portion of reported sales that a company with such a business would actually generate its profit on would only be the bit connected with distribution. Nevertheless, the pass-through cost would have the effect of making gross margins look lower.

Operating or EBIT margin

Operating margin or EBIT margin compares operating profit or EBIT (usually very similar or identical numbers) to sales. This is a very good measure of a business's operational strength and a go-to metric for most investors. It is also a great margin metric to use in stock screens.

A key issue we need to be alert to when looking at operating margins is a company's so-called 'operating gearing', which is also sometimes known as 'operating leverage'. This describes how sensitive a company's profits are to changes in sales. If a high proportion of a company's operating costs are 'fixed' (i.e., they do not increase or decrease much when sales do), then a change in sales will result in a much larger change in profit. While operating gearing can be fantastically beneficial when trading is strong, much like financial gearing (which we looked at when we explored RoE), it can devastate profitability should trading deteriorate.

When a company has high operating gearing and is also very sensitive to factors outside its control, such as the economic cycle, it can often look like a high-quality business based on margins and ROCE when times are good. However, it will quickly see profits plummet should trading turn. We'll see such a case first-hand when looking at a failure from our Quality screen in Chapter 16.

Usually shares in such companies can be easily spotted because they will have very low valuations compared with what we'd expect for genuine quality plays. It is extremely dangerous to mistake lowly rated shares in a highly cyclical company going through a purple patch for a bargain. Such shares tend to be cheap for a reason.

FCF margin

The final margin worth considering is the free cash flow (FCF) margin. This compares FCF to sales. This is very useful when looked at over time. It can be very erratic from year-to-year though, due to the changing capital expenditure needs of businesses. Also, in my experience, the FCF data available to use in stock screens tends to be very variable. For these reasons, while the FCF margin is very useful to consider, it is not something we'll find plugged into the stock screens we're soon to explore.

Quality #3: debt and cover ratios

Excessive debt can be incredibly dangerous for investors in shares. That's because, in the pecking order of claims on a company's assets, shareholders rank below a company's lenders. That includes quasi-lenders such as landlords and pension schemes. In practical terms, that means if a company gets into difficulty servicing its debt and debt-like obligations, the value of shares quickly gets wiped out in order for it to focus on satisfying the legally more important interests of lenders.

Some investors have a visceral aversion to debt due to the risks it presents. On an individual basis we should all ultimately take an approach to this issue that works best for us. But the use of debt is often a good thing. As we saw when we briefly looked at financial gearing, debt can play an important role in improving returns for shareholders. It's just a case of balancing the benefits with the potential risk.

Debt can be quite a tricky thing for screens to assess. First there is the question of what balance sheet items should be included as debt. While accounting rules mean companies must report their rental commitments as debt-like liabilities, many companies highlight debt excluding this item. I won't repeat the reasoning given during our quick tour through company accounts, but we can get into a lot of trouble if we ignore rental commitments.

There are two other reasons that assessing debt is a vexing issue, particularly for stock screens. The first of these issues arises because the appropriate way to measure debt for one business is not necessarily an appropriate way for another. For companies that have a large asset base against which debt can be secured, such as property companies, it makes sense to compare debt with total assets or NAV. This is generally known as a 'gearing' ratio.

However, comparing debt with assets will not make sense for companies that require little investment to churn out cash and profits. For these companies it is likely to be far better to compare debt with the amount of profit available to service debt. Often the comparison investors make is with EBITDA. However, another useful calculation that can be made is to work out a company's interest cover. Interest cover measures how many times EBIT covers the company's interest bill.

Let's put these ideas into some equations.

Debt measures for asset-intensive companies:

Net gearing = net debt* / NAV

*Net debt = debt − cash

Gross gearing = total debt / total assets

Debt measures for asset-light companies:

Net debt / EBITDA

Interest cover = EBIT / interest expense

A catch-all way to try to assess debt is to compare net borrowings with market capitalisation. This uses the market's valuation of a company's equity as a guide.

But this brings us to the second problem we run into when trying to decide on a method to screen for appropriate debt levels. What is an appropriate level of debt for one type of business can be inappropriate for another.

A bank with no 'leverage' would effectively be uninvestable because, as we've discussed earlier, the RoA of banks tends to be utterly puny. Fortunately, banks can leverage significantly because the value of their loan books tends to be relatively stable. However, if a real estate company took on the same level of leverage it would be likely to very quickly prove disastrous. That's because the potential for losses from a property portfolio is generally far greater than the potential for losses from a mainstream loan book.

Likewise, the dependable, regulated profits of a utility provider coupled with its solid asset base mean such a company can take on high levels of debt to boost returns. It can do so knowing a steady income stream is likely to be there to service its borrowings and also pay dividends to its shareholders.

By contrast, a company with high operating gearing and a business sensitive to external shocks would be foolish to try to juice shareholder returns by taking on high levels of debt. The tactic may prove hugely profitable for a while, but shareholders could be wiped out as soon as a downturn happens.

From a shareholder perspective, debt just magnifies the upside or the downside of an investment. Debt therefore needs to be seen in the context of the business's operating risks.

Sadly, all of this means there is no one-size-fits-all debt test we can plug into stock screens. All the same, balance sheet strength is a key consideration when it comes to assessing company quality. We just have to be judicious when we screen. Whatever approach we take, there are likely to be flaws.

Current ratio

A company's current ratio takes a more near-term view of its financial viability. This ratio simply tests whether the money earmarked to come in during the year (current assets) is more or less than the money expected to go out (current liabilities). It is a fairly broad-brush ratio but can be a useful, quick quality check. A number above one offers some reassurance based on the formula:

Current ratio = current assets / current liabilities

Dividend cover

One final aspect of quality to consider is dividend quality. Appropriate debt levels are one key consideration when thinking about the sustainability of dividends. But we can also get an idea of how capable company earnings are at covering dividend payments using a ratio called dividend cover. This simply compares dividend per share (DPS) with the earnings available to pay a dividend, the EPS. A similar calculation can be made using FCF per share. But it needs to be remembered that FCF tends to be more erratic from year to year than EPS.

Dividend cover of 1 suggests the DPS declared in a financial year matches that year's EPS. A dividend cover ratio of 2 would tell us DPS is twice covered by EPS. As a rough-and-ready rule of thumb, investors tend to get nervous about the sustainability of a pay-out when the cover ratio drops below 1.5.

Dividend cover = EPS / DPS

Quality #4: cash conversion

Given we earlier explored the matching exercise that takes place in accounts, we have some understanding that over time the profits reported by a company should roughly equal the cash that lands in its bank account. That money can then either be put to use growing and improving the business or can simply be returned to shareholders.

However, some companies are much better at turning their profits into cash than others. Cash conversion ratios try to identify whether companies are doing well or badly on this front. The most important principle when we consider how to judge cash conversion is that we should be comparing similar items from the P&L and cash flow statements.

My two favourite measures involve comparing EBITDA with cash from operations (i.e., operating cash flow before interest and tax are deducted) and FCF compared with shareholder profits. In both cases, cash conversion of 80% or more can normally be considered reassuring. However, cash flow can fluctuate quite a lot from year to year. This means it is useful to make a judgement based on several years of cash conversion rather than one year in isolation.

Another important consideration is that high-growth companies can consume a lot of cash. As with most ratios, the real value for an investor comes from understanding why the numbers have turned out as they have before making a judgement.

This is how we calculate the ratios:

EBITDA / cash from operations x 100

FCF / shareholder profits x 100

CHAPTER 9

GROWTH RATES AND MOMENTUM

AFTER PLOUGHING THROUGH so many ratios to measure quality, it may come as a bit of a relief that our exploration of growth rates and momentum will be less exhaustive. So much so that we'll explore both subjects in the same chapter.

However, that is not to suggest these considerations are necessarily any less important. Growth in particular needs to be considered alongside the quality of a company when assessing an investment case.

Growth rates

While understanding growth rates is relatively simple, there are a few wrinkles we need to pay attention to. We'll start with the one vital thing every investor needs to understand about growth: its value is completely dependent on the gap between a company's return on investment and its cost of investment. If the cost of investment is above return on investment, a company destroys shareholder value through growth.

We've looked at ways of measuring return on investment, but how do we calculate the cost of investment for a company?

The truth is, cost of investment is not something there is a nice easy formula for. There is also debate on exactly how it should be calculated. But fortunately, we do not need to go into the complexities of this issue as a rudimentary understanding should serve our purposes.

Just as companies make a return on their investments, there is also a cost attached to those investments. The most obvious is the cost connected to the interest a company pays on debt-funded investment. If a company was entirely funded by debt and could not create a return that was greater than the interest rate it borrowed at it would soon go under. Borrowing more to grow would only make its problems greater by creating a bigger EBIT shortfall versus interest due.

There is also a cost of investment connected with equity. This, though, is the thing that is a bit more nebulous in calculating cost of investment.

Essentially, the cost of equity can be thought of as the return that shareholders deem acceptable as compensation for the risk they are taking by backing a company. Some of this will be determined by the risk-free return we could get by investing in government debt. However, a large part of the cost will be down to company-specific risks.

The entire cost associated with all a company's investments is called the weighted average cost of capital (WACC). It is not something that's possible to accurately calculate because it has to be based on assumptions about the future, and the future is unpredictable.

The key thing to understand is that if ROIC is higher than WACC, then a company should create value for shareholders with its growth. The other way around and value will be destroyed.

As a very rough guide, we can think of WACC as running from a couple of percentage points above the risk-free rate for a very safe company in a developed market to some way into double digits above the risk-free rate for a rickety business in an emerging market. The risk-free rate is determined by government bonds in the local market. So, the yield on US bond would be used for a US company.

Because companies have lots of moving parts, and because management always has a plan to improve ROIC when it is low, making a judgement on whether value is being created or destroyed by growth is hard. Remember, we're interested in what ROIC is going to be on future investment made and that may differ from the past. All the same, it is worth being quite sceptical about historically low-quality companies pursuing aggressive growth strategies because it often ends in tears. That's especially true when big acquisitions are involved.

Average growth vs CAGR

It is always good to know how a company is growing and how it is forecast to grow across many different metrics. Key areas of interest for stock screens include sales, operating profit, EPS, FCF and DPS. It is important for us to remember that while profits can grow for some time thanks to operational improvements, sales growth is needed for profit growth to be sustained over the long term.

When looking at average growth over multiple years, it is important to focus on the compound annual growth rate (CAGR).

CAGR effectively tells us what percentage growth would need to have been achieved each year to take us from one point to another in a smooth trajectory.

This is different to averaging annual growth rates. Averaging annual growth rates can be extremely deceptive. An example can help illustrate this.

Take a company that starts out with EPS of 10p. In year one something bad happens and EPS drops to 5p. Then in year two EPS jumps back to 10p. In year three the company manages to grow EPS to 12.5p.

The three-year CAGR for this company is 7.7%. Growth looks alright over the period, which ultimately it was, even though this glosses over the stomach-churning roller coaster ride of those three years. Most databases used for stock screens will carry CAGR data like this which gives a decent idea of how a company has been growing and is forecast to grow over multiple years.

Averaging annual growth rates, by contrast, gives a very disingenuous picture. The EPS fall in year one was -50%. EPS doubled in year two to get back to its starting point, meaning 100% growth in that year. In year three we had 25% growth.

The average of those numbers (-50 + 100 + 25 / 3) is 25% annual growth. But the company only managed 25% EPS growth in the whole three years. The average of growth rates number is clearly rubbish.

Surprisingly, though, some databases do calculate multi-year growth in this way. It's also easy for us to unwittingly fall into this trap if we're not aware of the issue. Watch out!

Momentum indicators and trends

Some investors struggle with the concept of share price momentum, and for very understandable reasons.

The idea behind share price momentum is that prospects are usually better for a stock if the price is already rising and worse if it has been falling. Momentum acts as an indicator of both sentiment and the underlying performance of the company that has issued the shares. It is useful but imperfect.

But for investors heavily focused on bagging bargains, the concept can just feel plain wrong. If a share price has already gone up, it understandably makes us feel like we've missed the boat. If it has fallen, it can feel like it should now offer better value.

Sometimes this contrarian take will be true. But as we'll discover when we learn about screening for momentum stocks, more often than not the trend will prove an investor's friend. Momentum is one of the most significant and persistent known influences on future share price returns.

When things are getting better, they tend to carry on doing so. The same tends to be true when things are getting worse. And what is true of share price momentum is also true for many other fundamentals and trends.

My personal favourite way to plug share price momentum into stock screens is to simply look at price rises or falls over three months.

Another approach to momentum involves comparing a company's share price against the moving average. A moving average is usually calculated as the average closing price of a share over a specified number of days. Probably the most popular comparison is between the current share price versus the 50-day moving average. Broadly speaking, if the share price is above the moving average it is considered to be a good thing, and if it is below it is considered bad.

Forecast upgrades can be a brilliant indicator of momentum in a business. We will go into more detail on why this is when we look at our momentum strategy.

To test for forecast momentum, the method our momentum screen will employ is to compare forecasts today for a given point in the future (it could be the next financial year, for example) with forecasts for the same period from a number of weeks, months or even years ago.

The best way to make these then-and-now forecast comparisons is using an average of all broker estimates. This is known as the consensus forecast. But a problem can arise when there are very few brokers making forecasts for a company. In this situation, the appearance of one rogue forecast can show up as a major upgrade or downgrade when it is actually not reflective of any real change in the company's fortunes, just a new opinion, albeit an extreme one.

We can also get great insights into companies by tracking long-term trends in other fundamentals and ratios. Falling ROCE could indicate a business is becoming lower quality. Growth in gross margins could signal an improved competitive position. Rising net debt may indicate cash generation problems.

Looking for trends in fundamentals can alert us to important developments that are not immediately apparent when looking at a single year in isolation. Generally, such trends require further investigation to properly understand what is going on.

As far as stock screens are concerned, tests based on trends in fundamentals and ratios usually work best when used to support other key criteria.

CHAPTER 10

VALUATION RATIOS AND RED FLAGS

BEFORE WE GET on to looking at actual valuation ratios, let's quickly consider the hugely important but easily overlooked question of what we actually mean when we talk about a company's value.

Market cap

The value of a company is often thought of in terms of its share price or market capitalisation.

Market capitalisation is the value of all the shares a company has in issue at the current market price.

While this gives a clear-cut and transparent valuation, it only represents part of the picture. It tells us about the value assigned by the market to the claims of shareholders on a company's assets and cash flows. But it's not only shareholders who have claims on a company.

As we saw when we looked at the balance sheet in Chapter 5, shareholders' claims rank below those of lenders, landlords and pension schemes. It can therefore be quite misleading to focus on market capitalisation and share price alone when considering companies with high borrowings, lease liabilities and pension deficits.

Enterprise value

A more holistic view of value is provided by something that is known as enterprise value (EV). EV represents market capitalisation plus the value of other claims.

The most significant of a company's claimholders aside from its shareholders is usually its lenders. But lease obligations and pension deficits can also be massive items. The totality of these claims less a company's cash can be referred to as net debt. EV is calculated by adding net debt to market capitalisation.

It's worth being aware, sometimes the term 'net debt' is used in relation only to finance from lenders such as bank debt and bonds. It is always worth checking what exactly is being talked about when the term net debt is used and what has gone into an EV calculation.

The problem with EV is that unlike market capitalisation it is very hard to put a really good number on. That's because debt moves around during the course of a year and the figures investors see on the balance sheet only represent a period-end snapshot (as we've previously touched on, usually period ends are chosen to present the most flattering possible picture of debt). Additionally, if a company has issued bonds, the balance sheet value of that debt may be very different to the actual value of the bonds in the market – the price the debt could be bought back and cancelled at.

Meanwhile, other potential components of the EV valuation, such as pension deficits and leases, require a company or investor to make assumptions to estimate the size of the liability. They're best-guess figures.

What this means for stock screens is that we must accept that the EV data we will use is going to be rough and ready.

For valuation ratios, when we use EV, we must compare it with a measure of profit or cash flows that represents the money available to all of the company's claimholders. That's a long-winded way of saying we need to look at profit and cash flow numbers before interest payments are subtracted. Sometimes this means adding back interest, as was the case with the NOPAT formula we looked at as a component in our ROIC quality ratio in Chapter 8.

Profit ratios

One of the most ubiquitous ways to value shares is to make a comparison of company value against profits. Many of these profit ratios are so heavily scrutinised that it is questionable whether they can really highlight bargains with any reliability, even when used as part of a well-designed screen.

All valuation ratios can be calculated using either historical or forecast numbers. Forecasts are generally most useful as they tell us what the market thinks is going to happen. Things usually work out differently.

The most used comparisons between company valuation and profits are:

EV / EBITDA

EV / EBIT

EV / NOPAT

Price/earning (PE) ratio = P/EPS

With all these ratios, a lower number suggests a 'cheaper' share. When shares are cheap, it is best to assume they are cheap for a reason; which makes our first job to find out why. Quality, growth and red flag ratios will often provide a quick answer. So too can a quick assessment of the cyclicality of the company.

A spin on these classic earnings ratios is to combine them with a company's growth rate. The most basic of such ratios is the price-to-earnings/growth (PEG) ratio. This valuation approach has been expounded by three great investors: US fund management legends Peter Lynch and John Neff, and British investor and author Jim Slater.

The PEG ratio works best if neither the PE in the formula nor the growth rate are so extreme it suggests something suspicious is going on. A good rule of thumb is to exclude PEGs that look low due to growth rates above 25% and PEs below 7.

The ratio is a very quick and dirty way to compare valuation with growth and it ignores the question of quality, which as we have seen in Chapter 9 is key to the all-important question of whether growth creates or destroys value.

As a rule of thumb, a PEG of 1 or lower is often considered the sign of a bargain. It can also prove fruitful to look for PEGs which are low compared with valuations in the wider market.

A bit like the PE ratio, the PEG seems so obvious it probably shouldn't work. However, a number of the screens I've plugged the ratio into over the last decade have done extremely well. Perhaps the best of the bunch is my small cap screen inspired by Slater's excellent investment book *The Zulu Principle*.[14] This puts an emphasis on company quality as well as PEG.

The PEG formula is:

PE / Growth rate*

*Growth rate should either be based on historical growth to the period in which the company reported the EPS used in the PE ratio or the forecast growth rate beyond that period – i.e., don't double count the EPS used in the PE ratio.

The criteria I use for my Slater-inspired screen are as follows:

- A PEG ratio among the lowest quarter of all stocks screened (note that in my *Investors' Chronicle* column I screen FTSE All-Share, All-Small and AIM separately each year).

- Market cap of less than £500m but more than £10m.

- Net-debt-to-EBITDA ratio of less than 1.5.

- Cash conversion of 90% or more (this is based on operating cash to operating profit).

- Return on equity of more than 12.5% or an operating margin over 15%.

- Three-month momentum higher than the median average, or upgrades to forecast EPS of 10% or more over the past year.

- Forecast earnings growth in each of the next two financial years and average forecast growth of more than 10% but less than 50% (anything above 50% is considered an unsustainable growth rate for the purposes of this screen).

In the first seven years since I started to monitor the screen in June 2013, it produced a cumulative total return of 299% compared with 135% from the FTSE Small Cap and 91% from the AIM All-Share.

Sales and book value ratios

Rather than doing the obvious thing and valuing a company against its profits, it can be a better idea to look at a valuation against the source of those profits instead. This is an idea we'll explore in more detail when we look at our contrarian value strategy.

In most industries, the source of a company's profits can be considered to be its sales, but in some industries, like property and finance, assets are a more reliable guide. Valuing a company against its source of potential profits is particularly useful if profits are currently low or non-existent, but are expected to be much bigger at some point in the future, such as recovery plays or early-stage growth plays.

Sales can be compared against either EV or share price. EV is normally most desirable. Sales are also not affected by issues associated with the intangible accounting rules which we dared to delve into in Chapter 7. In the case of assets, we compare share price with NAV per share, which is often referred to as a price-to-book-value (P/BV) ratio. The ratios look like this:

EV/sales

Price to sales ratio (PSR) = share price / sales per share

Price to book (P/B or P/BV) ratio = share price / NAV per share

Cash flow ratios

We can also compare the value of a company or its shares with its cash flows. A company's cash flows also are not affected by intangibles accounting. As always with cash flows, it is worth remembering they are likely to be lumpy from year to year. When using cash flow forecasts, numbers are often adjusted a bit by analysts to give a smoother picture of what is going on.

Often cash flow ratios are expressed as a yield. In this form, the ratios tell us what cash flow is as a percentage of company valuation. This can be thought of a bit like an interest rate on a bank account, in the same way some quality ratios can. The difference is that the quality ratio is an indication of the interest rate a company is able to get by investing money into its own business, whereas a cash flow yield (or any other valuation ratio expressed as a yield) suggests the interest rate an investor may receive from buying the shares.

The higher the yield, the more investors are getting in cash flow terms from their investment. As with other valuation measures, any cheapness suggested by a high yield will normally be because investors are negative on future prospects whereas a low yield means they are probably positive.

When calculating an FCF yield using EV, we have to use something that usually goes by the name of either FCF from firm or unlevered FCF. The terminology here is as clear as mud. Fortunately, the meaning is actually pretty simple: interest payments have been added back into the FCF calculation, so we can make the comparison with EV.

Useful cash flow ratios are:

Share price / FCF per share

or as a yield...

FCF per share / share price x 100

EV / FCF from firm

or as a yield...

FCF from firm / EV x 100

And a final ratio...

EV / cash from operations

Dividend and shareholder yield

The last type of valuation ratio we'll cover is based on the amount of money companies pay out to shareholders.

It is questionable whether we should call this a measure of valuation. But this chapter is as good a place as any for us to address this important metric.

The cash pay-outs a company makes to its shareholders should really reflect cash it has left over at the end of a year and has nothing better to do with. We will delve into the reasons why in more detail when we look at dividend investing. But the main consideration for now is that assessing spare cash is not a very holistic basis on which to make a judgement about the valuation of a company.

Most investors focus on the dividend and a share's dividend yield when they think about pay-outs. However, an increasingly important component of the cash returns made by companies is share buybacks. A share buyback is when a company buys its own shares in the market and either cancels them or keeps them 'in treasury' for potential reissue.

The benefit to shareholder returns of a buyback is almost identical to receiving a dividend and reinvesting it straight back into the company's shares. This means it makes sense to think of cash returns as a combination of buybacks and dividends. It is important to consider buybacks alongside any shares issued, because share issues essentially reverse the effect.

Buybacks increase the amount of a company existing shareholders own by reducing the number of shares the company's assets and cash flows are divvied up between. When new shares are issued, assets and cash flows need to be split between more shares. This dilutes the claim of existing shareholders.

Ratios that consider buybacks therefore look at so-called net buybacks. This refers to the value of shares purchased by a company less the value of any shares issued during a year.

The valuation measure that factors in net buybacks alongside dividends is known as the shareholder yield.

While it is very easy to find information on dividend yield from data providers, shareholder yield information tends to be far harder to come by despite it being a far more useful measure of cash returns.

As with all our valuation ratios, these yields can be calculated using forecast or historical data. For buybacks, forecasts are hard to find.

Issues also arise when using forecast dividends. Dividend predictions often seem to be something of an afterthought. Brokers often forecast a dividend will be maintained when the actual historical yield offered by the shares is so high it clearly indicates the market thinks this is highly unlikely to be the case.

The formulas for the yield calculations are as follows:

Dividend yield = DPS / share price x 100

Shareholder yield = DPS + net buybacks per share / share price x 100

Avoiding intangible problems

A key advantage of using cash flow ratios, dividend yields and sales-based ratios is that they are unaffected by issues with accounting standards relating to intangibles.

These accounting standards can severely distort reported earnings and NAVs. This creates problems when looking at classic profit and book value-based ratios.

For stock screens that try to make comparisons across the whole market, having ratios that do not provide like-with-like comparisons for all companies is a major issue. That is a big reason to lean towards those ratios that circumvent these issues.

A silver lining comes from the fact that for the sectors where P/BV is most useful in assessing valuation, such as property and financials, balance sheets are mostly made up of tangible assets. That means the accounting standard is not such a problem within these sectors.

One tactic we can use is to screen different sectors with different valuation ratios. For example, one screen could be run using P/BV for property and financial companies, while other sectors could be separately screened for value using EV/sales.

High, low or don't know

Stock screen valuation tests often use rules of thumb. For example, we may ask to see all stocks with a PE ratio of 15 or below, or the stocks with PE ratios among the lowest third of shares screened. However, there are some major limitations to using these kinds of valuation tests in screens.

The reason we're exploring valuation after looking at ratios connected with three other key influences on share prices (quality, growth and momentum) is that most of the time valuation reflects sentiment about these other factors. Valuation is usually most useful in telling whether we are likely to be looking at a 'good' or 'bad' company rather than whether a stock is a bargain.

Really low valuations and high dividend yields are rarely a reason to pile in. They are more often a reason to approach with caution. Likewise, high valuations tend to be the marker of really great companies. You get what you pay for.

And as we'll see when we explore our quality screen, the law of compounding means it is surprisingly hard to overpay for high-quality companies with fantastic long-term growth prospects; it's just a shame such companies are so terribly hard to identify and rare to find.

The key question with valuation is whether there is a good reason to think the market will change its mind about how a stock should be valued in the future. Are there reasons to think sentiment could become more positive or more negative? Is that change already happening?

Most of the time it's fairly easy to appreciate the reason why a stock commands the rating it does based on the quality and growth on offer. The wisdom of crowds, as we will see in Chapter 25, means we should always be humble enough to take heed of the signals given by share prices.

But the power of a dominant narrative and the dynamics of the market can also deceive the crowd at times. Stock screens give us a way to break away from the crowd and see through consensus opinion.

So, while it is easy to get seduced by a low valuation ratio and the idea that we've found a bargain, more often than not stocks that look cheap are cheap for a reason. For value to exist, the wider market needs to be overlooking something that will alter the consensus view on a stock. The screens we're going to explore in this book are designed to seek out situations where the real attraction of stocks may be being overlooked.

Red flags

The central objective of the red flag ratios we'll look at is to test whether the profits a company is reporting may be over-egged.

Normally, dicey profits will show up as weak cash conversion over time. Aggressively reported profit numbers also often need regular adjustments for supposedly exceptional costs.

We should assess red flags ratios for cash conversion and profit adjustments over several years where possible to get a better picture of what is going on. The formulas below are useful to test for warning signs over the last five years.

5-year FCF conversion =

5-year cumulative FCF / 5-year cumulative shareholder profits x 100

Rule of thumb: worry if this is below 50% and a good explanation cannot be found

5-year profit adjustment =

5-year cumulative adjusted pre-tax profit / 5-year reported (also known as statutory) pre-tax profits x 100

Rule of thumb: worry if this is greater than 125% and a good explanation cannot be found

Other useful red flag ratios look at the components of working capital: inventories, receivables and payables. These are balance sheet items where cash costs can be hidden and with which non-cash sales can be created. It can be particularly instructive to look at the trend in these ratios. Even when these red flag ratios do not look worrying on their own, it is worth investigating if the trend is worsening. The specifics of different business models can also explain why some companies will naturally produce higher or lower ratio numbers.

The easiest way to gauge the level of working capital items is to compare them with sales. Sometimes we find these ratios expressed as 'days outstanding'. Inventories are also often compared with the cost of goods sold rather than sales.

The three key formulas are:

Stock / sales x 100

Receivables / sales x 100

Payables / sales x 100

Rule of thumb: worry if any of these ratios are greater than 25% and a good explanation cannot be found

We now have an extensive tool kit to use in our hunt for promising stocks and insight into how company accounts work. But how do we apply all this when faced with a stock to research? That's what we'll find out next.

CHAPTER 11

A LITTLE BIT ABOUT COMPANY AND STOCK ANALYSIS

ONE AIM OF this book is to encourage readers to do their own research. Stock screens are a beginning and not an end to the investment process. A good screen helps us marshal our research efforts in the most efficient way possible. Screens also provide a framework with which to understand stock ideas. But further research is essential. This chapter is about what we may want to consider in our research efforts.

In doing this, I'm also going to provide a view into the workings of the *Investors' Chronicle* magazines. That's because the lists of source material and points of enquiry in this chapter are the same as those I highlighted to new *Investors' Chronicle* writers for many years as the editor of the magazine's Ideas pages.

But before we get on to that, I'm afraid we need to get a bit cynical. Being too cynical can often cause us to miss out on great investment opportunities, but a little bit of rational cynicism can also be a good thing.

Never start at the beginning

There are two really important things to remember when reading a company's accounts.

First, always use the audited annual reports. These can be downloaded from companies' websites. Do not rely on the preliminary results a company releases on its results day. The prelims are a light-weight document and quite feeble when compared to the richness of the annual report.

The second thing to remember is to avoid reading accounts from the front. Sounds like odd advice, I know. After all, management has carefully laid out and ordered the document to tell the company's story. But that's the problem. Management will naturally tend to put the finest gloss on the narrative they present to investors. The directors will weave the story they want us to hear. That's what we get when we follow results from the front to back.

Some companies are better than others. But often investors find themselves greeted with the best (and frequently heavily adjusted) underlying numbers on page one of a company's annual report. The chairman will then speak of the year's achievements and fellow members of the board in glowing terms while giving a sympathetic spin to any bad news that cannot avoid being mentioned.

The baton is then passed to the chief executive, who is normally also found in an ebullient mood, waxing lyrical about the big strategic vision. Even the finance director, who has to explain the actual numbers in his or her contribution to the written statement, normally manages to focus on the positives while avoiding going into too much depth on the less savoury details.

Who could fail to be charmed by such an assault of niceties?

If the share price tanked on results day, but for the life of us we can't see why, it is probably because we read the accounts from the front.

And what is true of the written statements in an annual report is also true of the numbers-based statements. We've already seen how much estimation and discretion there is in the matching process used to create a profit and loss statement. This can be used to gloss and finesse. What's more, liberal adjustments that ignore things like write-downs, provisions and other 'exceptionals' can be used to distract from underlying performance rather than explain it better.

To use accounts to our fullest advantage, it is best that we start somewhere that makes our journey through the document slightly mysterious. A starting point where our interpretation is not being framed by the company line. A starting point that will raise questions rather than provide answers. Somewhere that will force us to scurry off for information into other parts of the document. We want our curiosity to lead us, rather than the company's investor relations teams. It's worth it even if it occasionally takes us to a dead end.

For me, the place to start reading an annual report is the cash flow statement. There's a narrative in the numbers but often a slightly confusing one. I find the numbers here tend to naturally lead me on a search for answers in the notes to the accounts, the balance sheet, the statement of key risks and the finance-director report. Also, making a point to look at certain items early on, such as auditors' reports, can quickly highlight important risks.

The notes in the annual report are a goldmine not to be overlooked. Here we learn things like: what the company's sales actually consist of; how costs break down; the make-up of working capital items and how healthy they look; when debt will need to be repaid or refinanced; the performance of acquired subsidiaries that may have large quantities of goodwill associated with them; and much, much more besides.

Investors are best served by trying to understand the narrative on their own terms before seeing how management wants to spin it.

Sources to use

Given what we've just covered, it will come as little surprise that the key source for research I'd recommend to anyone is annual reports. It is hard to think of more valuable documents for investors. But listed below are also some suggestions for a supporting cast:

1. Annual report (not unaudited prelims) – don't forget the notes and don't start at the front.
2. Historical financial and share price trends.
3. Company website ('about us'/presentations/conference-call transcripts etc.).
4. Recent news and announcements from the official listed-company news service, such as the Regulatory News Service (RNS) in the UK and Electronic Data Gathering, Analysis, and Retrieval system (EDGAR) in the US.
5. Any relevant industry data and information on competitors.
6. A few recent broker notes or in-depth articles aimed at investors, if possible.

Questions to ask

The most important part of the research process is asking good questions which we can then try to find answers to through our research. This is what really determines whether we'll end up finding out valuable information. There will be many specific questions that we'll want to ask based on what the screen that suggested a stock was trying to identify in the first place – as well as the specifics of the company we're looking at. However, below is a list of broad questions to help guide research. Some of the questions may at first appear obvious, but the process of properly answering them is often surprisingly complex and of huge value if done well.

1. What does the company do?

How does its business(es) make money from its activities; who are the customers and suppliers; where is money made geographically?

2. Is the company special?

Does the company have a 'moat' (intellectual property/scale/brand/regulation/network effect/sticky customer relationships); is management good (track record, quality of reporting, share ownership, incentives etc.); is the business operationally geared; does the financial performance suggest the company is special (high margins/high returns on capital/strong cash conversion over time)?

3. How does the company finance what it does?

Consider elements such as: working capital requirements; overall capital requirements; structure and level of debt and leases; pension obligations; cash generation.

4. What is the short-term and long-term outlook?

Are brokers upgrading forecasts; what's been said in recent outlook statements; is there a structural growth opportunity/risk; is there a cyclical growth opportunity/risk; is capacity in the industry rising or falling; what is the company's relationship with its buyers and suppliers; are the shares being shorted; are there any interesting buyers/holders of the shares (shrewd investors, activists, directors)?

5. In light of points 1 to 4, is there a valuation case?

Consider free-cash-flow yield, EV/EBIT, EV/NOPAT, EV/sales, P/BV, shareholder yield, PEG, DY, PE etc.

Process

We began this book looking at the huge advantage we can create for ourselves by having a strong process. These lessons do not only apply to the process of generating ideas through stock screens. The research process also benefits from having a clear structure. Here are some ideas.

Score it: we should try to create a scoring system that allows us to deconstruct and individually scrutinise the important judgements that go into making an investment decision.

As mentioned in Chapter 8, I like to score companies for Quality, Growth, Momentum and Value before trying to come up with a separate overall score. Given the importance of quality in determining the value of growth, these two considerations are interrelated in my scoring system (extra points for good growth prospects from higher quality companies).

Write it down: we should write down our thoughts and reasoning about key judgements in a clear and concise way. If we struggle to do this, the chances are we understand less than we think we do. As Albert Einstein is credited with having said, "If you can't explain it to a six-year-old, you don't understand it yourself." As someone who has built a career from putting words on paper, I'm almost embarrassed to admit how often I find gaps in my knowledge when I try to explain ideas in short, easy-to-understand sentences.

The clarity and succinctness of our written notes is also important because it makes them easier to review. When notes are easy to review, we are more likely to amend our judgements in reaction to new information and understand the mistakes we make.

Test it: we should actively seek out views that contradict our own. The human mind is hardwired to find supporting evidence for any idea it likes. If we indulge this habit we can easily overlook risks. One way to create this kind of push back for ourselves is to write a counter-argument to the case we have made for a stock.

CHAPTER 12

A LITTLE BIT ABOUT STOCK SCREENING TOOLS

Choosing a data service

To SCREEN THE market and whittle down thousands of stocks to a handful that really deserve attention, we need data and screening tools. That means we need to pick a data service to use.

In this chapter we'll go through some key considerations for choosing a data provider to power our screens.

We'll cover:

1. A reality check – to help us appreciate what we should and shouldn't expect from a data service.

2. The basics – core considerations about the data we need.

3. Understanding the data – the importance of properly interpreting what we are looking at.

4. Interrogating the data – the kind of functionality we want from a screening tool.

5. Spreadsheets – some helpful tools for manipulating data exported from a provider.

At the end of this chapter there are offers for two of the best data services available from UK companies focused on private investors. It is vital that readers try before they buy. Your opinion on the quality of these services may not tally with mine.

A reality check

You get what you pay for

As with many things in life, if you want a really good data service, you're going to have to pay for it.

There are some very good options for private investors which are available for a few hundred pounds a year.

Professional services, such as Bloomberg terminals, meanwhile, can costs tens of thousands. Not only is the price tag attached to these top-end packages way beyond the budgets of most private investors, the depth of content is also well beyond most people's needs. However, the price professionals are willing to pay for data tells us just what a valuable tool it is and having access to reliable information is vital for anyone thinking of investing in individual shares.

Free data sources are available, too. But what is on offer can be very limited. It can also be hard to find out how ratios are calculated and how raw numbers are sourced, which is an issue we'll look at more in a second.

You get what you're given

In previous chapters we've looked at ways to calculate certain ratios and financial metrics such as free cash flow (FCF) and return on capital employed (ROCE). There is no universally agreed method for these calculations. We may have a preferred method on which to base such calculations. However, data providers may differ on how they do things.

While some data providers may offer a degree of flexibility and a range of options for different ratios, users must generally be willing to accept a provider's way of doing things.

But we also need to understand what we're looking at when we're presented with a figure for FCF or ROCE, for example. Developing an understanding of how a data provider puts together its numbers can be time consuming at first but can also prevent costly mistakes in the long run.

We'll work through the calculation of a PE ratio in a minute to show just how dangerous it can be to assume we understand what we're looking at.

Nothing's perfect

In large datasets, there will always be some mistakes. We can't expect perfection from data providers, although the accuracy of many services can be extremely good. The good news is most mistakes in datasets will appear odd on sight or will quickly be revealed as we dig deeper into researching a stock.

When something jumps out as being weird, it is always good to check it is not just an error.

Most data providers are very grateful for a quick email to point out any such problems in their datasets. They are super keen to eliminate all the errors they can. This kind of correspondence can also help us learn about how the data is put together.

The basics

When choosing a data service, we want to be sure it offers everything we need before committing time or money. It is good to have a list of our basic requirements and to try to run a few screens, such as those we will look at in the next section of the book, to test the service. It is also worth distinguishing our must-haves from the nice-to-haves at the outset.

Sometimes we don't realise what we want until we're told it exists. A lot of thought will have gone into the construction of a good data service, and often its developers will have thought of cleverer ways of doing things than we've been able to imagine.

Coverage

One of the biggest costs incurred by most data services is the fees they have to pay to index providers for publishing key information on stocks. Generally, this means the more stocks covered, the more expensive the service is going to be.

It is good to have an idea of the stocks we will want data on and to check whether a data service covers them all. For example, do we want data on overseas markets as well as our home market? If so, which overseas markets? Are we only interested in blue chips, or do we also want coverage of mid-caps, small caps and even micro caps? Most services will have several pricing options depending on the level of market coverage their customers want.

With stock coverage, sometimes less is more. Even when searching for just a few gems, having too many stocks to consider can cause confusion and end up creating a lack of focus. Spreading oneself too thinly can be more costly than missing a few opportunities.

History

Looking at the historical performance of companies is invaluable. Data services are brilliant for this. When information is displayed well, we can see in seconds what it would take hours for us to find out by sifting through past annual reports.

The question is, how much history is enough? At the time of writing, to understand how companies performed in the last serious recession, it is necessary to track back nearly 15 years to see what happened during the Great Financial Crisis.

In share price terms, for many tech companies, 2000 remains an important market as it reflects a period of exuberance of which the markets of the early 2020s felt reminiscent.

While it is a case of the more financial history the better, my personal preference would be for at least 15 years of history but five years as a real minimum.

It is also important to understand how companies' financial histories are displayed. Companies are constantly buying new businesses and selling off subsidiaries. They raise new equity and reclassify their reporting divisions. They restate accounts, write-down assets and take massive exceptional costs.

Data providers have to find ways to deal with these issues, even if it is just reporting the statutory numbers as they appeared. It is important to understand what we are looking at.

Range

It is really important to know our data service has all the financial metrics and ratios we need. The previous chapters have already provided a long list of building blocks for financial analysis. The breadth of financial information we need in order to research a company makes it a major task to check if everything required is being provided by a data service.

The best way to decide whether a data service has a broad enough range of information is to take a deep dive into a company to see how much it is possible to find out. When doing this, we have to keep in mind that we'll never find all the answers we're after in the data. Even the very best products cannot replace the depth of information and explanations offered in a company's report and accounts (the best data services will normally link to report and accounts once a user has drilled down through the numbers to a certain level).

Support

The level of support offered to users of a data service is also very important.

We are highly likely to have questions about the data and how to use the service from time to time. Friendly and timely support is key.

These days, much of this support can be automated, and online tutorials can be invaluable. However, there are certain issues where we will need to get a real and knowledgeable person's advice through a live chat function, over email, or on the phone.

Understanding the data

Understanding data is vital. It is amazingly easy to misunderstand numbers if we are not tuned into how nuanced financial metrics can be. A quick example should help demonstrate the issue and provide food for thought.

Same ratio, different numbers

Let's take that most ubiquitous of financial metrics, the PE ratio. This is calculated simply by dividing share price by EPS. How is that possible to misunderstand?

Here's how:

Let's say we are looking at a company call Widgets PLC with a share price of 100p

We know 100p should be on the top of our data provider's PE ratio, but what should be on the bottom? Here are some EPS figures that the data service could choose from to create the ratio's bottom half:

First half EPS for last financial year: 5p.

EPS for last financial year: 10p.

First half EPS for current financial year: 7.5p.

Forecast current financial year EPS: 15p.

Forecast next financial year EPS: 20p.

There are at least four ways the PE ratio could be calculated from these EPS numbers, all of which would be considered standard. To make these calculations easier, we will assume this company is exactly halfway through its financial year. (In reality companies don't tell the world their first-half EPS on the day the first half closes, but this is an example, so we'll use a bit of artistic licence.)

Calculation method one (PE=10)

We could look at the historical PE ratio based on Widgets PLC's last financial year. This would mean dividing 100p by 10p to give a PE of 10.

Calculation method two (PE=8)

Another very standard way to calculate the historical PE would be to use earnings achieved over the last twelve months (LTM). Given we are halfway through Widget PLC's current financial year, we would do this by taking first-half EPS (7.5p), adding it to last year's EPS (10p) and then, so as not to double count first halves, subtracting the first-half EPS from the last financial year (5p).

That means EPS is: 7.5p + 10p − 5p = 12.5p.

If we divide 100p by 12.5p, we get a PE of 8.

Calculation method three (PE=6.7)

Because investment is always forward looking, it is also quite standard to calculate a PE based on forecasts.

One way to do this would be to take the forecast EPS for the next full financial year. This is 15p. So in this case the PE is 100p divided by 15p, or 6.7.

It is worth noting, we are assuming the PE is being based on consensus forecasts. For most companies there will be several different analysts predicting different numbers, so there is a different PE relating to each of those forecasts. As a rule of thumb, the consensus number is always the best one to look at unless there are good reasons for thinking otherwise.

Calculation method four (PE=5.7)

The final standard PE calculation would be based on forecasts for the next twelve months (NTM). Generally, this is done by simply taking the proportion of the forecast EPS for the remaining portion of the current year and the rest from the forecast for the following financial year.

For example, if a company was a quarter of the way through its current financial year, the NTM EPS figure would be based on three quarters of the forecast for the current financial year and a quarter of the forecast for the following year.

As we have assumed we are exactly halfway through Widget PLC's financial year, that means our NTM EPS will be: (0.5 x 15p) + (0.5 x 20p) = 17.5p.

Using 17.5p as our EPS figure means we would have a PE of: 100p/17.5p, or 5.7.

So there we have it, four PEs for the same company, all of which would be considered standard calculations, which range from 10 to 5.7.

But we're not done. There are two other considerations which may mean these PE ratio are not quite what we think.

Adjustments

A striking thing about the PE ratios we've calculated for Widget PLC is that they are very low, especially in light of expected EPS growth from 10p to 15p and then 20p.

Remember, as we explored when looking at valuation in Chapter 10, the most likely reason for a low rating coupled with high growth rate is not that we've found a massive bargain that everyone else has missed, but rather that the company itself is a bit rubbish.

A possible explanation for the problem being highlighted by the low valuation is that this company makes returns on the money it invests that are lower than the cost of its investments. This means the company would actually destroy value as it grows, which is an issue explored in Chapter 9.

One way such torrid situations often become evident in company accounts is through large adjustments to report earnings (warts-and-all numbers).

For example, past investments that are unable to cover their costs will ultimately need to be written down in value. However, these write-downs may be treated as a one-off cost and excluded from what Widget PLC presents as its adjusted earnings. This means a PE based on adjusted earnings, which is often also the basis of broker forecasts, will ignore a key indicator that growth is actually coming at great cost to shareholders.

We need to know if our data service is calculating its PE using adjusted or statutory figures. Some data providers will also standardise numbers themselves, which introduces another type of adjustment.

The best data providers will allow us to see all the various permutations.

Dilution

Another key consideration with the earnings number is whether the company has committed to issuing new shares. For example, there may be debt that is set to convert into shares or a large amount of 'in-the-money' warrants that are likely to be converted into new shares.

In such circumstances, EPS will be expected to fall in the future when the new shares are issued and Widget PLC's profits need to be divided between more shares. This means it is vital to know if EPS and other 'per share' numbers are calculated using the 'basic' or 'diluted' number of shares. The diluted number tells us what per share numbers will be once all the new shares a company has committed to issuing are issued.

So, even the most ubiquitous numbers and ratios used by investors need to be properly understood to avoid unwelcome surprises further down the line. The best data services will provide clear explanations of how their numbers are arrived at and also multiple options for key numbers and ratios.

Interrogating the data

It is vital that screening tools have good functionality. The most basic free screens offer options to look for stocks based on multiple ratios that fall between two values. This will be woefully inadequate for creating a decent screen. A good way to test a screening tool's functionality is to try to run some sophisticated screens, such as those we will look at in the next section of the book. However, here are a few key considerations.

Quantifying

The most intuitive way of thinking about numbers is in absolute terms.

For instance, I want to see stocks with a PE of less than 10.

The trouble with using this kind of rule of thumb is that the market changes all the time. In the worst bear markets, a PE of 10 may not be that cheap, whereas in hot markets a valuation this low may simply point us towards value traps (shares that are cheap and keep on getting cheaper because the issuing company is going down the tubes).

While we will sometimes want to deal in absolute numbers it is also incredibly useful to screen for numbers relative to the market as a whole. It is therefore preferable that a stock screening tool offers the following options:

Percentiles

A very useful way to define the most attractive stocks on a particular metric is to ask to see those that fall within an appropriate range of values. For example, rather than asking for PEs of 10 or below, we could ask for PEs in the bottom 20% among the stocks we're screening.

We could couple this with a test for quality, asking for return on capital employed (ROCE) being in the top 50%, for example.

And then maybe we want to see whether our cheap and reasonable quality stocks are being noticed by other investors. So we could throw in a test for three-month share price performance in the top 25% of the stocks we're screening.

If instead of using percentiles, we simply put our finger in the air and set absolute numbers, it would be very hard to tell whether the bars we were setting for stocks were too low, too high, or just right.

Ranking

Ranking stocks based on different metrics can be a very useful technique, especially if we are able to create a combined ranking.

A famous screening technique that uses this method is the Magic Formula, created by veteran hedge fund star Joel Greenblatt. Greenblatt's recommendation in his classic book *The Little Book That Beats the Market* was to create annually reshuffled portfolios of 30 stocks ranked for valuation and quality.

To create a combined Magic Formula ranking, the two rankings for every stock on each criterion are simply added together and then a new ranking is created from that. Combined rankings can also be created by giving different weightings to several different ranked criteria.

There's no end to the number of rankings that can be combined, but the risk with screens is always that we overcomplicate things and lose sight of what we're really after. Combining lots of rankings, while fun, can easily result in a confused mess.

Alternative questions

A key problem stock screens encounter is that certain types of businesses have different financial characteristics. What may appear exceptional for the market as a whole may be typical for a certain sector. This can lead to the results from some screens becoming dominated by certain types of companies. That's something we have to live with to an extent, but we can also tailor screens to provide more relevant tests for certain sectors.

Either... or...

We sometimes will have two criteria that both point us in the direction we want to go. For example, we may decide that a company can be considered to have a low level of debt either if net gearing (net debt as a percentage of net assets) is below 50% or if net debt represents less than 2.5 times EBITDA. We could therefore choose to screen for companies that qualified on either one or the other of these criteria or both.

The net gearing test is useful for companies which are asset focused – such as real estate companies or utilities – while the net debt to EBITDA test works for companies that need few assets to generate sales and profit – such as software companies.

If... then...

Another way to approach the fact that different stocks have different characteristics is to make tests provisional on the type of company we're looking at.

Again, taking the example of asset-heavy and asset-light companies, we may want to test for valuation using different ratios. For asset-heavy companies we may want to use a price to book value (P/BV) ratio and for asset-light companies enterprise value to sales (EV/sales).

To do this it is good to be able to tell a screen to treat different sectors differently. In the case of our asset-heavy companies, we may want real estate, financials, and utilities to be tested for valuation using P/BV and everything else EV/S.

Likewise, to test for quality we may want to look at RoA for asset-heavy companies coupled with a test for leverage (assets to equity), whereas our asset-light companies may simply be tested based on margins.

If... and...

When screens struggle to produce results it is useful to start loosening up some criteria. We'll see in the next section that my approach to screening is to focus on core criteria that must be satisfied and non-core criteria which only need to be partially satisfied.

To do this we need to tell our screen that a stock should represent a positive result *if* the core criteria are all met *and* a given proportion of our non-core criteria are also met (e.g., four out of six tests).

In my experience this kind of functionality is rare to come by in standard screening tools. A good way round this is for us to roll up our sleeves and deal with data outside these limitations.

Spreadsheets

One of the easiest ways to ensure maximum flexibility when screening is to pull data into a spreadsheet package such as Microsoft Excel, which is what I have always used for the screens I run.

If building a screen in a spreadsheet, the ideal scenario is to have a data service which will automatically update in the spreadsheet itself. This will usually require some kind of software plug-in. However, the more likely option open to private investors is to download data from a data provider.

It is important that the data is as clean as possible when used. This means it needs to be made up of numbers only and not symbols, which a spreadsheet will struggle to recognise. Formulas can be used to clean up messy data.

The internet is full of tutorials about doing all kinds of wonderful things with spreadsheets; most of the knowledge needed is just a Google search away.

My Excel skills are basic and have all been learnt on the hoof with the assistance of an *Excel Data Analysis for Dummies* book and the aforementioned Google searches. The formulas I use are probably extremely inelegant for anyone schooled in spreadsheets, but they work, and for those who are filled with fright by the thought of using computer spreadsheets, a quick run through of the basic and most useful formulas I use should help show they are not that fearsome.

Spreadsheet formulas generally work by using familiar language like 'IF', 'AND', 'OR' and 'RANK' followed by instructions in brackets. The order things are written in has to be one that the computer understands.

Spreadsheets themselves are structured in numbered rows and columns labelled with letters.

Once a formula is in a cell, the formula can be 'dropped down' some or all of the spreadsheet.

If you've read this far in this book you are more than capable of getting to grips with these technicalities, but reading a book on the subject or watching a course to learn the basics will save lots of time and frustration. It is beyond the scope of this book to try to cover this detail.

For now, here are some of the most useful Excel formulas I use to screen stocks. All these formulas assume the data item we are interested in doing something with is in column A of the spreadsheet and row 1. That means the cell is called 'A1'.

Cleaning

As mentioned, when data is downloaded it is often a bit of a mess.

A cell where there is no result may appear as 'N/A', for example. This will result in errors when we try to apply formulas on the cell.

Alternatively, an absent result from a database may display as a 0, which can play merry hell with our screen if we're calculating percentiles (e.g., the cheapest quarter of stocks based on PE).

We may also be served up negative numbers when negatives are irrelevant. For example, negative PEs signify loss-making companies rather than super cheap ones. We normally just don't need to know about these values.

If we turn these values into dashes, Excel will simply ignore them when performing other calculations. Here are a few formulas that allow us to do just that:

An easy way to get rid of non-numeric values is to tell Excel to turn the cell value to a dash, should dividing it by 1 produce an error. If it is not an error, then we tell Excel keep the original A1 cell value.

This is how we ask Excel to do this for us.

=IF(ISERROR(A1/1),"-",A1)

Similarly, if we want 0s to turn into dashes:

=IF(A1=0,"-",A1)

And if we want anything that is valued at 0 or less to turn to dashes we use the mathematic notation for this in the formula which is =<. So we get:

=IF(A1=<0,"-",A1)

We can also do a combo clean up. One thing to note is that we have to pile up closing brackets relating to each individual request at the end of the formula. So:

=IF(ISERROR(A1/1),"-",IF(A1=<0,"-",A1))

Screening

Once our data is cleaned up, we can screen it. All the following formulas will give stocks a score of 1 if the test is passed and 0 if it fails.

It is also good to be sure our dashes get a score of 0, so we'll start every formula with a prefix to tell Excel that dashes are zero scores:

=IF(A1="-",0,...

Absolutes

If cell A1 is a PE ratio and we want to test if it is equal to or less than 10 we could write the formula like this.

=IF(A1="-",0,IF(A1=<10,1,0))

Percentiles

One thing we will frequently want to do is see where a stock lies relative to peers. If we wanted A1 to be in the bottom 25% (in Excel 25% is written 0.25) of all values in the A column (in Excel terminology the A column would be written "A:A") we could write the formula like this:

=IF(A1="-",0,IF(A1=<PERCENTILE(A:A,0.25),1,0))

Alternatively, if we wanted A1 to be in the top 25% of values in column A we could use the following formula:

=IF(A1="-",0,IF(A1=>PERCENTILE(A:A,0.75),1,0))

Ranking

To ask Excel to rank a cell relative to the values in a column, we use the following formula to rank from high to low:

=RANK(A:A,A1)

Or from low to high we use:

=RANK(A:A,A1,1)

To create a combined rank, we can add our rankings together and then re-rank. However, we have to be sure we exclude dash values when we are summing together the ranks, otherwise dashes will be treated as zeros rather than invalid results.

That means we will start our formula telling Excel that if any of the cells we are adding together are dashes, we need to see a dash as our result. If we are adding together ranks in cells B1 and C1 we would tell Excel that if B1 or C1 are dashes we want to see a dash with the following formula:

=IF(OR(B1="-",C1="-"),"-",...

After this we just add a formula to ask Excel to add cell B1 and C1 if it hasn't already put down the result as a dash. The formula for doing this is:

=IF(OR(B1="-",C1="-"),"-",SUM(B1,C1))

If the results appear in column D, we can then use the ranking formula on that column or just order the column from low to high as is.

It is worth facing the initial and inevitable annoyance of making a few mistakes with spreadsheets to get to a point where they become easy to use, as they can open up great possibilities for screening which may not be available when working inside the tools provided by a data service.

That's the end of Part Two. We've now had a full tour of the tools, techniques and data we will need to screen the market for stocks. What we need now are some clear ideas about what to screen for. That's where we're going next in Part Three, which will explain not only the mechanics of four powerful screening strategies, but more importantly, why they make sense.

Two of the best data services I know that are available to UK investors are Sharescope and Stockopedia. These are British companies but also offer access to data on international stocks. They also both provide versions of the screens listed in this book, and readers of this book can get an introductory discount using the code **algyhall** at www.sharescope.co.uk/algyhall for Sharescope and code **ah25** at stk.pe/algyhall for Stokopedia. However, before you dive into any subscriptions, please make sure you trial the service well. Selecting a data service you understand and feel comfortable using can significantly benefit investment returns.

PART THREE

THE SCREENS

In Part Three, we're going to look at four screening strategies and develop a deep understanding of how and why they work:

1. Quality

2. Value

3. Dividend investing

4. Momentum

For each, we will look at a screen that has exploited the key ideas of the strategy to produce returns substantially better than the market. This is how the screens have performed in the first 10 years since they appeared on the pages of the *Investors' Chronicle* magazine. The start dates are March 2011 for the dividend screen, July 2011 for the value screen, August 2011 for Quality and December 2011 for Momentum.

Table 5: Summary of screen performance

	Quality	Value	Dividends	Momentum
10-year cumulative total return	508%	330%	346%	371%
10-year index total return	120%	88%	79%	109%
10-year outperformance of index	388%	242%	267%	262%
Screen CAGR	20.0%	15.7%	16.1%	16.7%
Index CAGR	8.2%	6.5%	6.0%	7.7%
10-year cumulative total return with 1.5% annual charge	422%	270%	284%	305%

Source: Thomson Datastream.

Building your knowledge about why these screens have been successful will empower you to tinker with criteria and make up your own screens from scratch.

More broadly, understanding the factors that make investment strategies work makes it easier to spot stocks with the potential to generate strong performance, while also weeding out those that only offer false promises.

How screen performance is calculated

Performance data for the screens is based on the closing price of all the stocks highlighted by a screen on the day the screen results were first published on the *Investors' Chronicle* website to when the screen was updated the following year.

The performance numbers are based on total returns data (share price plus dividends) from Thomson Datastream. This assumes all dividends are reinvested. It is assumed there is a full reshuffle once a year when the results from a new screen are published.

In every case, the performance is compared with the index that the screen was conducted on. I have also provided a 'with charges' performance number, which assumes an annual 1.5% dealing cost.

The start dates of the 10-year performance periods are arbitrary and not cherry picked. They mark the date on which the screens were first officially published in my *Investors' Chronicle* column.

Where screens fit in

While the performance data based on the annual warts-and-all results from the screens is impressive, the real value of the screens is to produce ideas that can be researched further.

As well as the ideas behind the strategy and criteria, we'll look at the qualitative considerations needed to assess whether shares genuinely deserve a place in your portfolio.

While the screen performance is based on yearly portfolio reshuffles, there is no reason why a one-year holding period would necessarily be the right holding period. In fact, as we'll see in a second when we look at quality shares, a key objective for investors should be to find a share that will compound forever. A buy-and-hold wonder stock.

So, when at the end of each strategy section we look at examples of shares the screens have picked, we will not confine ourselves to assessing a 12-month time period. We'll be looking at how the share has done in the time between being highlighted and my writing this book.

Learning from mistakes

For each screen we will look at one stock that has been a success and one that has been a failure. Assessing the failures is perhaps more important than gloating on the successes. Knowing what to avoid is one of the most profitable skills investors can develop.

By way of example, research conducted by O'Shaughnessy Asset Management has shown that between 1964 and 2015, reconstructing the Russell 2000 to simply exclude the half of stocks that were ranked lowest on basic quality measures boosted annual returns from 11.6% to 15.0%.[15]

So if we can learn to spot the stocks that are likely to be poor performers, we can improve our own investing performance.

When the strategies work best

Before we learn about our four strategies, it is worth knowing when they have been at their most effective in the past. Long-term studies into the performance of different investment styles offer broad clues, although history can only ever provide us with a rough guide. We also can't predict the future, so trying to hop between styles is normally not a great idea.

Generally, we're best off finding an approach to investing that gels with our psyche and sticking with it. Knowing that no strategy should be expected to outperform all the time can help build our resilience as investors when things are not going well. Resilience is a key attribute for successful investing.

Based on a 50-year study by investment firm Research Affiliates,[16] the following table gives a very broad overview of the economic conditions that tend to be best and worst for the strategies we are going to look at.

Importantly, we are talking about good or bad performance versus the broader market. So, a strategy that does badly during an economic recovery will likely make positive returns, but just not keep up with a market. Likewise, a strategy that does well during a recession may just lose less money than everything else. The table represents my own crude interpretations of the findings, but it is not a bad approximation of what we can expect.

Table 6: How the four strategies perform in different economic conditions

| STRATEGY | Economic conditions | | | |
	Recession	Slowdown	Recovery	Growth
Quality	Great	Good	Bad	Good
Value	Bad	Good	Great	Good
Dividends	Great	Great	Bad	Bad
Momentum	Ok	Great	Bad	Good

Source: Research Affiliates.

How to use the screens

Screens should not be a straitjacket. They're there to help. That means we need to be clear on our objective while allowing a degree of flexibility about how we get there. Here are some key considerations:

- We need to understand the strategy and the type of investment we're hoping to find. This *is* something to be rigid about when constructing and running a screen.

- Screens can be applied to any index or selection of stocks. Keep in mind, though, different indices have different characteristics. For example, the US market is more growth-orientated while the UK has many mature dividend-paying companies.

- Be flexible on the fundamentals used. For example, if choosing between using RoE, ROCE and ROIC to test for quality, the most important consideration is likely to be which we have the best data on, combined with which measure we have the best feel for. Picking fundamentals is as much an art as a science.

- When market conditions mean our original screening criteria have stopped producing enough ideas, relax non-core criteria. This could mean only demanding stocks pass three out of five non-core tests, for example. Valuation tests based on absolute values (e.g., a PE of less than 15) are rarely worth having as core screening criteria as they mean radically different things at times when the market PE is high or low.

When we explore our four screens, it is therefore important to keep in mind that there is no need to strictly stick with the way I've applied them over the 10-year periods we will be looking at. And there is no reason to think these screens need to be conducted on the same specific indices I've used over the decade.

Certain market conditions have sometimes caused these screens to stop producing a sufficient number of ideas. We'll explore some of the criteria changes I've made in response. This includes changing the fundamentals tested for and the nature of the tests themselves.

We will also identify each screen's core tests. These are the tests that go to the heart of the strategy, while the non-core tests can be more freely relaxed, only partially met or dropped altogether.

The important point is that there is nothing sacrosanct about the precise criteria used. The key objective is to try to embody the investment strategies we're aiming to emulate.

The other thing that is not sacrosanct about the screens is their relative standing in terms of performance over the last 10 years.

Different investment styles go in and out of favour with great regularity. The dominant style of the last decade can become the most challenged style of the next decade.

But there are many reasons to think all four strategies featured in Part Three are good. We explored this point in Part One, but it is worth recapping why we can expect these strategies to continue to deliver over the long term:

- There is a clear common-sense logic behind them, which we will now start to explore in depth.

- There is a lot of evidence from academic and industry research indicating that stocks that exhibit basic characteristics sought by our four strategies outperform over time, on average.

- Finally, there is the performance of the screens in the 10 years since I began to follow them in my *Investors' Chronicle* column.

QUALITY INVESTING

WE'RE ABOUT TO meet the kind of company every investor should aim to own shares in. The kind of company that over time can make its owners spectacularly rich. We'll also look at a way to screen for this type of stock that delivered total returns of 508% over a decade compared with 120% from the market.

I am referring to quality companies, and our first screen is the High Quality Large Cap screen.

A quality company is one that can produce exceptional returns on the money it invests in its own business. These returns need to be enduring, which requires the company to have a strong competitive advantage. The larger the growth opportunity available to such a company, the richer it will make its owners.

There is one key concept investors in quality companies need to understand. It is a concept that is also one of the most important ideas in personal finance. It is the gateway drug to saving and investing, and something Albert Einstein is reputed to have called "the eighth wonder of the world". It is compounding.

To get an appreciation of the power of this idea, we're going to start our exploration of quality investing with a detour into the world of personal finance and video games. For those who want to cut ahead to the practical screening action, feel free to skip to Chapter 14, where we will look at the screen and then move on to how to interpret its results.

CHAPTER 13

THE EARNING CURVE: WHY QUALITY INVESTING WORKS

COMPOUNDING IS SOMETHING that creeps up on us. It happens in increments that are small enough to go unnoticed but create vast changes to wealth over sufficient periods of time.

In 2020, Nintendo's wildly popular *Animal Crossing: New Horizons* computer game inadvertently gave its avid players a crash course on how compounding works. A glitch in the game allowed savvy players to harness and fast-forward the power of compounding to make their *Animal Crossing* selves fantastically rich.

Let's look at what happened.

Animal Crossing is what gamers call a social simulation. In a world of anthropomorphic animals, players do very life-like stuff, such as going fishing, collecting fossils and making their houses really nice.

For an uninitiated child of the 1980s who grew up playing games like *Commando* and *Barbarian: The Ultimate Warrior* (me), it all sounds a bit weird. But for today's more rounded and considered youngsters (my son), such games are great fun.

The lesson in personal finance and compounding came thanks to *Animal Crossing's* Bank of Nook. For a brief and happy time, players could deposit Bells, the *Animal Crossing* currency, at the bank and earn a monthly interest rate of 0.5%.

While 0.5% a month may be much better than anything available from banks in the real world, for those who don't know about the magic of compounding, it probably doesn't sound like very much. It's a small number. However, compounding turns small numbers into huge ones over a long enough time frame.

Compounding works like a snowball rolling down a hill. A money snowball. The snowball may start small, but with each turn it picks up a little bit more snow. The ever-increasing surface area of the snowball means the amount of snow it picks up increases with each and every turn. The effects may not be very noticeable at first, but it doesn't take too long for the snowball to get big enough that it is picking up increasing multiples of its starting mass with each new rotation. If the slope goes on for long enough, you end up with a gigantic snowball at the bottom.

Back to those gamers and how they created their own high-speed money snowball. The Bank of Nook's 0.5% monthly interest meant an owner of 100,000 Bells on deposit earned 500 Bells in the first month. In month two the compounding starts. That's because 0.5% is now earned on all 100,500 Bells – the original sum plus last month's interest. So that means 502.5 Bells interest in month two.

Even for the most avid *Animal Crossing* fan, an extra 2.5 Bells is hardly likely to sound like the eighth wonder of the world.

Watching compounding in action in real time is even more boring than watching paint dry. The process feels glacial even when returns are actually very attractive, such as the 0.5% a month offered by the Bank of Nook.

That's where the glitch in the game came in. By resetting the system clocks on their consoles, players found they could time travel. That meant they saw the power of compounding in minutes rather than decades. Delayed gratification became instant gain.

Players who deposited 100,000 Bells in the bank and skipped ahead in time 38 years logged back in as millionaires. In the final year of the 38 they would have earned nearly 60,000 Bells interest compared with just over 5,000 Bells in year one. That's the magic of compounding.

Nintendo quickly got wise to what was going on as more and more people exploited the glitch. In Spring 2020, as part of a Nature Day update, players received a letter from the Bank of Nook's manager. It told them interest rates had been slashed and maximum payments had been capped at 9,999 Bells.

It was a fun and educational way to see the power of compounding while it lasted.

Real-world compounding

Over the past three decades, real-world investors have been able to build their wealth even faster than *Animal Crossing* players, even if they have not been able to time travel. For British investors in the MSCI World index, compound annual returns, while hugely erratic on a year-to-year basis, have averaged a bit under 10%

over the 30 years to the end of 2020. Compounding means a return of 10% a year is enough to double your money in a little over seven years. If returns stay at 10%, the time to double will remain the same even though the amount of money now being doubled has itself doubled.

Doubling your money twice means quadrupling your original investment. That would take about 14.5 years. Doubling again, which at 10% means a 22-year wait, means an eightfold increase from your starting point. And for those prepared to leave compounding to do its work for a full 30 years, doubling would have happened about four whole times. That would mean a 16-fold return – i.e., doubling-on-doubling-on-doubling-on-doubling. And we could go on. It's another money snowball.

Based on actual historical returns, a British investor who put £100,000 into the MSCI World index would have become a millionaire in about 28 years to the end of 2020. This does not account for the very real drag from inflation. Adjusted for this, it would take 37 years for the equivalent of £100,000 invested into the MSCI World index in 1983 to have turned into a bit over £1 million at the end of 2020. An amazing outcome for just patiently waiting.

How compounding works inside a quality company

While compounding is best known as a personal finance concept, it also occurs inside good companies. The caveat is, no company has limitless growth prospects, and the power of compounding will tail off sooner than it does for an entire stock market.

To understand how compounding works inside a company, let's take an example of one that can generate a 20% return on every pound invested in its business.

The defining characteristic of company quality for investors is the ability of a company to generate high returns on investment and sustain high returns in the face of competition and changing economic circumstances.

For simplicity we'll also assume the company has no limits on its growth in the period we're studying, and its assets require no maintenance spending to keep them productive. We've very much entered the world of the hypothetical for a moment.

The company is set up with an initial £1m equity investment. Equity is the bit of a company's capital that has been funded by and belongs to shareholders. Beyond this initial bit of external financing, the company makes all future investment in the business from its own profits. Given the limitless growth on offer, all profits are ploughed back into expansion.

What happens as this company grows?

In year one it generates £200,000 of profit. In other words, 20% of that initial £1m investment made by shareholders. This is reinvested in the business. So in year two the company generates 20% from equity of £1.2m (the original £1m plus the £200,000 added from last year's profit). It therefore makes a profit of £240,000 in year two, and we will start year three with £1.44m of equity to generate profit from.

We've heard this story before. It's our money snowball. The process of value creation is now happening inside a company rather than in a Bank of Nook savings account or from an investment in the broader stock market.

Amazingly, it only takes 38 years for this company to create equity worth £1 billion from the initial £1m investment, as Figure 1 illustrates. A 1,000-fold increase. It's easy to see why investors who believe they have found a genuinely high-quality company with exceptional growth potential don't tend to quibble too much about the price they pay for its shares. If the magic of compounding really works, shares can prove great value even when they trade at seemingly outlandish valuations.

Figure 1: How a 20% annual return turns £1m into £1bn

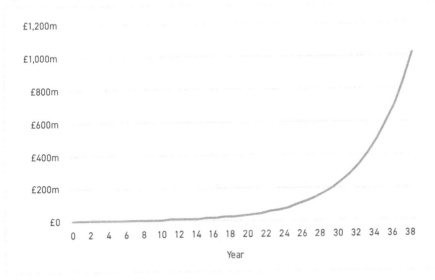

Paying up for quality

Top-performing, quality-focused fund manager Terry Smith provided a prosaic illustration of the eye-popping valuations quality stocks are able to justify in his 2021 New Year letter to investors.

He looked at 25 high-quality companies of the type that his fund invests in. Based on the returns the stocks actually achieved, he calculated what maximum PE an investor could have paid in 1973 to achieve compound growth in the value of their investment of 7% a year in the 46 years to 2019. That return represented a good chunk of outperformance over the MSCI World Index's annual 6.2% over the same period, measured in US dollars.

While one of the 25 stocks justified a PE of zero, for the rest of the sample group the multiples investors could have paid and outperformed ranged from 16 to a massive 281. The median justified PE was a wince-worthy 64. Nine of the 25 companies, or 36%, were able to justify a PE of over 100 in 1973.

Smith was not looking at any old list of companies though. He was looking at resilient businesses with significant competitive advantages. A lot of companies can go through periods of looking like they may fit this bill, but few manage to deliver over the long term.

Smith's solution is not to be tempted to try to buy quality at bargain prices by looking for the winners of tomorrow. Rather, he looks for companies that 'have already won'. That's the type of approach of the High Quality Large Cap stock screen. We will look at how the screen works in the next chapter.

Why we overlook quality

It is incredibly hard for us to properly appreciate the money-making magic of quality companies for two reasons. First, we struggle to spot the real thing and, second, as we've just seen with Smith's PE study, we struggle to correctly value it when it is in plain sight.

Both can be explained by what was termed the 'straight-line instinct' by Hans Rosling. Rosling was a much-celebrated physician, best-selling author, data-visualisation pioneer and founder of Gapminder, a 'factfullenss' education organisation. His observation was that while progress rarely takes the form of a straight line, our brains are hardwired to expect it to.[17]

Our brains also tend to over-extrapolate recent events, whether good or bad. The downside of these instincts is that we see amazing periods of growth as continuing in a straight line, and we are gullible to a great story. We are easily convinced the companies we have fallen for will be able to produce high returns on their investments and growth.

We overlook the fact that high growth rates often quickly decelerate or even reverse. We also easily forget that most companies produce pedestrian returns on investment in the long term. On the flip side, though, when we do find a genuine, high-quality growth story, we struggle to appreciate the true potential. We continue to view things in terms of a straight line and fail to appreciate that real progress is best regarded as an upward sloping curve, like our company that turned £1m of equity into £1bn in 38 years Our minds simply hit a roadblock when trying to contemplate the exponential effects of compounding and the valuations this justifies.

In some regards this is very reasonable. No one can see the future, and all companies at some point can expect to see their competitive advantage disappear.

But this also means value is often left on the table for investors, even when companies have long displayed all the hallmarks of being the real deal. There is amazing money to be made from backing true compounding machines.

So, despite being so hankered after, those companies that are clearly delivering persistent high returns and growth can often turn out to be underappreciated even when their shares command what appear on the surface to be high valuations. We're now going to look at a screen that attempts to hunt out this exact type of stock.

CHAPTER 14

SCREENING FOR HIGH-QUALITY STOCKS

IN THIS CHAPTER, we look at the High Quality Large Cap screen.

First, let's have a quick recap of what we have learned about quality investing:

- Quality companies create value for shareholders by achieving a high return on the investments they make in their business.

- Quality companies possess an enduring competitive advantage that will allow them to continue to make high returns long into the future.

- The bigger the opportunity such a company has to invest in growth, the more significant the effect of compounding will be.

- We are prone to overestimate the number of quality growth plays available to invest in.

- We are also prone to undervalue real quality growth plays.

- There is a big opportunity for investors that is often hidden in plain sight.

Why start with a quality screen?

There's a reason we're starting our exploration of screens with one that looks for high-quality compounding machines. It's because, no matter what strategy we pursue, this is the type of stock we ultimately want to unearth.

Some of our other screens try to find stocks that are being more obviously overlooked than the quarry of the High Quality Large Cap screen. All the same, for these other screens, finding an overlooked high-quality stock is hitting the jackpot.

The advantage of finding a high-quality stock that is not widely recognised for being as exceptional as it really is, is that its price can appreciate massively when other investors wake up to its charms as its valuation multiple balloons.

But investors do not have to hunt for hidden gems to profit from high-quality companies.

The screen we are going to look at in this chapter looks for companies that display credentials that already clearly suggest they are high-quality businesses.

There can be high price-tags attached to companies that have genuine and well-recognised competitive advantages alongside well-recognised growth opportunities. Such stocks can still deliver exceptional returns. They are often worth paying up for. That's how my High Quality Large Cap stock screen managed to deliver a six-fold return over its first decade of life.

Track record

In the 10 years from its inception in August 2011, the High Quality Large Cap screen produced a cumulative total return of 508% compared with 120% from the FTSE All-Share Index in the same period. The FTSE All-Share is the index the screen combs through to select stocks. This performance is shown in Figure 2.

The cumulative performance is based on the assumption that each time a new screen was published on the *Investors' Chronicle* website, which was annually, the entire portfolio was reshuffled.

Details of all the annual selections of stocks can be found in this book's appendix.

Even though the performance numbers are notional, it is nice to inject some real-world considerations into the mix. That means accounting for costs associated with share dealing. If we assume a 1.5% annual charge, the cumulative performance from this screen drops from 508% to 422%. The difference between the two figures illustrates why the compounding of costs should always be a major consideration for investors as well as the compounding of gains.

This screen has also proved very dependable over the decade. At its worst, the average peak to trough fall from its stock selections was 26%, compared with 35% for the index.

Figure 2: High-quality large caps

Source: Thomson Datastream.

While looking at cumulative performance is a helpful indicator that this screen is useful, the stocks highlighted are intended as a source of ideas rather than to provide off-the-shelf portfolios.

There are also two things to keep in mind when considering the performance. This screen is designed to have a manageable output to encourage further research into the ideas it spits out. That means in some of its most fallow years, it has only highlighted four stocks. Furthermore, I feel the screen lost its way a little bit for three years between 2015 and 2017. I changed the criteria in 2018 with excellent results. We'll see why the screening criteria needed changing in a bit. But the overarching lesson is that market conditions change with time, and screens have to adapt.

Paying up for quality

In order to buy into fantastic companies it can be necessary to pay up. And as we have seen, it can be well worth doing so. But when paying up for stocks it is important to keep in mind that high share prices do create valuation risk, even when business risks are low.

If a company's shares are priced for perfection, even a minor disappointment can be quite devastating in share price terms. And as we will see when we look at momentum investing, the market has a habit of getting carried away with great stories, even if the story is genuinely backed up by an excellent investment case.

This is a major consideration for investors in quality stocks today. A good illustration of this can be seen in the re-rating experienced by the five stocks that made up the first ever selection of the High Quality Large Cap screen in 2011 (there were actually six stocks identified by the screen at the time, but one has been taken over during the decade). These five companies are shown in Table 7.

Based on a forecast next 12-month (NTM) PE ratio, the re-rating experienced by the stocks has been almost three times the re-rating experience by the index. So while the FTSE All-Share has experienced a 52% re-rating, the five High Quality Large Cap shares have on average re-rated by an incredible 148%.

Table 7: The first six stocks selected by the High Quality Large Cap screen in August 2011 and their subsequent PE re-rating

	NTM PE 11 Aug 2011	NTM PE 11 Aug 2021	10-yr re-rating	10-yr total return
Spirax-Sarco	14.4	47.1	227%	1024%
Halma	13.8	46.3	236%	854%
Experian	13.4	34.2	155%	434%
James Halstead	16.3	28.0	72%	259%
Rotork	17.0	25.3	49%	164%
FTSE All-Share	8.9	13.5	52%	120%

Source: FactSet.

As it happens, the total return from buying and holding the original six stock portfolio, at 507%, would be almost exactly what the return was from switching between portfolios each year, before accounting for any dealing costs.

This illustrates one of the other beauties of targeting quality compounders. Done right, the best trading strategy is simply to buy and hold, and then keep holding. Finding the right company to buy and combining this with inactivity tends to be richly rewarded.

But higher valuations in this area mean there is less potential upside for investors today than there was 10 years ago as there is less room for re-rating upside.

A similar story to the one told by the re-rating of the stocks selected by the first High Quality Large Caps screen is told by the overall valuation of the flagship fund of Terry Smith – the star fund manager we just met in Chapter 13.

His Fundsmith Equity fund has seen the average free cash flow (FCF) yield of stocks held plummet from 5.8% to 2.7% over the 10 years from the end of 2011 to the end of 2021.

Criteria

While a stock screen can attempt to sniff out signs of a competitive advantage in a business, it cannot be expected to do all the work. Trying to understand if a company has a robust competitive advantage – also known as an economic moat – is a largely qualitative process.

We will look at some of the key features of a business that suggest a moat exists a bit later in this chapter. But first, it's time to play the numbers game.

The High Quality Large Cap screen's criteria draws heavily on the quality ratios we explored in Chapter 8. The tests are:

- Higher than median average (mid-ranking) return on equity (RoE). **CORE TEST**

- Higher than median average operating margin. **CORE TEST**

- Operating margin growth over the past three years.

- RoE growth over the past three years.

- Higher than median average operating margin in each of the past three years.

- Higher than median average return on equity (RoE) in each of the past three years.

- Interest cover of five times or more.

- Positive free cash flow.

- Operating profit growth over the past three years.

- Earnings growth forecast for each of the next two years.

- Market cap over £1bn.

How it works

Let's think about the two core criteria the screen uses.

These are the two quality tests for above median RoE and operating margins. If a company has a strong competitive advantage, these metrics should be high. When I've needed to boost the screen's output of ideas in the past, I've allowed stocks to fail one or more of the tests, *except these two core tests*. These two tests really need to be passed in my opinion.

Something to note about these core tests is that it may not sound that demanding to just ask that stocks exceed the median (mid-point) average. However, experience has shown this is a high enough bar to produce sensible results when combined with at least some of the other non-core tests.

These core tests are also a bit tougher than they may first appear because loss-making companies, which have negative RoEs and operating margins, are excluded before medians (mid-ranking metrics) are calculated.

Core tests

RoE

The test: Higher than median average return on equity (RoE).

We've talked a lot (in Part Two) about the importance of the amount of profit a company makes from the investments it makes in its business in determining its quality. The RoE test is the key method this screen has for assessing this.

When looking at the RoE ratio in Chapter 8, we saw how its major weakness is that it can be flattered by companies taking on large amounts of debt. We'll also briefly explore the reasons for this again when looking at the screen's interest cover test.

For our quality test, the main implication is that high levels of debt generally increase risk and thereby reduce business quality. That's not what we're after here.

But the ratio also has advantages for screens comparing companies from many different sectors. The key benefit of RoE is that it provides a broad sweep on the question of quality. For some companies it can make a lot of sense to take on debt to boost profits. Financial gearing can be an important and sensible contributor to a company's returns if end markets are defensive and the underlying business is strong.

Bearing in mind the weaknesses of RoE, though, it is important that this test is supported by the other core test for operating margins. The interest cover test, which we will look at in more detail shortly, also attempts to check the balance sheet is not loaded with excessive debt. Meanwhile, the consistency test, requiring above median RoE for three years, is also important to check the robustness of this quality measure.

Operating margins

The test: Higher than median average operating margin.

The limitations of RoE make a second test for quality especially useful for this screen. The RoE test is backed up by a test for high operating margins. High margins are a great indicator that a company may have a strong competitive advantage. It needs to have qualities special enough to make people pay up for its wares, or business processes advantageous enough to let it operate at a lower cost than its competitors, or potentially both.

However, the margin test does restrict the type of quality company our screen is going to highlight. The screen essentially excludes businesses which make excellent returns on investments by generating lots of sales from their assets but at relatively low margins. On our journey through quality ratios, we discovered companies with high capital turn ratios (producing a lot of sales from capital employed) often generate great returns from high sales even if margins are low.

To broaden this screen out we could introduce an *either/or* test to replace the high margin test. Stocks would pass *either* if they displayed attractive margins *or* if they displayed attractive capital turn. Or we could just run two separate versions of the screen looking for these different kinds of quality stocks.

While I can't quibble with the High Quality Large Cap screen's 10-year performance, in some ways I wish I'd been savvy enough to have included such an *either/or* test when I devised the screen 10 years ago. Still, a central aim of my stock screen column has been to try to stay as consistent as reasonably possible with the criteria of each screen. In doing so, my hope has been to build up a better long-term understanding of how each screen creates value. Although as we'll see in a second, I have had to take cues from the market and make some pragmatic changes.

Another alternative approach would be to just screen for companies with an attractive return on invested capital (ROIC) or return on capital employed (ROCE). These were the first ratios we looked at when exploring measures of quality. These are great ratios because they are not influenced by a company's financing decisions, and they also capture the impact of both capital turn and margin.

One of the problems I've had with taking this approach historically is that I have not been able to get consistent data. Often, devising stock screens is about finding a way to achieve an end goal in the best way possible based on the data available.

Ultimately, RoE and operating margins have great strengths as quality indicators and have done very well for this screen over a decade.

Non-core tests

Consistency over three years

The tests:

- Operating margin growth over the past three years.

- RoE growth over the past three years.

- Higher than median average operating margin in each of the past three years.

- Higher than median average return on equity (RoE) in each of the past three years.

As well as screening for attractive quality ratios, we want ratios that have both improved and been consistently strong over the last three years. The idea here is to avoid stocks that are showing signs of quality that may just be a flash in the pan.

Ideally, we'd look back over a full market cycle to understand how robust a company's performance has been against a range of economic conditions. However, stock screens need to keep things simple to be most effective.

Looking back over a full cycle could lead us to needlessly eliminate opportunities. This kind of long-term analysis is often nuanced and usually more valuable when undertaken after the screening process.

When testing for consistency, we also have to think hard about how to deal with genuine one-off events, such as Covid-19. We could take one of two views about the significance.

Firstly, we could view it as exceptional. We don't want to miss opportunities to invest in quality compounders because something totally unforeseen has muddied the track record... or do we?

The other view to take would be that a defining characteristic of real quality is a business that is resilient regardless of the slings and arrows it encounters. A quality business is one that is so relevant to its customers it can seize opportunity even from adversity. We saw many companies do just this in the depths of the Covid-19 pandemic. The trouble is, when it comes to the pandemic's corporate success stories, it's extremely hard to say how much was down to the luck of being in the right sector at the right time as opposed to genuine resilience.

Fortunately, there is always the option of running two variations of a screen in order to capture both perspectives. For me as a journalist, the constraint of writing a single column means for clarity's sake I needed to take a single view on this subject in 2020. My post-Covid screen struck a compromise. While it still required growth from RoE and margins, it dropped the screen's tests demanding that ratios be consistently better than the median over each of the past three years.

Interest cover

The test: interest cover of five times or more.

Our screening criteria tries to ensure high RoE is not a reflection of a company taking on excessive balance sheet risk by loading up on debt.

RoE compares profit to net asset value (NAV). As net debt is subtracted from total assets to get to the NAV figure, the more debt a company has, the smaller the NAV number will be. In turn, because we divide profit by NAV to calculate RoE, the smaller NAV is the higher returns will look.

The earnings number used in the equation will also shrink due to the company having to pay a higher interest charge. But when times are good, this will not be as pronounced as the reduction in the NAV number.

The screen tests for interest cover to get an indication of whether debt appears to be at a reasonable level and is not the main reason for high RoE. The test in question is that interest cover is five times or more. And because the interest reported in company accounts includes amounts relating to rental liabilities and pensions, this test usefully covers a lot of bases.

Cash generation and balance sheet strength

The test: positive free cash flow.

As we've already seen in Chapter 5, quality is not only about the profits a company makes on its investments. Cash generation and balance sheet strength are major considerations too. The interest cover test provides the dual function in this screen of supporting the RoE test while also signalling that debt is unlikely to jeopardise the business.

The cash generation test the screen uses is soft. All we're asking for is that free cash flow (FCF) is positive. It's a kind of bare-minimum test. Part of the reason for setting a low bar here is that FCF can be quite variable from year to year, as has been discussed in previous chapters.

But there is another practical stock-screening reason. It is often counterproductive to ask for too much from a screen. If we're too prescriptive we miss out on opportunities, and we can also quickly reduce the output of ideas from our screens to zero.

Profit growth

The tests:

- Operating profit growth over the past three years.

- Earnings growth forecast for each of the next two years.

The other soft test used by this screen is for growth. We want the companies coming through the screen to have grown profits in the past and to be forecast to grow profits in the future. But by how much, we don't care.

This is not to suggest growth is a minor consideration for quality compounders. In fact, it is one of the two vital ingredients that make the magic of compounding happen, the other being high returns on investment. However, growth lends itself well to qualitative assessments. It is also infuriatingly hard to forecast, as we'll see when we look at our final market-beating screening strategy based on momentum.

Perhaps more fundamentally, this is a screen looking to identify companies with quality businesses. It therefore puts quality first in its list of priorities. And let's not forget, when companies lack growth opportunities, they should return more cash to shareholders, either through buybacks or dividends that can be reinvested. Both types of cash returns allow the magic of compounding to occur, albeit in another way.

Size

The test: market cap over £1bn.

While all quality companies started out small at one point, and there can be good results screening for quality small caps, size does have significance for quality. Large companies tend to be more established and robust. And as we've seen, one of the strengths of this strategy is that it looks for companies that have already proven themselves rather than trying to identify the next big thing. The latter is a risk we just don't need to take.

The screen is still prepared to fish in a part of the market that many would regard as containing small fry, but its £1bn market cap cut-off avoids the tiddlers which may lack real substance as quality plays. It also reflects the more diminutive size of the UK market compared with the corporate titans that can be found elsewhere, especially in the US.

Adapting this screen

The High Quality Large Cap screen has not always been so blind to issues of valuation as it is today. When I originally came up with the criteria, markets were still getting over the fallout from the Great Financial Crisis. Investors could buy into quality plays on the cheap. The screen therefore employed tests to try to bag shares in great companies at bargain prices. It did this using the price to earnings growth (PEG) ratio, which seeks to balance the considerations of valuation and growth prospects.

To recap from Chapter 10, the formula for the PEG ratio is:

PEG = price earnings (PE) ratio / EPS growth rate

However, things changed. For the three years from 2015 to 2017 (inclusive), the output from the screen didn't seem to pass the smell test. The screen was finding attractively valued stocks that looked as if they belonged to quality companies based on the numbers, but on closer inspection things did not add up. There were too many companies dependent on strong economic conditions to generate their returns, otherwise known as cyclicals. This type of company tends to be lowly valued when times are good in anticipation that it will suffer badly as soon as the business cycle turns. We'll meet one of these properly in Chapter 16.

In 2018, I dropped the screen's valuation tests, although I did continue to monitor how the old version of the screen performed. The screen that paid little attention to valuations has gone on to perform extremely well. My ghost monitoring of the original screen found it performed very poorly by comparison. But more importantly than the improved performance of the new screen, the companies the revamped screen highlighted on the whole did look like a high-quality bunch.

The other adaptation made to this screen over the years is, as already mentioned, to allow stocks to fail one or more of the non-core tests at times when the output is low.

It is easy to assume that there is nothing worth investing in when a trusted screen produces no results. In my experience, though, this is rarely the case. We must always be prepared to adapt to circumstances.

So, having screened for quality stocks, how do we go beyond the numbers in assessing whether a company really does have a sustainable competitive advantage? That is what we'll look into next.

CHAPTER 15

FROM QUANTITATIVE TO QUALITATIVE – HOW TO IDENTIFY REAL QUALITY

WHILE OUR High Quality Large Cap screen looks at some of the key ratios that are helpful in highlighting quality plays, to understand if a company really lives up to the 'quality' billing, we must understand its business and where it may possess a competitive advantage.

In the real world, companies are far more complex than our example of a company turning £1m of equity into £1bn from Chapter 13.

The road to profitability is also normally much less straightforward. However, wonderful feats of compounding do happen. Corporate poster children for what investors often refer to as quality compounders include the likes of Amazon, where shareholders would have made about 500 times their money over the last two decades, and Costco, which has managed a 180-fold return over the same period.

But for this kind of insane value creation to take place, companies need something extremely special going for them. They need both huge growth potential and a formidable 'moat' to protect their high returns on investment from competitors. We should not move on under false pretences: such situations are extremely rare. While we all know of Amazon, it is easy to forget the droves of dot.com carcasses it has left in its wake over the years.

Normally, when companies make fantastic profits, they quickly attract a lot of attention from entrepreneurs and investors. Competitors set out to mimic what they're doing. Investors throw cash at these rival ventures. As competition and supply increases in an industry, pricing power and profitability tend to rapidly deteriorate. Returns quickly go from the spectacular to the average. In fact, in many industries that rely on large, up-front, long-term investment, spending splurges can cause massive value destruction.

Take British mobile telecoms company Vodafone. When its shares first started to trade on the London Stock Exchange in the early 1990s following a demerger from a listed electronics group called Racal Electronics, it boasted a return on assets (RoA) of over 30%. The returns diminished during the decade as the group spent heavily to fund its breakneck growth and as competition increased. However, RoA remained healthy and was still over 20% in 1999.

But as is often the case, bust followed boom. Profits plunged when the dot.com bubble popped. RoA went negative. And while the company did manage to claw back some ground, with the mobile phone sector now mature and fiercely competitive, the company was never again able to make anywhere near the money it did during the 1990s.

For the last five years, Vodafone's RoA has bobbed between low single-digit positive and negative numbers (see Figure 3).

Figure 3: When 'Quality' is fleeting – Vodafone never reclaimed its dot.com mojo

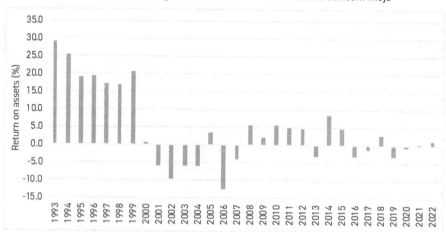

Source: FactSet.

More often than not, moats are breached or are found to have never really existed in the first place. They also usually prove to be weaker than we realise when a company is doing well.

Sources of competitive advantage

There are six main types of moat investors should stay on the lookout for. None are permanent, but they can protect profitability for a long time. Knowing what to look for makes assessing a company's competitive position far easier to understand. Here's a whistlestop tour of the key sources of competitive advantage:

1. Scale

When companies become large, they can often find ways to do things more efficiently than rivals. Examples include the ability to: invest in state-of-the-art factories; better fund research and development (R&D) and product innovation; bargain down suppliers; establish a geographic footprint that creates superior distribution; and fund nationwide advertising campaigns.

While scale advantage sounds like something that is the preserve of vast corporations, it can also exist when a company dominates a small niche. We'll see one such example in Chapter 16. If a market is not big enough to support more than one player, the incumbent can generate really spectacular profits.

For businesses like this, the only opportunity for growth is often through acquisition. Many small acquisitions in highly fragmented markets tend to serve shareholders better in such circumstances than a single big 'transformative' deal.

2. Switching costs

Sometimes it is costly for a company's customers to switch their business to another provider. Such companies find themselves with a 'sticky' customer base. That means a steady stream of sales from customers that won't quibble too much about price increases.

Critical business software is an example of a product with high switching costs. It can be a huge faff to switch from a familiar software programme to a new, unfamiliar one. That's especially true for corporate software packages which are used throughout a firm.

Other types of company, especially in the industrial space, try to work closely with customers at early stages of product design. This can make a company integral to its customers' businesses. The stickiness of these relationships increases if what is being sold to the customer is a relatively small proportion of the overall product cost and the end market is fragmented.

3. Network effect

Some products become more valuable the more they are used. While this type of moat used to be chiefly associated with physical distribution and branch networks, in the digital age, virtual networks are where the action really is.

A good example is social networking sites, where a user's proximity to other users makes for a better experience and more lucrative ad sales opportunities for the site's owner.

4. Cost advantages

Some companies have a particular attribute that makes them the lowest-cost producer. This could apply to the owner of a particularly high-yielding gold mine, for example.

Cost advantage can also come about due to superior business processes that allow a company to outcompete rivals. Processes can be easy to copy, but the advantage from developing a business culture based on the pursuit of excellence can be surprisingly enduring – even if it does sound terribly cheesy!

5. Brand

People pay more for big brands and often show tremendous loyalty towards branded products, even during economic downturns. Breakthrough brands can produce spectacular growth for their owners.

Franchise businesses, which allow franchisees use of a brand in exchange for a fee, are perhaps one of the purest examples of the exploitation of brand value.

6. Intellectual property and regulation

The final well-recognised way to keep competitors at bay is through legal means.

Companies that successfully gain patents on must-have products, technologies and processes can keep a market to themselves for many years. This is key to the business model of pharmaceutical and biotechnology companies.

However, we need to keep in mind that few of the many millions of patents granted create any meaningful competitive advantage for their owner.

Superior R&D can also be used by companies to keep an intellectual property (IP) advantage even if there is no legal backing.

Regulatory barriers and official licences can also keep competition at bay. The sky-high margins of tobacco companies stand testament to the advantages of being an incumbent in a highly regulated industry.

From theory to practice

Knowing what to look out for to determine whether a business model has an enduring competitive advantage is incredibly valuable in assessing the output of screens. We're now going to try to get a deeper, hands-on understanding by looking at a couple of the stocks highlighted by the High Quality Large Cap screen over the last decade.

CHAPTER 16

STOCK SELECTION FOR HIGH QUALITY LARGE CAP

WHAT SEEMS CLEAR in theory can often be a lot more confusing to understand in practice. We're going to look at two stocks selected by the High Quality Large Cap screen over the last 10 years to get a better flavour of what we need to look out for. The stocks have been chosen because I believe they offer great examples of some of the key considerations in understanding the results from this screen. We'll start with a success story and then move on to a failure.

The success: a compounding epic

Fantasy figurine and game maker Games Workshop (GAW) has twice been highlighted by the High Quality Large Cap screen. It's delivered a total return of 485% since being highlighted on 26 September 2017 and 122% since being highlighted on 3 September 2019, both to the end of the 10-year performance period monitored by this book. Despite such strong numbers, over those years the stock has demonstrated both the highs and lows of a strategy focused on quality and makes a great case study for that reason.

The other reason for picking Games Workshop is because it is a great example of the value that can be created by a strong brand and intellectual property. It also boasts scale advantages because while it is not a big company, it operates in a niche hobby market. That means despite its size, its manufacturing activities, which involve making miniature figurines, can provide an edge.

These characteristics were key clues for investors that this company really had something special when it was originally highlighted by the screen.

Games Workshop was founded by three fantasy fanatics in 1975. After a spell of private equity ownership, it floated on the London Stock Exchange in 1996.

While the company's products have enjoyed an enduring popularity with its customer base, for a long time investors were less interested in its shares. From an investment perspective, a key issue was that the company seemed very erratic.

Its schedule for launching games paid little heed to the market's desire for regular, incremental sales and earnings growth. Meanwhile it paid its dividends based on what made sense for the business, not what tallied with shareholders' wants. That's to say, it distributed surplus cash regardless of whether it was less or more than it had handed out the previous year.

While there is good reason to applaud these best-for-the-business tactics, such behaviour is nevertheless frowned on by owners of public companies. The shares consequently traded at a feeble rating for many years, bobbing between a high single- and low double-digit forecast PE ratio between 2009 and the time when the High Quality Large Cap screen first highlighted Games Workshop in 2017.

Its underlying quality credentials – based on its brand, loyal customer base and dominance of a niche market – were being overlooked by investors, but with the help of the screen highlighting the situation, were evident to those who took time to take a closer look.

By the time the screen next highlighted the stock in 2019, it was well on the way from being a recovery/growth play in the market's eyes to a fully fledged quality compounder. What had happened?

Let the quality shine through

For a long time, the immense value associated with Games Workshop's dominance of a niche market lay dormant. However, a new chief executive appointed in 2015, Kevin Rountree, managed to unleash it. By the time the screen highlighted the stock in 2017, his influence was already becoming clear.

The potted history of this transformation is that following a five-year period of cost-cutting and reorganisation, Games Workshop made a big push towards customer engagement starting in 2015. The company started to make use of digital media and mobilised its highly engaged and loyal fan base as a marketing machine, partly through fan-created content.

Turnover and profit growth started to turn up sharply. The company was now selling more of its traditional miniature figurines and games through both its own shops and third parties. It also saw royalty revenue start to take off. Royalty revenue includes things like licensing intellectual property for computer games and film. Royalty revenue is almost pure profit. It was also another reassuring sign of brand quality at the time the stock was highlighted by the screen. Figure 4 shows what growth looked like by the time the screen highlighted the stock for the second time in 2019.

Figure 4: Games Workshop sales and EPS growth (2010–2019)

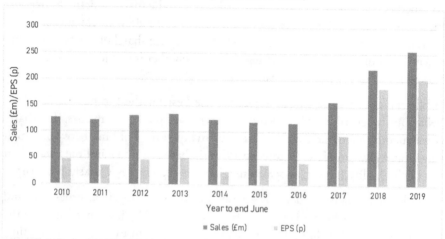

Source: FactSet.

Rountree also made the company pay more attention to investors as well as fantasy fans. A key element of the investor charm offensive involved making the cycle of product launches come more into line with the financial reporting cycle. This made the excellent margins and returns the company was able to achieve far easier to appreciate.

Furthermore, as sales increased, the company's margins and return on investment ballooned because a large amount of its cost base is fixed. It benefited from so-called operating gearing. It was able to make more use of its existing manufacturing and distribution facilities.

Investment was needed to meet growing demand. Big investment in new capacity increases the amount of capital employed by a business. Until a good amount of the new capacity is utilised, this can temporarily push down a company's overall return on capital employed. But as long as margins are maintained, returns on the investment should once again become very attractive in the longer term. As Games Workshop has the ability to keep margins high, shareholders have had reason to applaud every penny ploughed into expansion. This is what makes compounding work.

And there was certainly a growth opportunity. The UK market for Games Workshop's products was already relatively mature when the screen spotted it, but based on its penetration on home shores, there was significant room for expansion in Europe and North America. This was only helped by fan engagement and the wider cultural penetration of the brand through those ridiculously profitable royalty deals with media companies.

There is a blue-sky element to the royalty deals, too. As has been witnessed with iconic pop-culture fantasy brands such as Marvel, the ability for the right owner to create value can be immense.

The only way isn't up

But it has not all been smooth going for the business. One of the reasons this is such an interesting company for us to look at is because as well as illustrating the virtues of competitive advantage, it also helps us understand the dangers associated with valuation risk.

The experience of Games Workshop shareholders since the autumn of 2021 has illustrated the blows that quality investors can endure and why it makes sense for investors to seek diversification even when they are buying seemingly robust companies.

Towards the end of 2021, brokers began to make small downgrades to EPS forecasts due to post-Covid supply chain difficulties. This coincided with news that fans were unhappy with a new zero-tolerance policy on the production of fan-created games, animations and videos, which was announced in July 2021.

The shares' valuation dropped from a forecast PE of nearly 33 in February 2021 to just under 25 by October. That is still a lot better than the PE of 15 when the High Quality Large Cap screen first highlighted the stock in 2017, but a painful de-rating for anyone who bought at the top. For such buyers, a minor disappointment from a trading perspective and forecasts has meant a major share price drop.

The share price fall not only demonstrates the risk of high valuation. The large fixed-cost base that creates positive operational gearing when times are good goes into reverse when sales growth slows. This means reactions to surprise trading news are always likely to be more extreme for a company like Games Workshop.

Figure 5, which runs from the publication day of the 2017 screen to October 2021, illustrates the whole investment journey. It charts Games Workshop's forecast PE, forecast EPS and total return.

Figure 5: Games Workshop's ups and downs

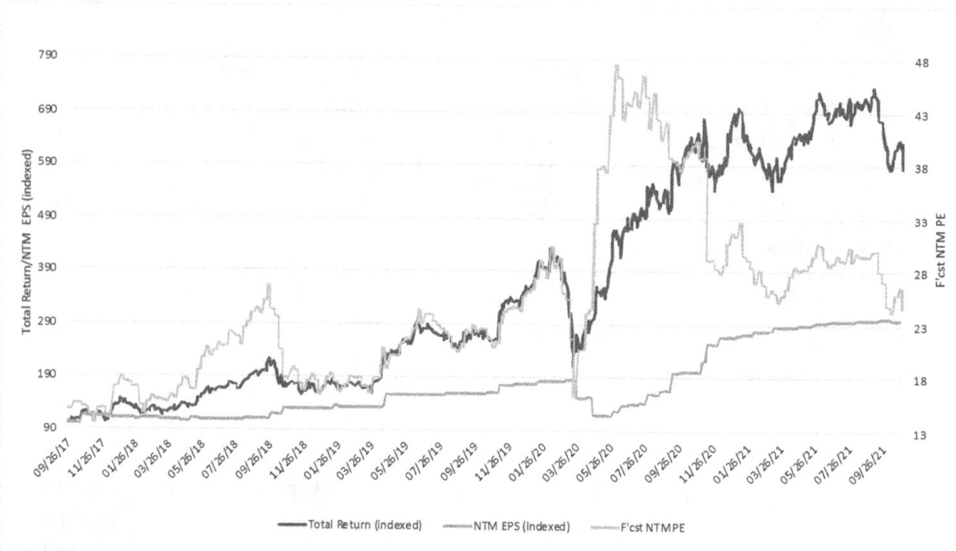

Source: FactSet.

The failure: cyclicality compounded

Crest Nicholson is a house builder. A house builder is not the type of company one would normally look to in search of a quality investment. These companies are highly sensitive to conditions in the housing market and carry huge amounts of risk on their balance sheets connected with money invested in ongoing development projects. It is a great example of how a quality screen can be fooled.

The balance sheet risk reflects the fact these companies have to invest huge amounts in working capital – land, bricks, labour, etc. – in order to get their high-priced end products to a point they are ready to sell. This working capital is the source of profit as well as risk, so is a necessity.

If, once a new house is ready to sell, the market has bombed, it will not be possible to cover the huge amount of cash costs stored on the balance sheet associated with the build. That will result in a loss on each home sale. It could also result in insufficient cash flows to finance the balance sheet's significant requirements.

The real rub is that everything turns down at the same time for house builders. Cash is harder to come by when the housing market turns south because selling prices drop at the same time as the number of transactions plummets. This requires house builders to write-down the value of their working capital and the plots of land they hold to ensure future supply. At the same time, their banks, which normally secure lending against these assets, can get nervous and stop advancing new loans.

Things can go horribly wrong for house builders over a typical business cycle. They are not quality companies.

This is exactly what we mean when we refer to a company as being cyclical. Its fortunes are not consistent throughout the business cycle, but dependent on external circumstances.

An argument could be made that the UK government's policy of consistently backstopping the housing market improves the quality of these plays. We could even argue that the reliance of the UK banking sector's own balance sheet on the health of the housing market means the government has little choice but to continue with its backstopping policies. In addition, we could argue that the discipline the sector has shown in avoiding overexpansion since its credit crunch calamity makes these companies higher-quality prospects than they were during the last housing market cycle.

However, none of this can make house builders high quality plays, despite their ability to produce fat margins and returns on investment when times are good.

Lower of the low quality

There are higher and lower quality house builders. And that adds insult to injury when it comes to Crest's appearance among the stocks selected by the High Quality Large Cap screen on 26 September 2017. At the time Crest was highlighted, it looked one of the lowest-quality listed house builders.

As we saw when we had a brief look at Du Pont analysis in Chapter 8, a company's all-important return on investment can be broken down into how quickly it turns investments into sales (capital turn) and the amount of profit it makes on its sales (margin). And as discussed in the last chapter, a potential weakness of the High Quality Large Cap screen is that it does not look at capital turn. For companies that use a lot of capital in their operations, especially working capital in the case of house builders, this can be a particularly telling measure.

Capital turn was where Crest's performance was weakest relative to peers in 2017. However, margins were not great compared with the competition either, as can be seen in Table 8.

Table 8: Capital turn, margin and RoA for house builders (2017)

Company	Asset turn	Pretax magin (%)	Pretax RoA (%)
Persimmon	0.79	24.7	19.5
Bellway	0.87	21.9	19.1
Berkeley	0.58	27.5	16.0
Taylor Wimpey	0.79	19.9	15.7
Redrow	0.78	18.9	14.7
Crest Nicholson	0.75	19.6	14.7
Barratt Dev	0.71	15.9	11.3

Source: FactSet. Based on last published annual results as of 26 Sept 2017.

But when things are bad, there is always the potential for them to get better, right?

This is what appeared to have been happening with Crest over the previous five years. The improvement in quality measures is what attracted the attention of the High Quality Large Cap screen. Capital turn and margins were both improving, which in turn meant far healthier levels of profit were being generated from all that working capital. This is shown in Figure 6.

Figure 6: Crest of a wave?

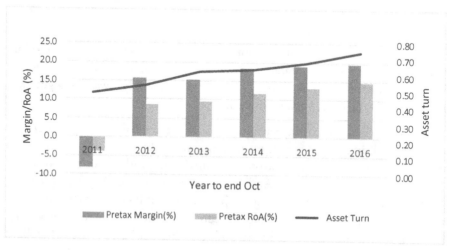

Source: FactSet.

The trouble is, 2017 demonstrated why progress by cyclical companies is so often built on weak foundations.

Crest went into reverse and the shares tanked. The shares delivered a 24% negative total return over the next year. An investor who bought the shares in 2017 was down nearly 70% before the share price bottomed in early 2020. As it happens, the shares then went on to double after being selected by my Contrarian Value screen later in 2020. We will look at this value screen next. A value screen is an altogether far more fitting place to alight upon the shares of a house builder.

There was something of a clue to the future deterioration in Crest's performance when it was selected by the High Quality Large Cap screen in September 2017. This came from a succession of small downgrades to forecast earnings in the preceding months (illustrated in Figure 7). However, more fundamentally, Crest was a high-risk cyclical stock and therefore never deserved consideration as a high-quality pick.

This is where the investor needs to exercise their own judgement once they have the screen's results. If a quality screen produces stocks which you know are not in quality companies – such as cyclical companies like house builders – these should be eliminated from consideration.

Figure 7: Early signs of trouble...

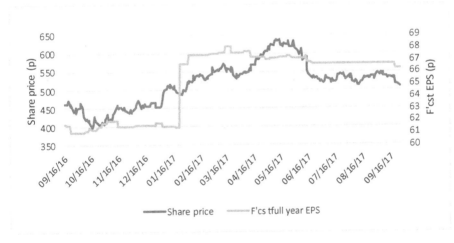

Source: FactSet.

In summary

We've looked at why quality investing works, the financial hallmarks of quality stocks we can exploit with screens, and the qualitative analysis to find out whether a company is the genuine article. Our two examples have added meat to the bones.

There is no guarantee we will always get it right when trying to assess whether a stock fits the quality mould. In fact, we will almost certainly get it wrong sometimes. However, the in-depth knowledge we've developed should significantly improve our chances of identifying high quality plays and avoiding those companies that look like they fit the bill, but only on the surface.

CONTRARIAN VALUE INVESTING

ON A STILL and freezing night in April 1912, a man broke away from a crowd moving across the deck of a ship. Afterwards, he could never quite say why he did it. It was lucky he did, though. His contrarian move took him in the opposite direction to his fellow passengers, and after a bit of time, he heard noises from the ship's side. Looking down he saw a partially full lifeboat about to be lowered. With calls for women or children going unanswered, he was hastily told by the crew to jump aboard.

About an hour and a half later he watched the ghastly sight of the ship he'd been on, along with the crowd of people he had been among, sinking beneath the sea.

The ship was the *Titanic*. The contrarian decision to break away from the crowd was not only of great value for the man involved, it was also of inestimable value to me personally. The guy was my great grandfather.[18] Were it not for his peculiar decision to break away from the herd that night, I would not be. Nor would this book.

Going against the crowd can be a highly profitable strategy in markets, too, as we are about to see. Contrarianism is at the heart of the value investing strategy we are about to explore.

As profitable as the strategy can be, it can also be very risky. However, the performance of the screen we will be finding out about suggests the rewards are often worth it. The cumulative total return over the first 10 years since inception has been 330%, compared with 88% from the FTSE All-Share.

Those 10 years held a different fate for traditional value strategies, though. Traditional value's torrid run has left many people asking whether the game is up. Has the pace of growth and technological innovation simply made focusing on cheap stocks an exercise in targeting moribund companies? Or have changes to accounting standards made it impossible for investors to accurately measure value?

Both are possibilities.

However, from a more prosaic standpoint, the screen we are going look at has continued to bring home the bacon. So maybe, armed with well-designed screens and a thorough understanding of the deeply ingrained human behaviours that make value investing work, all is not lost.

We'll start our exploration of value by looking at the ideas that underpin this style of investing. Readers who want to get straight down to business can, of course, skip this chapter and move straight onto the screen itself. We will also revisit the accounting issue we looked at in Chapter 7 to see why it particularly dogs traditional value measures, before getting onto the screen itself and how to interpret its results.

CHAPTER 17

AVERAGING UP: WHY VALUE INVESTING WORKS

What is value investing anyway?

SOME PEOPLE HOLD the line that all investing is value investing.

This is an argument largely based on semantics. The point being that almost all credible investing strategies take account of valuation.

As we saw when we looked at quality investing, quality plays can be valued on what appear very high multiples but can still be very undervalued based on the high returns they go on to generate over many years.

Some investors try to model this type of scenario using something called discounted cash flow (DCF) models. DCF models are very useful in theory as they can tell us the intrinsic value of any company. In practice, though, the heroic assumptions about the distant future needed to construct such models make them very subjective.

The kind of value investing we'll be screening for is rather more earthy. It has no interest in disappearing down a DCF rabbit hole. For our screen, all investing definitely is not value investing.

We're interested in 'regression-to-the-mean' value investing. Or to be more colloquial, contrarian value investing. This kind of value investing requires us to make a judgement about whether sentiment has gone too far against a stock. If we think there is a good chance it has, we can take a bet on things improving.

But before we move on, it's important to understand the idea of regression to the mean. To do so, we're going to take a trip back to the 1950s and the Israeli Defense Force.

Regression to riches

Remember Daniel Kahneman? He's the pipsqueak 21-year-old Israeli army lieutenant who went on to win a Nobel Prize. We met him in Chapter 2 when we found out about how he revolutionised the way Israeli army recruits were assessed.

Kahneman's army days were a fecund period for insights featuring heavily in his seminal book *Thinking, Fast and Slow*. One of the experiences he found most notable from his military years related to regression to the mean. It came about when he attempted to share evidence with air force flight instructors that rewarding good work was a more effective way to improve performance than punishing mistakes.[19]

A salty instructor stood up to dismiss young Kahneman's speech. What the instructor told the room was that when he praised cadets for doing well they usually did worse next time. By contrast, when he screamed at cadets for doing badly, they usually improved.

This prompted a 'eureka' moment for Kahneman.

The young lieutenant marked a chalk target on the floor and told the instructors to throw coins at it while facing in the opposite direction. This was a game in which luck determined a significant portion of the outcome.

The distance of each instructor's coin from the target was measured and the throws were ranked on a blackboard. Kahneman then had the instructors repeat the game. More often than not, the highest-ranking instructors from the first round did worse in the second round and the lower-ranking instructors did better.

Something similar was going on with the cadets on their training flights. If they'd performed particularly well on one set of exercises, it was likely to have been partially influenced by good luck. Regardless of whether they were rewarded for the performance, the luck would probably not be repeated during their next flight. By contrast, the poor performers were likely to have experienced some bad luck before being screamed at. That meant it was odds-on the next flight would be better no matter how they were treated.

When listed companies underperform, their shares are punished. Sometimes mercilessly. This normally happens when earnings decline due to external shocks or internal problems.

But companies are much the same as air force cadets or flight instructors throwing coins blindly. Luck plays a role in determining how good or bad their fortunes are. While some businesses do enter a state of terminal decline, many will experience a change of fortune and recover to reclaim their past form. This is regression to the mean. The mean refers to a long-term average.

Regression to the mean is also often evident in the valuation of shares. When companies get into trouble, they can see their shares priced as if they will always be in dire straits. But if the company does experience an improvement in its underlying trading, it is also likely to experience a marked improvement in valuation, which gives investors the double whammy of a re-rating and a recovery in profits.

So, while contrarian value investing can be risky and can involve long waits, it can also produce huge gains relatively quickly when it goes well.

Mean means

The real difficulty when assessing a company's regression-to-the-mean potential, is that it is hard to know exactly what the 'mean' is.

We can regard the mean as the steady state of sales and profits through a whole business cycle. That cycle could be linked to economic ups and downs, managerial ups and downs or something else. The difficulty is that the long-term prospects of companies and markets are themselves dynamic. The steady state is not steady. Things change, from business models, to competition, to end-markets. Sometimes significant changes happen abruptly. Sometimes a new 'mean' steady state for a company can be bankruptcy!

This makes the recovery potential of a distressed company hard to predict. Contrarian value investing is risky. This is why balance sheet strength is usually a key consideration for value investors.

There are usually a huge number of variables involved in determining if and how a recovery will take shape. Many of these can be well outside a company's scope of influence and beyond the ability of even the sharpest minds to forecast.

However, what is predictable is the human instinct to overreact to bad news.

Above all else, contrarians put their faith in the ability of other investors to under-appreciate the power of regression to the mean.

Doing this can require value investors to put faith in the ability of a company to recover even when there are few tangible signs that it will. Indeed, the most profitable time to target contrarian value situations is when the outlook is bleakest.

The risk of investing at such times is very real, and the fear of putting money on the line can be visceral.

Fear and loathing

There are many reasons we feel fear and revulsion towards underperforming shares and companies. These are a mirror image of why it's all too easy to get over-enamoured with growth stocks. If you flip the investor psychology we're about to explore on its head, you have a set of reasons why momentum exists.

Again we can turn to the work of Kahneman along with his long-time colleague Amos Tversky for some explanations. The duo identified a common human behaviour they termed the endowment effect. Essentially, people value things differently when they own them.[20]

The default position people have is to put a higher value on something when it comes into their possession. Many experiments have been done to confirm this. One well-known example involves students refusing to buy mugs and pens for a certain amount of money, but after being given the objects, they are unwilling to exchange them for the same amount.[21]

Something else happens to our ownership-attachment when prices start to move. If the price of what we own goes up, we love it even more. If it goes down, though, we start to hate it more than is warranted.[22] We take price movements personally.

However, shares don't normally get sold quickly when they start to fall. Another psychological phenomenon gets in the way. Something called loss aversion.

People have been found to hate losses almost twice as much as they like equivalent gains. In fact, people hate losses so much when it comes to investing, that researchers have found they struggle to even accept the value of their holding in a random basket of stocks is likely to fall in line with the market.[23]

For investors holding a sinking share, this often means hanging on in the hope that it will rebound in value and retrace to the original buying price. This can cloud our consideration of whether there is a superior investment we could make with proceeds from a sale, albeit a sale at a loss.

Meanwhile, loss aversion for non-holders means steering clear of catching the proverbial 'falling knife'. The process often ends in capitulation for the broken-spirited holder of the stock close to the bottom. The agony is so much, shares are often ultimately sold with little consideration for price.

This is likely to be a key factor at play in the finding that professional investors on average reduce the overall returns they achieve through the timings of their sales.

The worst sellers of shares have been found to be fund managers that are focused on fundamentals and have higher-conviction portfolios.[24] These are the precise type of people we'd expect to experience the most psychological tug to hang on to a losing position.

Along with loss aversion, there are several other deep-rooted human behaviours that keep us away from beaten up shares. So called availability bias and recency bias are noteworthy contributors. Availability bias describes a common tendency to focus excessively on the most attention-grabbing information that is available. Recency bias refers to our habit of focusing too much on the most recent events. Together, these factors make it very hard to see beyond a bad-news story and imagine a brighter future.

One of the great things about stock screens is that they can jolt us out of this loss-averse stupor and make us look at a potential recovery opportunity afresh.

When the fundamentals don't work

Of the strategies explored in this book, value investing has the most illustrious history. Academic recognition of this investment style stretches back to the 1930s, a time when accounting standards had only recently been invented. Many of the techniques were formally laid out by Benjamin Graham and David Dodd in their classic investment book *Security Analysis*. Their teachings provided the foundations for Warren Buffett's early investment career.

However, over 15 years from the mid-2000s, traditional value strategies performed terribly.

While value investing started to underperform in 2007, it wasn't until midway through the 2010s that investors seriously began to question whether the strategy was broken.

The uncomfortable truth is that classic value investing had until recently been on an epic losing streak. Figure 8 shows the MSCI World Value Index has eaten the dirt of the Growth version of the index over many years to the end of 2021, although, in 2022 the tide turned a bit.

Prior to 2007, the long-term track record had been so strong, and the evidence for regression to the mean so compelling that it raises the question "why would a classic value approach stop working?"

There are plenty of hard-to-quantify reasons that we could use to explain this. Most notable would be that the pace of innovation and disruption means investors' hopes for growth stocks, which have historically always run ahead of reality, could

Figure 8: MSCI World Growth vs MSCI World Value

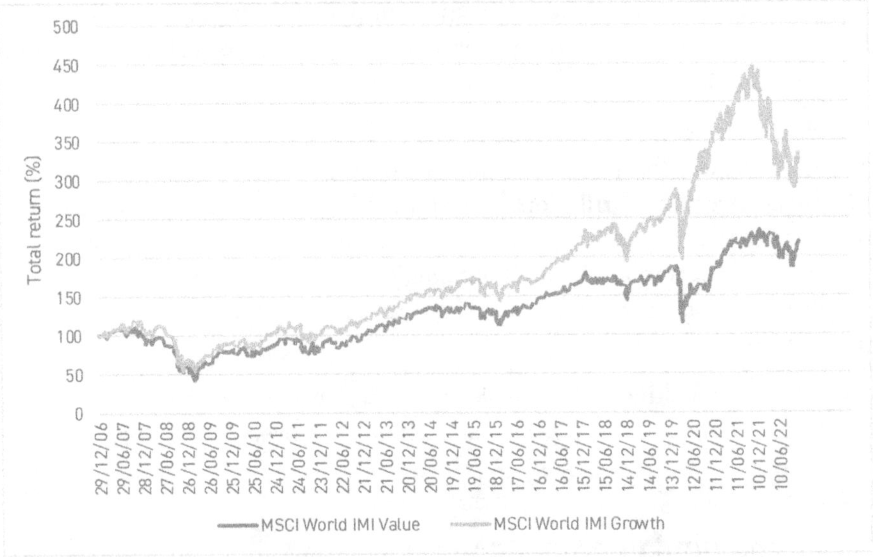

Source: FactSet.

have finally been overtaken by the tremendous pace of technological change. This sounds somewhat overblown, but as we'll find when we look at momentum investing, we are genuinely seeing unprecedented growth from the world's most successful companies.

Another far more mundane and readily quantifiable force has been at work: misleading accounting standards. We've already explored the bizarre way intangible investments are treated by company accounts. Most of these investments are not matched against costs over their useful life. Instead, they are treated as an upfront cost. This artificially depresses profits for intangible-intensive companies when they are investing in growth. It also leads to these companies' accounts understating the real size of the balance sheet.

The balance sheet is the foundation of the price-to-book-value (P/BV) ratio. This ratio was a favourite of Graham and Dodd. It was also the ratio academics Eugene Fama and Kenneth French used in a famous academic study that really put value on the map as a go-to strategy.

Over recent years, a lot of evidence has emerged indicating that the key numbers on which traditional value investment strategies are based – profits as well as book value – have become distorted as intangible investment has grown in importance to companies.

How would value investing strategies have performed had this accounting issue not existed? Investment firm Research Affiliates has done some number crunching to try to find an answer.[25] Other studies have made similar findings.[26]

Research Affiliates added back companies' intangible investments to their balance sheets. They did this by treating research and development (R&D) spending in the same way as tangible investments in things like property – in finance jargon, R&D was capitalised and then amortised against profits in later periods. But many intangible investments are also hidden inside companies' operating costs, such as spending on brand and software development. Research Affiliates therefore took a portion of these costs, too, and gave them the same treatment as would be given to tangible investments.

Tracking a classic value strategy of selling short the most expensive fifth of stocks based on P/BV and buying the cheapest fifth, a value strategy adjusted for intangibles had not done nearly as badly as appeared to be the case without the adjustment. In the period Research Affiliates tested, its adjusted value strategy did underperform over later years, but held up way better earlier on, as demonstrated in Figure 9.

Figure 9: Research Affiliates' intangible adjustment test

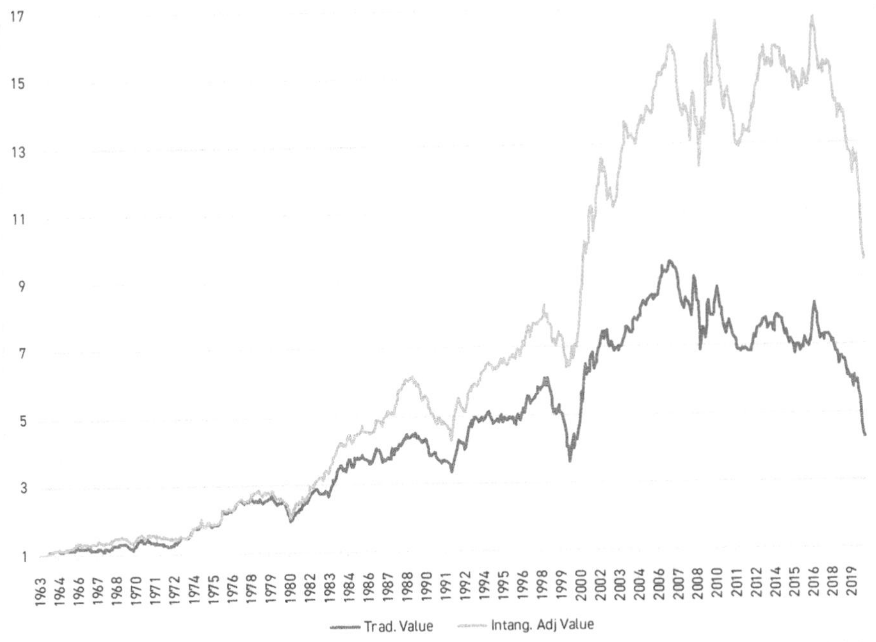

Source: Research Affiliates.

But investors do not need to make whizzy adjustments to get around the problem created by these accounting standards. As we have already touched on, some parts of a company's accounts are not affected by this issue. That is particularly true of companies' cash flows, which make no attempt to match spending with revenues. Cash flow simply takes sales and spending as it comes in hard cash terms.

A US value investment firm called Distillate Capital has focused on cash flow in its attempt to get around the intangibles issue. It uses enterprise value to free cash flow (EV/FCF) to measure value. It combines this with its own measure of quality to create portfolios for its US and international exchange traded funds (ETFs). At the time of writing its inaugural ETF, which launched in November 2018, has consistently been ahead of the S&P 500 Index, despite much of that period being characterised by the chronic underperformance of value strategies.

Amazingly, Distillate Capital has also found that for most of the last decade, based on its own favoured valuation measure, the MSCI World Growth Index was cheaper than the MSCI World Value index.

Another measure of value that is not affected by the issue with intangibles is EV/sales. That is because the sales line of the P&L account appears before any of the distortions caused by intangibles accounting standards take effect.

The screen we will look at in the next chapter uses EV/sales to highlight value. I would love to say that I was prescient about the intangibles accounting issue when I devised the screen. However, the truth is I was pretty ignorant to the extent of the problem. EV/sales appealed to me greatly though on another level. It's luck that this also helped our next screen dodge the intangibles bullet.

CHAPTER 18

SCREENING FOR CONTRARIAN VALUE

L ET'S HAVE A quick recap of what we've learned about value investing:

- Regression to the mean is a ubiquitous force that influences the trading of companies and the valuation of their shares.

- When companies do badly, investors tend to become excessively pessimistic.

- Capitulation can create amazing bargains.

- Contrarian investing is very risky.

- Intangible accounting standards have created major problems for traditional valuation measures based on profits and book value.

If not profits, what?

The valuation ratios that are most used by investors compare either share price or EV to profit. The PE ratio is ever popular. Over the last decade EV/EBITDA has started to give it a run for its money in the ubiquity stakes.

As we've explored, the way companies are made to account for their investment in intangible assets has created major problems for these valuation measures.

However, there is another reason why contrarian investors are best off ignoring valuation measures that use profits. In fact, when hunting for deep value situations, recent profits and forecast profits are often the last place investors should look.

That's because, the best value opportunities are in companies that are in real trouble. Such companies are likely to have seen profits shrink substantially or even be totally obliterated. These kinds of situations are likely to look very expensive on profit-based valuation measures.

We also should not expect forecasts to alert us to the approaching sunny upland of a recovery. Analysts usually only start to put in buoyant recovery forecasts sometime after a change of fortunes has started to become apparent. They need something substantial to base their predictions on, after all.

That's not to say low PE or EV/EBITDA ratios can't sometimes highlight overlooked situations. They're just not a very reliable guide. In fact, when these ratios look very low, they often highlight companies that investors rightly expect to experience sharp profit falls. The issues such companies face will be known in the market, but the problems have yet to filter through to the reported numbers or analysts' expectations.

This kind of faux value is not something we want our value screen to identify.

So where should investors look to see if value exists in a would-be recovery situation? The approach taken by the Contrarian Value screen is to look at the source of a company's potential future profits. It's sales.

Track record

The Contrarian Value screen we're now going to explore has profited over 10 years by looking to sales as a key indicator of value. Significantly, as we've seen, this has been achieved during a decade in which traditional value strategies have chronically underperformed.

In its first 10 years since inception on 27 July 2011, the screen managed to produce a cumulative total return of 330% compared with 88% from the FTSE All-Share. While the screen has been devised to be a source of ideas rather than an off-the-shelf portfolio, if I factor in a notional annual dealing charge of 1.5%, the cumulative performance comes in at 270%.

Details of each year's stock selection can be found in the appendix.

Something to note about the performance is that this screen has really delivered when the market was rebounding strongly from a fall. This is exactly when we would expect this kind of value strategy to outperform.

Recovery situations tend to appear in great abundance in challenging markets. The upside at these times can be excellent. When conditions are more clement, there is a greater chance that stocks that scream value are really barking dogs.

Whatever the backdrop, though, targeting recovery plays is a risky game. It's not without good reason that most value investors want to see a margin of safety in the stocks they buy – something we will look at in more detail in a bit. Furthermore, if you do not feel discomfort buying into a contrarian value situation, you may want to go back and check there isn't something you've missed in your research. Value normally exists for a discomforting reason, and it's best to know what that reason is.

The risks of this strategy are reflected in the fact that the biggest peak-to-trough fall from a portfolio selected by the Contrarian Value screen over the 10-year performance monitored was 51% compared with 35% from the FTSE All-Share Index (as shown in Figure 10). Ouch!

Figure 10: Contrarian Value screen vs FTSE All-Share

Source: Thomson Datastream.

Criteria

The Contrarian Value screen sets out to find potentially cheap shares in companies that are performing worse than they have in the past. The implicit assumption is that these businesses can return to past form. That means that when we look at the screen's results, we need to be very conscious of asking the question of whether something fundamental has changed.

The other big question for value investors is whether a company has the financial health to survive the wait for its fortunes to improve.

Historically I've conducted the Contrarian Value screen on FTSE All-Share constituents. It uses a two-step process. Step one tests whether a company is of sufficient quality, and step two tests for value. The criteria are as follows:

Step one

- Five-year compound average annual sales growth rate that is the lower of

  - 7% or more or;

  - in the top two-thirds of stocks screened. **CORE TEST**

- Forecast sales growth in each of the next two years. **CORE TEST**

- An average five-year operating profit margin that is the lower of (i) 10% or more over the past five years or (ii) in the top two-thirds of stock screened. **CORE TEST**

- Positive free cash flow.

- Gearing (net debt as a percentage of net assets) of less than 50% or net debt of less than two times cash profit.

Step two

- Select the cheapest five stocks based on EV/sales from those that pass step one

How it works

Putting faith in regression to the mean reflects a belief that the performance of a company is more likely to rectify itself over time than not. So when the return a company makes on its sales – its margin – has dropped, we need to think there's a good chance it'll rebound.

The screen we're looking at starts out by trying to identify companies that have a track record strong enough to suggest they may recover from a setback. So, while the screen's main objective is to identify value situations, the first step is to identify quality, albeit a different kind of quality than what our High Quality Large Cap screen looks for. It is only after establishing whether a company has what we are after that we move on to the question of value.

Step one – core tests

Sales growth

The tests:

- Five-year compound average annual sales growth rate at lower of

  - 7% or above, or;

  - top two thirds of stocks screened.

- Forecast sales growth in each of the next two years.

One of the most important considerations among the criteria is the question of whether sales look healthy. Are there signs the company is selling something people still want?

If sales are declining, we are more likely to be looking at a moribund business. We have two core screening tests that try to assess whether a company's top line is healthy.

The first is based on the historical growth record over five years. Ideally a company will boast a compound average growth rate (CAGR) of 7% or more over this period.

The decimation of past performance records caused by Covid-19 lockdowns forced the introduction of an alternative version of this test in 2021. This alternative simply requires the historical growth record to be within the top two thirds of stocks screened. At a minimum, though, the historical sales growth rate still needs to be positive.

This test is intentionally quite demanding. Not only does setting a high bar reduce the chance of deeply troubled companies making the cut, it also means that should these companies' fortunes improve, investors are likely to get more excited about prospects. There could be a viable growth business lurking beneath the surface.

When we look at a past success of the screen in the next chapter, we will focus on one such business that illustrates why this criterion can be so powerful in helping us find stocks with massive re-rating potential.

The other sales growth test is simply that forecasts for sales growth are positive in the next two financial years. It is a lower bar than the historical growth test. We are after all chiefly focused on finding companies that are troubled but could see a return to form. We therefore should not expect analysts' views of the future to be too bright at the time the stocks are highlighted. We do still want to see expectations that sales will hold up, to give us an indication of business strength even in the face of adversity.

Also, we do not actually need strong future sales growth for this strategy to work. What's most likely to be the key first step in realising value from our recovery situations is an improvement in profitability.

Profitability

The test: an average five-year operating profit margin that is the lower of

- 10% or more over the past five years, or;
- top two-thirds of stock screened.

While we do not need to target companies producing strong profits now, we want an indication that sales could potentially be profitable in the future. This is what regression to the mean is all about.

The five-year average operating margin test provides us with a pointer that this may be the case. If a company has produced decent margins in the past, it could do so again.

As with the historical sales growth test, a top-two-thirds margin test was introduced in response to Covid-19. The same logic applies.

This test does not preclude companies that are still reporting high profitability, although the fact that we will later screen for cheap shares means these are unlikely to be the stocks we ultimately alight on. But if a company does happen to come through this screen and margins appear to be high, it is important to understand what other factors are making the valuation low. There is a strong chance it will have something to do with the balance sheet or problems that have yet to show up in the P&L.

The profitability test also serves this screen in another way. Sometimes a company will report sales that include a lot of costs which get passed directly to customers – so-called pass-through costs. The company will have limited risks associated with these pass-through costs but will also not make profit from them.

Such companies often appear to be very cheap compared with sales, but as far as this screen is concerned that would be a false positive as a good chunk of those sales will never be profitable. However, by the same logic, these types of companies will also have low operating margins because they only turn a profit on a small portion of their revenues. The profitability test therefore helps filter out this kind of situation, although it is not always totally effective in doing so.

Non-core tests

Free cash flow

The test: positive free cash flow

A key concern with recovery situations is whether a company can keep afloat until a turnaround kicks in. The timing of recoveries is usually unpredictable.

If a company is producing positive free cash flow it suggests it should be able to cover its most pressing expenses. It is important to understand how cash flows are being supported by companies. For example, cash outflows may have been kept artificially low by holding off on essential maintenance spending and the like. This can hamper a business's recovery potential.

However, positive free cash flow provides an indication that the company may not need to go to its lenders or shareholders with a cap in its hand.

Debt

The test: gearing (net debt as a percentage of net assets) of less than 50%, or net debt of less than two times cash profit.

Debt is what tends to make or break troubled companies. It is the biggest threat to shareholders in recovery situations. Remember, the claims of lenders rank above those of equity holders. That means when disaster strikes it is equity holders who take the first hit. Investors in shares of recovery plays can face the very real danger of being totally wiped out to better protect the interests of lenders.

We want to reduce the chance of this happening, which is why we have a strict debt test. As some companies will not be profitable at the time of the screen, they can pass either a test that compares debt against the balance sheet or one that compares debt to profit.

An alternative debt test could involve comparing net debt to market capitalisation or an interest-cover test. For companies where valuations and profits are depressed, though, finding a suitable measure to compare debt with is not altogether straightforward.

We'll look at danger signs to look out for, and how to spot them, in a minute.

Step two

Valuation

The test: select the cheapest five stocks based on EV/sales from those that pass step one.

Once we've established the list of companies that fit our quality criteria, we can move onto the question of valuation. To do this, the screen simply selects the five companies meeting the quality criteria that have the lowest EV/sales ratios.

As already discussed, the virtue of the chosen valuation measure is that it looks at the source of profits rather than profits themselves, which may be very depressed. It also avoids becoming embroiled with the accounting issues relating to intangibles that bedevil profit-focused ratios.

In 2021, investors in high-growth, loss-making companies started to use EV/sales and price/sales ratios to make valuation arguments. The last time I am aware of this being so popular was during the dot-com boom. The fallout from both periods suggests EV/sales can be a dangerous and misleading yard stick to try to value expensive companies. The key issue is that it is hard to say how valuable sales are before there is a clear indication of how profitable those sales are likely to be for the companies involved.

Personally, I only feel sales-based valuations are really useful in trying to identify cheap stocks. I think we are better off with other valuation tools when trying to make sense of popular, high-priced investments.

This view about when EV/sales is useful is in part borne out by my experience with the Contrarian Value screen. It would be nice if the screen were able to highlight more than five companies on each outing. So nice in fact, that I've even monitored a different version of the screen based on the 20 cheapest stocks.

The problem is, using this screen in the UK market, once you go beyond the cheapest five stocks the shares stop really being that cheap at all. As a rule of thumb, a stock can be considered interesting when the EV/sales ratio is around one or lower.

Beyond the cheapest five shares, the screen usually ends up with companies valued at EV/sales of two or more. This cheapest-20 version of the screen has performed significantly worse than the cheapest-five version.

Adapting the screen

The main adaptation I've had to make to the Contrarian Value screen over my decade of monitoring it has involved adapting to the massive blow to company sales and profits from the Covid-19 pandemic. Details have already been given when discussing the individual criteria.

The important thing to bear in mind with this screen is that we want to include companies that are likely to be vulnerable to external events. It is therefore important to adapt the screen so we can continue to identify them when a far-reaching event does occur.

CHAPTER 19

FROM QUANTITATIVE TO QUALITATIVE – WILL IT RECOVER?

FOR A STOCK highlighted by the Contrarian Value screen to be of real interest we must have some confidence that the company will be able to recover and produce decent profits from its sales at some future point. The quality criteria used by the screen increase our chances of finding such situations. But the screen can only take us so far.

What we really need to understand is why the shares are so cheap in the first place. Only once we're confident about the risks that are being priced in can we evaluate whether worries are overblown. So, the most important questions we need to ask of the stocks highlighted are not what could go right, but rather what is going wrong and how much worse things could get. This is key to identifying what value investors often refer to as an investment's margin of safety.

There are several questions worth asking when trying to understand a recovery play. The best place to start is with the issue that can wipe out shareholders faster than anything else: debt.

Debt

To really understand a company's debt, there are six things we should think about: amount, covenants, maturities, cost, ratings and paydown. We will now explore each of these elements in further detail.

Amount

On the face of it, the question of how much debt a company has sounds like quite a simple one to answer. But there are complications around what constitutes debt and how much is appropriate for a given company.

While debt often takes the form of money advanced by banks and bondholders, companies can have other forms of borrowing and debt-like liabilities.

Supply chain financing, such as early supplier-payment schemes, invoice factoring and inventory financing can be hidden among less obvious balance sheet items. Leases are also best considered as debt as these claims sit above the claims of shareholders. Underfunded defined benefit pension schemes also represent a very debt-like liability that is likely to drain cash.

Significant assumptions need to be made to assess companies' pension liabilities, which draw on best-guesses about the lifespans of scheme members and future interest rates, inflation and investment returns. It is worth knowing the total size of what is owed as well as how much is underfunded. The larger the liabilities, the more significant changes in assumptions are likely to be to a company's balance sheet health, and the more significant the inherent uncertainties are.

A key consideration with debt levels is assessing whether a company's operations are cash-generative and resilient enough to keep on top of interest payments and repayment. For example, companies, such as utilities, which have reliable trading and very valuable assets, can support much higher debt than companies with low margins and cyclical end-markets. Reliable companies also find it much easier to refinance borrowings when they are due for repayment.

Covenants

When companies borrow, they agree to stay within certain parameters. For example, lenders may specify that interest cover cannot fall below a given level. If companies fail to comply, there will usually be consequences that are bad for shareholders. Often very bad. Waivers are usually agreed to deal with truly exceptional circumstances, such as the Covid-19 pandemic.

It is worth knowing what a company's debt covenants are, assessing how close a company is sailing to them, and thinking what the likely consequences of a breach could be.

Maturities

When companies raise debt, they must agree with lenders when they will pay it back. If debt is due to mature soon, and trading is bad, the negotiations to refinance the borrowing can be fraught. When companies manage to raise debt under such circumstances the terms can be harsh, and clauses may be put in that can dilute the interests of existing shareholders.

If companies are unable to find lenders to refinance debt, they may try to get money off shareholders on terms that are very disadvantageous to anyone unable to participate. Private investors tend to be particularly vulnerable in such circumstances.

Companies may also resort to selling off assets and subsidiaries to bring down debt that is approaching maturity. When a company is a forced seller, it is often the crown jewels that get sold first.

Checking debt maturity dates in the notes to the accounts can be very important.

Cost

Some companies have very expensive fixed-rate debt agreements. This can be good for shareholders if the company is able to refinance such borrowings on better terms, which is sometimes a welcome bonus as a recovery unfolds. But high debt costs may also simply be a warning that no one has been willing to lend to the business on standard terms.

What's more, if high-cost bond holdings have a long time before they can be redeemed, a company will incur high costs to cancel its expensive borrowing.

Ratings

A clue about the general health of a company can come from the rating assigned to its debt by ratings agencies such as Moody's and S&P. The direction of travel as well as the rating itself is of significance.

The pricing of publicly traded debt can also offer investors clues to the financial health of the company.

Many perceive debt investors to be ahead of the game compared with equity investors. Large and widening spreads between the yield on a company's bonds and the safe yield represented by government bonds can be a warning sign that a company is in trouble.

Paydown

In the early 2010s, two finance students at the University of Chicago called Brian Chingono and Daniel Rasmussen, sought to create a numbers-driven investment strategy that would emulate private equity returns by investing in the shares of listed companies.[27] The premise for the endeavour was a belief that the alchemy of private equity came from buying companies on the cheap using loads of debt and then paying down the borrowings.

While buying heavily indebted value situations goes entirely against the grain of having a margin of safety, there's no question it should turbocharge returns if it works.

Take the example of two companies with enterprise values (EVs) of £100m. They are identical in every way, but one has £75m of net debt and market cap of £25m making up its £100m EV while the other has a market cap of £75m and net debt of £25m. Both companies somehow get their hands on £25m to pay down debt.

Now let's assume EV stays at £100m for each. The more heavily indebted company has added £25m to its original £25m market capitalisation by reducing debt to £50m. The value of its equity has doubled. The impact on the value of the other company's equity is the same in absolute terms – a £25m increase – but in percentage terms it is far less impressive. Increasing the market cap from £75m to £100m represents an increase of only one-third compared to the doubling experienced by its near-identical peer.

Given these mechanics, a key question for Chingono and Rausmussen was how to identify companies that were going to reduce debt in the future. Extensive testing of stocks over the 50 years to 2014 revealed a rather prosaic answer. Companies that had paid down debt in the recent past were the ones most likely to do so in the future. If a company had the ability to generate surplus cash one year, the chances were it would repeat the trick.

The other factor that the pair found significant in determining whether a company would pay down debt was improving capital turn. This makes sense because, all other things being equal, if a company needs less capital to generate each pound of sales, it makes more capital available to devote to other things, such as paying down debt. Alternatively, improving capital turn suggests that from the same capital base, a company can produce more sales from which to generate cash to pay down debt.

It is always worth watching the trajectory of debt. But it is also important to understand how a company is making inroads into its borrowings. For example, if it's selling off cash-generative business units to shore up its balance sheet, it may just be a case of running hard to stand still. The disposals may mean it is losing the cash flows that service its borrowings.

If a company is selling new shares to pay down debt, this too is less desirable. It is just shifting the burden onto shareholders and reducing the proportion of profits accruing to each share. Sometimes, though, it can be the best option.

Still, debt paydown is an important trend to look out for and can sometimes justify taking more risk in the hope of a higher return.

Other considerations

While it would be hard to put a definitive list together for factors to watch out for when targeting recovery situations, here are four other considerations aside from debt which we should pay attention to.

Supply not demand

Cyclical companies can frequently make great recovery plays. Mining companies, for example, see their fortunes wax and wane with metal prices. House builders are very sensitive to the housing market. Recruitment companies are very sensitive to job market activity. The list could go on.

The cyclicality of companies can be significantly increased by certain business characteristics, especially their level of indebtedness and the proportion of costs that are fixed.

If we take our first example of miners, a fall in the price of the metal being mined does not make it any cheaper to get the stuff out of the ground. Operating profits therefore can be severely squeezed.

Falling metal prices also don't make the interest due on borrowings any lower. And because the cost of developing and opening a new mine can be immense, miners can hold large amounts of debt. Regardless of metal selling prices and volumes, interest payments still need to be made on that debt and borrowings need to be paid back when they come due.

What all this means is that, for some companies, the lowest points of the cycle can be very low indeed. Share prices can get to lows that suggest the market thinks shareholders will probably be wiped out.

The market can sometimes be right with its dire prognosis. But when it is wrong, the upside can be gargantuan even when the future simply begins to look viable rather than necessarily good. And as we've already seen, there are many reasons why investors are likely to become overly pessimistic during a company's darkest hours.

When trying to gauge the potential for a cyclical stock to recover, many people pay a lot of attention to the outlook for demand. This is something that is highly unpredictable and very hard to forecast.

What gets less attention is something that can be far more influential on prospects, and which is observable in the here and now: supply.[28]

When industries experience prolonged slumps, the bottom is usually characterised by mergers and acquisitions as players seek safety in scale alongside the collapse of weaker players.

These corporate events are signs that capacity is being removed from the market. Supply is falling. In itself, this is enough to improve the pricing power of the remaining players. And when end-market conditions finally improve, demand is concentrated on a few names and the survivors face less competition which means they can achieve greater profitability.

Even companies in moribund industries can benefit for long periods from last-person-standing upside. Mature industries are also normally characterised by long periods of consolidation as companies try to create value long after genuine growth opportunities have disappeared.

So, when it comes to cyclicals, pay attention to demand but let supply be the primary guide.

Disruption

A key dynamic at play in the supply cycle we've just looked at is the ebb and flow of competition in an industry. However, sometimes new competitors fundamentally change an industry. These competitors are known as disruptors, and they tend to have special features.

The mechanics of disruptive competition were formally set out by Clayton Christensen in the 1990s in his seminal book *The Innovator's Dilemma*.[29] Studying the fast-moving disk drive industry, he found industry incumbents were actually very good at exploiting what he called 'sustaining innovations'. These represent improvements that make existing products better.

What incumbents struggled with were innovations that offered something different, and in many ways inferior, to what was already being produced but had applications in small, less-profitable markets. Incumbents had no rationale for chasing the business being won by the innovators of such disruptive technology.

At first this was not a problem, but as the disruptive technology rapidly evolved and improved, it soon found inroads into incumbents' markets. The disruptive innovation stopped being inferior to incumbents' products while still offering the advantages that had originally helped it find a way into its original niche markets.

Disruption has run rife over the last few decades. A prime example has been online retail. These virtual shops lack the tactile experience of traditional retail and normally generate far lower margins, making them unattractive propositions for incumbents. Yet as online services have improved, the convenience and choice they offer has trumped bricks and mortar rivals.

For value investors, the problem caused by disruption is that it permanently reduces the viability of established companies in an industry. In these circumstances a fall in profitability is not something that will be recovered from but will either be a new normal or a step on the road to decimation. Value investors need to be alert.

Acquisitions

One of the quickest ways to turn a good business into a bad one is through a mega acquisition. The word 'transformative' when linked with the word 'acquisition' should set off alarm bells. It is not that all big acquisitions end badly, but it is scary how many ultimately destroy value.

For value investors, a big acquisition gone bad creates two problems when trying to judge the potential for a recovery.

First, it can be very hard to judge how deep the self-inflicted wounds are and the pain can stretch out for many years. Past profitability may never be regained.

Second, big acquisitions can significantly alter the nature of the enlarged company's balance sheet. This is especially the case if a lot of debt has been taken on to fund the deal. After all, the borrowings were taken on based on the rose-tinted view of the future at the time of the grand acquisition, rather than the grimmer reality that followed.

Dodgy numbers

Sometimes companies are very aggressive in how they report profits. In the case of fraud, they tell outright lies.

If a company has been cooking the books or goosing the numbers, then past levels of profitability may never be recaptured for the simple reason that they were a fiction. Value investors need to be very wary of this type of situation.

Looking out for high levels of short interest can provide a good indicator that all may not be as good as it seems at a company. For UK shares, shorttracker.co.uk is a very good, free resource. The red flag ratios we looked at in Chapter 10 are also very helpful.

In the next chapter we will see how one red flag ratio provided a major warning of the dangers of would-be recovery stock Ted Baker. The fashion retailer was highlighted by the Contrarian Value screen as a recovery play but, as we'll see, proved to be anything but.

CHAPTER 20

STOCK SELECTION FOR CONTRARIAN VALUE

ASSESSING RISK IS key to being a successful contrarian value investor. To help illustrate how we can do this and put the lessons from the last chapter into practice, I've chosen an example of a share the Contrarian Value screen highlighted in 2014 that illustrates a nice balance of risk versus the potential for recovery. After looking at this success, we'll look at a share the screen highlighted that appeared screamingly cheap at first glance; however, it held huge risks on closer inspection.

The success: cheap for a season

Engineering company Hill & Smith may not be the most noteworthy success from the Contrarian Value screen's past picks. However, the way the shares' 320% total return has been achieved since it was first highlighted on 29 July 2014 can teach us a lot about the type of situation the screen aims to unearth.

The company makes heavy-duty infrastructure products, such as pipes and crash barriers, for the transport and utilities sectors. This accounts for about 70% of revenue and half profits. The remaining sales and profits come from several galvanising plants it owns and operates. Galvanising is an industrial process used to weather-proof metal objects, often very large and heavy ones, usually for use by the construction industry. This is done by dipping the objects in chemicals.

Powering a re-rating

Since Hill & Smith was highlighted by the Contrarian Value screen, it has made a smart pivot towards the US, where there is a huge pent-up need for infrastructure investment. When the screen highlighted the shares back in 2014, 46% of sales were from the UK and 25% from North America with the rest from other parts of the world. Fast forward to 2020, and 25% of sales were from the UK and 71% from the US, with just 3% from elsewhere.

This has been a noteworthy factor in changing how the company is perceived, which in turn has been reflected in how the shares are valued. When the screen highlighted the stock back in 2014, it traded on a forecast PE of just 11.7. Prior to the Covid-19 pandemic the shares were trading at 17 times forecast earnings. That's a re-rating of about 45% (the PE jumped during the pandemic, reflecting an earnings hit but expectations of a sharp recovery). The re-rating compares with a 15% de-rating by the FTSE All-Share Index over the same period.

On an EV/sales basis the re-rating was 83%. We'll see in a minute why our sales-based valuation has told us so much more about the re-rating upside on offer than the PE. But first, why were investors able to buy at what proved such bargain prices in summer 2014?

Manageable risks

Hill & Smith is a somewhat cyclical business. When the screen first highlighted the stock, the world was experimenting with austerity economics. That meant many of the government agencies that buy infrastructure products from Hill & Smith were tightening their belts. Meanwhile, commercial customers, not least those in the construction industry, were still feeling the pain from the credit-crunch-induced recession.

But while Hill & Smith is a bit cyclical, things never seem to get all that bad for the company. That's down to its focus on multiple regulated industries, essential products, and countries where there's long-term growth in infrastructure spending.

Figure 11 shows that while sales, profits and margins have had ups and downs with the economic cycle over the last 20 years, things have never gotten too bad. And the company has always been profitable.

Very importantly, given external factors can cause some fluctuation in sales and profits, management has also historically been conservative with borrowings. Net debt stayed below two times cash profits throughout the last decade.

Beyond the cyclicality, the company's businesses have some very attractive attributes. Its infrastructure clients need trusted suppliers that can comply with

Figure 11: Hill & Smith is a bit cyclical

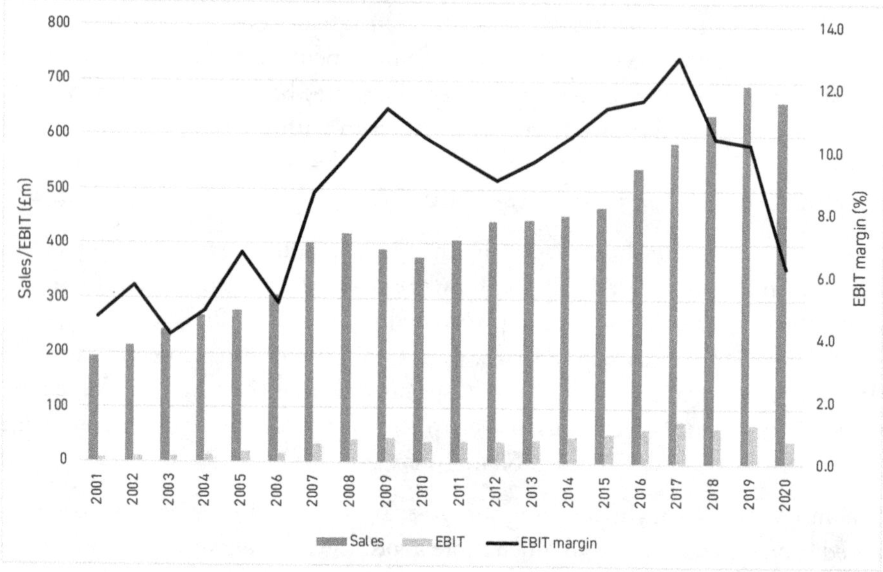

Source: FactSet.

ever-changing regulation. That puts a more significant focus on quality of service and product rather than just price.

Meanwhile, the high operating margins boasted by the galvanising business (galvanising operating margins in 2020 were over 30%) reflect the fact that each site has a local mini-monopoly. That's because sites cost a lot to set up, and there is a relatively predictable level of demand in each geographic area. This is due to a captive customer base. Customers need to go to their closest centre due to the high cost of transporting heavy metal objects to be galvanised. The cost of transport is a significant consideration alongside the cost of galvanisation.

For galvanising site owners, the high setup cost means there is no point in competitors building facilities too close to each other and splitting the local market. All this would do is create two uneconomical sites. The fact demand is cyclical also means plant owners are incentivised to be conservative in the distance they put between each other. This is especially true in a country with a vast land mass such as the US. The mini-monopolies of galvanising plants create pricing power and high margins.

Let the good times roll

Investors seem to focus on the attractions of companies like Hill & Smith – good but cyclical businesses – more when trading is strong. When times are bad, the long-term virtues can be quickly forgotten. Indeed, it is not only credit-crunch and Covid-19 travails that have seen the valuation of the shares bomb. The same happened in 2018 when the company experienced a poor year due to currency movements and order delays, some of which were due to terrible weather.

Shares in companies like this have a habit of throwing up buying opportunities.

But despite its ups and downs, the company has continued to grow. Margins have also by-and-large improved over the years. That means the share price has not only risen on the back of growing sales. The effect of growing sales has been magnified by rising profit margins. The benefit to shareholders has in turn been magnified further by the shares' rising valuation as a multiple of profit.

This dynamic is what explains the more pronounced re-rating based on EV/sales which captures both the margin gain as well as the PE re-rating (see Figure 12).

Figure 12: Hill & Smith – everything points up (indexed)

Source: FactSet.

And all the time, healthy dividend pay-outs have been feeding into the overall total return from the shares. As we will see in the next chapter, healthy dividends can be a hallmark of quality that the market finds easy to overlook.

Underlying its short-term cyclicality, Hill & Smith has long-term strengths. The mispricing of this by the market when the screen highlighted the stock in 2014 has allowed contrarians to bag excellent gains.

The failure: cheap for a reason

As one would expect from a screen that hunts for contrarian value, the stocks it highlights have often been under the cosh for quite a while. That was certainly true of fashion retailer Ted Baker when the screen highlighted its shares on 24 July 2019. The trouble was, things were about to get much worse.

For those on the lookout for risk, there was one massive warning sign alerting shareholders to the trouble ahead.

A contrarian set up

The riches-to-rags ride Ted Baker's shares had been on prior to being highlighted by the Contrarian Value screen helps illustrate the downside of buying quality stocks with lofty valuations (something touched on when looking at our Quality screen).

For a long time, Ted was considered a retail business of exceptional quality. In 2015 its shares had commanded a rating of 30 times earnings. However, slowly but surely sentiment had soured.

During the 2010s, trading conditions for traditional retailers worsened as e-tailers progressively ate more and more of their lunch. While Ted's sales had appeared to hold up well to the onslaught, it looked vulnerable based on the many concessions it operated in department stores. As the future of these outlets began to become more uncertain and weaker department store chains started to go to the wall, so sentiment darkened towards Ted.

The mood wasn't helped when the company's founder and chief executive was accused of overseeing a 'hugging' culture. It was after he resigned that the profit warnings started. The first warning was in February 2019 and it was followed by another in June 2019.

All in all, this made for a suitably contrarian backdrop for our screen to pick up on the stock in July that year. By this time, the 2015 earnings multiple of 30 had dropped back to one of just 10, and the shares had lost two-thirds of their value from their highs.

Could things get any worse?

Absolutely!

Things can always get worse

The real warning sign that there was more trouble ahead came from the levels of stock being reported by the company. For Ted, stock chiefly consists of unsold clobber sitting in warehouses and on shelves.

When we looked at red flags in Chapter 10, we saw how helpful it can be to compare a company's stock levels with its sales to try to assess whether its goods will end up in the bargain bin or worse. Remember, stock represents costs that have been incurred already but have not yet been recognised in the P&L statement. Today's hard-to-shift stock is tomorrow's losses. For fashion retailers, ageing stock can prove particularly pernicious, as trends change quickly.

Not only was Ted's stock-to-sales ratio absurdly high when it was highlighted by the Contrarian Value screen, but the trend in the ratio was a textbook example of what investors do not want to see. Over 10 years stock-to-sales had risen from the reasonable (just over 20%) to the astronomical (nearly 37%), as Figure 13 demonstrates.

Figure 13: Ted Baker: a decade of rising stock to sales

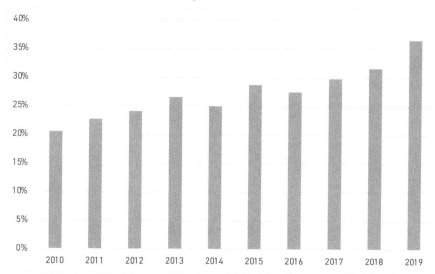

Source: FactSet.

By the time it was highlighted by the screen, Ted had already started to write-down the value of stock in its previous profit warnings, but the real shocker was yet to come.

Two more profit warnings landed in 2019, along with the revelation that the value of stock had been significantly overstated. When the bill finally came in, the size of the write-down to stock value was a massive £58m, double what had originally been expected. As for the shares, they lost nearly another 90% of their value from the level where the screen originally highlighted them.

Screens are not designed to dig all that deep, but as individuals we can.

In summary

We've learned how we can use the pervasive force of regression to the mean to our advantage in investing and the stock characteristics we can screen for to find shares that look like they're ready to bounce back. However, we've also seen there are pitfalls that value investors can easily fall into. It can be a dangerous game. By looking beyond the numbers, including at example stocks, we should be in a better position to avoid these traps and enjoy the benefits of value investing and our screen.

DIVIDEND INVESTING

WE HEAR A lot about something called income investing. Many funds have been launched under the banner, especially in the UK, and many professional investors profess to be followers of the approach. But calling this section of the book Dividend Investing is not a case of confusing terms. It is done purposefully to draw a distinction between what we will explore and what the finance industry often means by income investing.

The big difference is that while the strategy we're going to explore does use dividend yield to find promising stocks, generating income is not central to its objectives. Income is just a by-product. In some ways, it is an unfortunate by-product. It would be nicer if these companies were able to invest in profitable growth opportunities rather than having nothing better to do than hand money back to shareholders.

As we will see though, conservatively managed companies that opt to hand back cash rather than spend it on misguided glory projects may be dull, but they can also be very profitable to own over time. And backing them is likely to help us sleep well at night.

In terms of outperformance, my dull-but-dependable High Yield Low Risk screen has done very nicely. It managed a 346% cumulative total return in the 10 years since its inception in March 2011 compared with 79% from the FTSE All-Share Index.

The reason for the outperformance is well known to the investment industry, but the nature of its dullness means few professionals bother exploiting the strategy.

Readers who want to get straight to the practicalities of the screen can skip ahead to Chapter 22. For those who want to understand the strategy in a bit more depth, we're going to start on the baseball pitch.

CHAPTER 21

BRILLIANTLY BORING: WHY DIVIDEND INVESTING WORKS

AT THE START of the millennium, a man called Billy Beane stunned the world of baseball. Beane was the general manager of the Oakland A's, a team whose major claim to fame was having one of the most diminutive payrolls in the top-flight game, about one-third that of leading rivals. That's a major obstacle in a sport obsessed with star players.

Nevertheless, Beane created a team that racked up the longest winning streak in top-flight baseball history and won playoff places in the World Series, which ultimately saw him offered what at the time was the fattest ever general manager paycheque to defect to a rival (he turned the job down).[30]

He achieved this feat by doing something which sounds obvious. He looked for what attributes made players win games. To do this he turned to a fan-compiled stats system called Sabermetrics that was originated in the 1970s by a man called Bill James.

What James had found was that game-winning attributes were not the type of flashy things baseball talent scouts looked for, such as good physiques and powerful hits. More important was a lot of dull stuff, such as staying on base.

When Beane ran the numbers to try to find such players, he found they were chronically overlooked by professional teams. He could snap up winners for peanuts. The fact some were fat, some were scrawny, and one even had a club foot made his team something of a laughing stock at first. But eventually the success became so overwhelming no one could continue to put it down to fluke.

As in baseball, dull and overlooked can be a devastatingly effective combination for investors. However, unlike baseball, where Beane popularised the strategy of buying unlikely winners, dull companies continue to get neglected by investors, for reasons we will explore in a minute. That creates a great opportunity for those who are prepared to go against the grain, as Beane did.

A finance heretic

Around the same time as Bill James started to explore his revolutionary ideas about baseball in the 1970s, an academic called Robert Haugen was establishing himself as a similarly heretical force in the world of finance.

Haugen was a man who raged against the conventional wisdom of the Efficient Market Hypothesis (EMH). The central idea behind EMH is that the interaction between market participants means all known information about an investment must be in the price. The conclusion is that trying to beat the market is futile. And for those who must try, the only way to outperform the average is to take more risk than average. It is this last point about the trade-off between risk and reward that Haugen had a particular problem with.

In fact, Haugen torpedoed this central EMH idea in 1972 when he released a study with James Heins that had the not-so-catchy title of: 'On the Evidence Supporting the Existence of Risk Premiums in the Capital Market'.[31]

To understand the conventional wisdom that Haugen and Heins overturned, we have to first understand what the finance industry means by risk. In finance, risk is not based on how much money someone can expect to lose from an investment. Rather, risk refers to the amount of volatility an investment experiences on the way to its end point. This is usually measured against the volatility of the broader index it is part of and is known as a stock's beta.

This understanding of risk is different to an intuitive take but captures a sensible idea based on human behaviour which we explored when looking at value investing. Investors tend to feel most compulsion to sell up when they are losing money and prospects appear bleak. This compulsion to head for the exit is greatest when markets and stocks hit the bottom. This is by definition the maximum pain point. It is also ironically the worst time to sell and the best time to buy. Very volatile stocks produce very pronounced pain points which increase the likelihood of poor selling decisions.

For EMH proponents, a logical idea was that investors should be rewarded with higher returns for buying more volatile – i.e., riskier – shares. The idea is logical, but it also is wrong.

With financial data becoming more readily available, Haugen and Heins set out to test the theory. Taking the period of 1926 to 1971, the academics tested what returns from stocks had been based on their monthly volatility. The findings were the reverse of what the EMH anticipated. To quote from the paper: "The results of our empirical efforts do not support the conventional hypothesis that risk – systematic or otherwise – generates a special reward. Indeed, our results indicate that, over the long run stock portfolios with lesser variance in monthly returns have experienced greater than average returns than their 'riskier' counterparts."

Many studies have since confirmed Haugen and Hein's findings across different markets and different time frames.* So despite the logic, less risk seems to not only be good for investors' nerves but also for their bank balances.

While the relationship between risk and performance is broadly inverse (less volatile shares perform better than more volatile shares), it is not entirely linear. Rather, returns initially tend to rise as risk reduces. This is quite marked at first, before tailing off with returns dipping slightly from the peak for really low-risk stocks.

What's going on?

Quite a few of the explanations that have been proposed for the unexpected real-world relationship between volatility and performance are painfully technical. But there are also more intuitive explanations based on human behaviour. One of the most compelling of these centres on people's love of high-risk bets.

The popularity of lotteries illustrates this. In lotteries the odds are wildly against a player making more money than they spend on tickets. However, while there is no rational financial sense in playing the lottery, the small price of a lottery ticket is probably worth it for most people, for an entirely different reason. The possibility of winning mind-blowing riches gives us a thrill.

Studies into the behaviour of gamblers suggest that when it comes to long-shot bets, like the lottery, the thrill is based on a genuine misperception of risk.[32] This psychological phenomenon is known as 'longshot bias'.

Other studies have shown that what is true of lottery players and gamblers is also true of investors.[33] The excessive appetite investors display for shares that offer a low-probability chance of extreme upside is often referred to in finance as 'skewness'.

---

* Such studies include those by Baker and Haugen (1991), Chan, Karceski and Lakonishok (1999), Blitz and van Vliet (2007), Nielsen and Aylursubramanian (2008), Carvalho, Xiao, Moulin (2011), Blitz, Pang, van Vliet (2012).

Investors generally put an excessive proportion of their portfolios in investments that offer highly skewed returns and also routinely overpay for the privilege by buying in at high valuations. On average, these investors and investments underperform the market. There will naturally be some lucky winners. These exceptions are the people we tend to hear about, which adds to our perception that longshots are more reliable than is really the case.

There are other common human traits that encourage us to indulge in our love of longshots. Studies show we're an endemically overconfident species. This leads us to overestimate our understanding of investments and their risks. We are also extremely good at finding evidence to support what we want to believe while ignoring things that go against our desires.

To bring this back to the story of the Oakland A's, we tend to overvalue the glamorous but risky players, and in turn we ignore and undervalue the dull plodders. But dull plodders can have game-winning attributes in the stock market as well as on the baseball pitch.

When it comes to investing, the kind of dull plodders we want to build a team around are often the type that not only have less volatile share prices, but also advertise their lack of glamour by paying reliable dividends. And if our objective is to look for stocks that are overlooked because they are considered dull, then it stands to reason that they will have a relatively attractive valuation in the form of a healthy dividend yield.

Looking for attractive dividends brings us closer to our quarry in another way. For a company's management to have the confidence to pay a decent dividend, the company should really have a sound and stable balance sheet and a sound and stable business. These are things we want from dull and reliable companies.

The existence of a strong dividend record also increases the chances that the low volatility of the shares reflects a genuinely low-risk business. That's because, if management are choosing to return capital to shareholders rather than spend it on glory projects, it increases the chances the company is conservatively run.

Eugene Fama and Kenneth French, two rockstars of finance academia (if that's not too much of an oxymoron), analysed mountains of data to offer an interesting explanation of the low-volatility anomaly based on only two company characteristics. These are that companies with less volatile share prices tend to have decent levels of profitability coupled with conservative levels of investment.[34] What a dull and reliable combo.

The low-volatility open secret

In his book *High Returns from Low Risk*, Dutch quant Pim van Vliet recounts one of the most surprising discoveries he made when moving from academia to fund management: there are two kinds of risk in finance.[35]

The ability to achieve higher returns from lower-risk stocks was something that had fascinated van Vliet as he worked on his PhD. He wanted to offer this sleep-at-night investment strategy to the masses. However, after joining fund manager Robeco in 2005, he quickly found out that adopting the strategy professionally could see him and his colleagues out of a job. The problem was that finance professionals are judged based on their performance relative to the market over short time periods.

In finance, risk is a two-way street. Even if low-risk stocks outperform in the long term, the fact that almost by definition they are likely to underperform the market when it is rising fast represents a big danger for professionals. Professionals who underperform during a bull market get short shrift. That's a particular concern for them because bull markets are the time when money tends to flood into funds.

From an investing perspective, a low-risk strategy really earns its keep by protecting investors' wealth on the downside. But when markets are falling, it is hardly a killer sales pitch to suggest investors will lose money but hopefully less than the wider market.

While it is broadly accepted by most investors that market timing is not possible, no one wants to lose money. And we are psychologically predisposed to think the downside of investing does not fully apply to us.[36]

Table 9 shows the kind of economic conditions that have led to outperformance and underperformance of a low-volatility strategy based on the work of quantitative investment firm Research Affiliates.[37]

Table 9: Low beta's excess return from six months before a period of economic...

Recession	Slowdown	Recovery	Growth
9.40%	2.30%	−9.20%	−1.30%

Source: Research Affiliates.

As long as private investors are not obsessed with consistently beating a benchmark (and there is little reason why they should be) this is great news. It leaves the field open. Match-winning players can be picked up on the cheap because big-money investors are disincentivised from bidding up prices.

In the next chapter we will find out how we can screen for these overlooked stars of the stock market.

CHAPTER 22

SCREENING FOR HIGH YIELD AND LOW RISK

L ET'S RECAP WHAT we've learned about dividend investing:

- Dull but reliable stocks are often overlooked and undervalued.

- Low volatility and low beta shares suggest dullness.

- A decent dividend yield can be an indicator of an overlooked stock.

- A strong dividend record can suggest that:

  - a company has limited growth opportunities and is indeed dull,

  - management is conservative,

  - the business is cash generative,

  - and finances are solid.

- Low risk, high yield stocks outperform over the long term, but because they tend to underperform during hot bull markets, they are not popular with professional investors.

Dividends, not income

One of the most important characteristics of the screen we're now going to explore is its focus on dividends. However, the reason for this focus is to find a certain type of company rather than because of any great virtue in generating dividend income.

In the next chapter, we will look at why focusing too much on income generation can create problems for investors and undermine the strengths of a dividend-focused strategy.

Another key danger for our strategy is that paying ever-increasing dividends can become the focus of management ego. When this is the case, the misallocation of cash towards dividend payments can be just as bad as spending money on dubious growth projects or dud acquisitions. A strong record of historical dividend payments can represent a destabilising influence on a company's finances, which increases the riskiness of its shares.

With our screen, we want to avoid this kind of situation while increasing our chances of highlighting consistent dividend payers who back their pay-outs with earnings and ultimately cash flows. These are more likely to be the kind of conservatively managed, good businesses with overlooked virtues that we're after.

The High Yield Low Risk screen's track record suggests it has generally been very effective in highlighting this type of situation.

Track record

Over its first 10 years since featuring in the *Investors' Chronicle* magazine, the High Yield Low Risk screen racked up a cumulative total return of 346% compared with 79% from the FTSE All-Share (the index that stocks were selected from).

We can see how this has been achieved in Figure 14, and details of historical stock selection can be found in this book's appendix.

The cumulative return from the screen assumes annual reshuffles of the portfolio. If we factor in a 1.5% charge to represent dealing costs associated with reshuffles, the total return falls to 284%. The primary function of this screen, though, is to highlight promising ideas rather than to create off-the-shelf portfolios.

These 10 years, which run to March 2021, were not altogether easy ones for dividend investors. While dividend-focused investment styles started out strongly, the final five years were challenging. The Covid-19 market collapse in 2020 was particularly tough.

Many overlooked companies with higher-yielding shares have an element of cyclicality to their businesses. Such a seismic economic event as the pandemic lockdowns therefore hit share prices hard even when companies looked robust in other ways.

Figure 14: 10 years of high yields and low risk

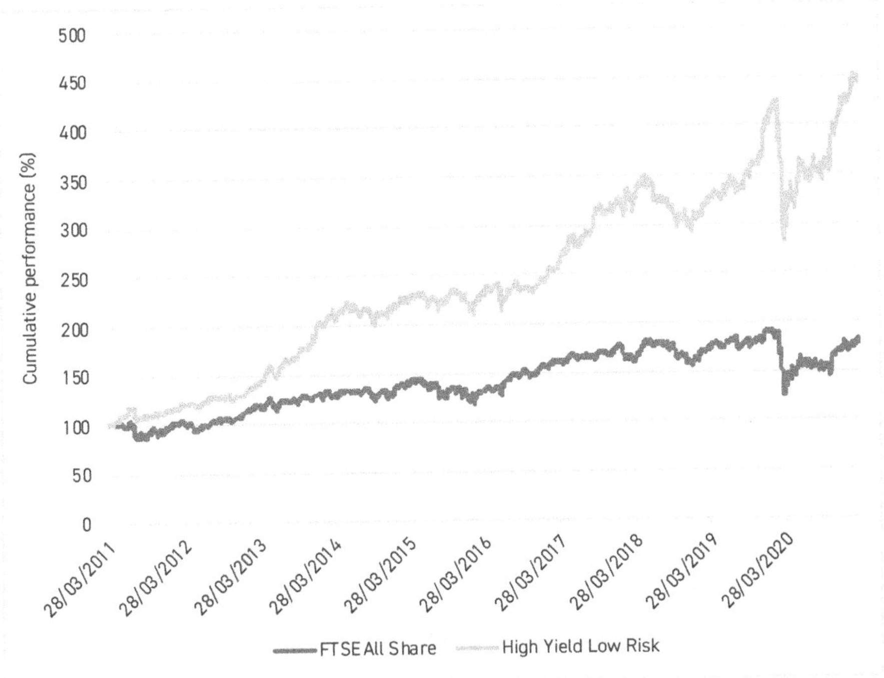

Source: Thomson Datastream.

This may help explain why the focus on low volatility only offered limited solace for the High Yield Low Risk strategy during the early 2020 market meltdown. During this tumult, the maximum drop experienced by the screen was 33.8%, based on total return. That was better than the negative 35.3% from the index, but not by much.

Criteria

In many ways we can consider this screen a quality screen, but of a different type to the one we looked at previously.

In contrast to our other quality screen, the kind of quality our dividend-focused screen looks for is a type that is easy to miss. It is not necessarily reflected in consistently high returns on capital and reliable growth.

With the companies we're now hunting for, there may be limited opportunity for growth. There could be some cyclicality. Perhaps returns on capital are decent rather than great. Or maybe the business model is just hard to understand.

The type of quality we want to find is based on a company's long-term reliability and robustness. Ultimately, this is likely to boil down to it being a decent business that is conservatively managed. That is something that can often make a company seem dull, despite conservative management being effective at producing superior long-term outcomes for shareholders. Family-owned businesses with multi-generational management perspectives often fall into this category.

Let's have a look at what the High Yield Low Risk screen looks for:

- A forecast dividend yield for the next 12 months above the median average for dividend-paying shares (the 'high yield' test). **CORE TEST**

- A one-year beta of 0.75 or less (the 'low risk' test). **CORE TEST**

- Dividend payments covered 1.5 times or more by earnings.

- Ten years of unbroken dividend payments.

- Ten years of positive underlying earnings.

- Underlying earnings per share (EPS) higher than five years ago.

- Dividend per share (DPS) higher than five years ago.

- A return on equity of 12.5% or more.

- A current ratio (current assets to current liabilities) of one or more.

How it works

As the screen's name suggests, the main focus is on high yield and low risk. These are the core tests we really want stocks to pass. The other tests the screen uses are fairly soft. If we make them too demanding we run the danger of making the screen one no stock will pass.

Some fundamentals that should be important considerations for dividend hunters are intentionally ignored by the screen. We'll look at the reasons why as we go through the logic behind the tests the strategy does use.

But when we look at how it is possible to adapt the screen, we'll see how another screen has also achieved good results by including some of the omissions from this screen's criteria and ignoring other criteria. Happily, it seems there's more than one way to skin a cat.

But first, let's take a closer look at the High Yield Low Risk screening criteria.

Core tests

High yield

The test: a forecast dividend yield for the next 12 months above the median average for dividend-paying shares.

If a share has a decent yield, it suggests people are not falling over themselves to buy it. Normally this is for good reason. But importantly for us, this can sometimes also mean the virtues of a stock are being overlooked. By looking for yields that are over the median (mid-ranking) average, we're not requiring stocks to have extremely high dividend yields. This means we're less likely to find our screen highlighting troubled companies.

The fact we are looking for a yield that is better than the mid-ranking yield of index constituents rather than the index yield itself is an important distinction.

An index yield is calculated as a weighted-average yield of the constituents. A weighted average yield for a collection of stocks, such as an index, is calculated in proportion with each company's size, as measured by market cap. So, an index where large constituents are mature, slow-growth companies that pay very big dividends is likely to have a higher weighted-average yield than its median average. This is the case with the UK's FTSE All-Share Index, which I've historically conducted this screen on.

The reverse would be true for an index where the biggest companies were high growth, because high-growth companies tend to have better things to do with their cash than return it to shareholders. This is true of an index such as the S&P 500.

When the weighted average is high compared with the median, using the index yield would mean we increase the risk of identifying low-quality, low-growth companies, because these are normally the type of companies that have very high yields.

When the weighted average is low compared with the median, using the weighted average yield is going to reduce the likelihood that we identify genuinely overlooked stocks.

The median is therefore best for our purposes. It is an important distinction to be aware of.

One change we could make to this test is to replace the dividend yield criterion with one based on shareholder yield (dividends plus net buybacks). However, it is hard to access reliable data on shareholder yield.

Low risk

The test: a one-year beta of 0.75 or less.

A beta measures how volatile a share price is compared with the index it is a part of. A beta below one suggests that when the index rises and falls the stock does so by less, while above one suggests more.

This is far from a perfect measure of risk, but in practice it doesn't do a bad job of highlighting stocks in companies with more defensive characteristics including more conservative balance sheets.

Knowing the way your data provider calculates beta and getting a feel for the data is important, as the level where this test is set may need to be changed depending on the data.

The key thing to keep in mind is that we're interested in stocks that roughly occupy the lower two-fifths of the risk spectrum.

Non-core tests

Dividend cover

The test: dividend payments covered 1.5 times or more by earnings.

Dividend cover is a very important consideration for dividend hunters. It compares a company's EPS with DPS. It does this because dividends are paid from earnings. So for pay-outs to be sustainable, dividend cover must be at least greater than one.

The test used by the screen requiring dividend cover of 1.5 times or more is not a tough one. That's because dull, reliable companies may pay quite a lot of their earnings out as dividends. They may not have much else to do with their money. They should also already have their balance sheets in decent nick to put them in a stronger position to hand out large chunks of surplus cash.

One issue with measuring dividend cover is that companies are not always good at turning reported earnings into cash.

There can be many reasons for this.

For example, it can also be due to money getting tied up in a business's working capital (work in progress, stock on shelves, unpaid bills etc.). And mature companies with high-yielding shares can face big bills to maintain and improve a doddery asset base. Whatever the case, cash is the ultimate king when it comes to dividends. That means a big omission from the High Yield Low Risk criteria is that there is no test to see how effective companies are at turning profits into cash.

This judgement is based on the fact that cash flows can be very lumpy. In a year when cash is unusually scarce, a dividend may look less secure than is really the case. If there is a large amount of capital expenditure a firm has to undertake in a given year, for example, its cash flows could look terrible. However, that is not necessarily reflective of the long-term picture.

The job of earnings is to try to provide the smoothed-out and more far-sighted picture of how a company is doing, by matching a company's spending against sales in the actual period those sales are generated. This means a big capital project which will benefit a company for many years to come will have its cost spread out across those years.

So, earnings-based dividend cover can provide a truer picture of a company's dividend-paying ability. That should be particularly true of the kind of conservatively run company our screen is after. This kind of company is far less likely to employ aggressive accounting techniques.

So, while the cash flow section of a company's accounts is ignored at investors' peril, the judgement for the purposes of this screen is that more would be lost than gained by testing for cash generation.

What's more, the screen's tests for dividend track record, which we will look at next, should help increase our likelihood of identifying cash-generative companies.

Still, the omission of a cash conversion test is something we need to keep in mind when we look at the screen's results on a case-by-case basis.

Dividend and earnings history

The tests:

- Ten years of unbroken dividend payments.

- Ten years of positive underlying earnings.

- Underlying earnings per share (EPS) higher than five years ago.

- Dividend per share (DPS) higher than five years ago.

The screen uses four criteria to assess whether a stock has a track record that suggests it may be a resilient business.

We can also think of these four tests as a way for us to ask whether stocks really are low risk or just low beta.

That probably needs some explaining.

A danger for investors targeting low beta is that this measure of volatility can simply imply a company's business cycle and share price movements are out of sync with the rest of the market. If a stock zags when the market zigs, it may well have a low beta. But such companies can still have yo-yo share prices. They can be very risky and unreliable businesses that simply dance to a different tune to the majority of an index's constituents.

This is often the case with commodity stocks, such as shares in mining and oil companies. They can pay very high dividends, too, at least when times are good. The trouble is that for investors looking for reliable plays, the profits of such companies are highly sensitive to the price of the commodities they produce. Commodity prices often perform differently to broad stock-market indices but are also very volatile.

That means we can have a combination of low beta and high dividend yield but also high share price volatility and low underlying business reliability.

However, consistent profitability and dividends, alongside growth in EPS and DPS over the last five years, suggests a business is more likely to be genuinely reliable and have shares that are genuinely low risk.

It's worth noting that the screen's criteria put no requirement on companies demonstrating particularly strong growth. The ability of a company to grow its earnings and dividend can be very important in creating value for shareholders, but we're primarily after dull companies here. Dull companies often grow at a pedestrian pace.

If you ask too much of a screen, it simply won't bring back any results. We can assess growth prospects for ourselves when we get down to examining the screen's results.

Quality
The tests:

- A return on equity of 12.5% or more.

- A current ratio of one or more.

The return on equity test (RoE) used by the screen is there to tell us whether a company is of decent quality. As previously touched on, there are some sound reasons for investors not to like RoE as a measure of quality. However, it is a useful ratio for the kind of broad sweep that stock screens need to make.

There is also one particular benefit RoE has when it comes to screening for dividend stocks.

RoE takes into account how debt influences shareholder returns. Often this is seen as a weakness of the ratio. However, when it comes to reliable dividend payers, it can make sense for such companies to take on relatively high levels of borrowing, although even the most reliable of businesses can take on too much.

The benefit of a genuinely reliable income stream can usually be greatly enhanced for shareholders if debt is used sensibly to fund the purchase of more income-producing assets. This also brings us on to another omission from this screen's criteria. There is no test for debt levels. The judgement here is simply that what would be lost by including a debt test (reliable companies that can justify relatively high borrowings) could be greater than what would be gained (eliminating dangerously indebted stocks).

Also, given we have identified this as a noteworthy omission from our criteria, we know we need to look at debt on a case-by-case basis when we look more closely at the stocks passing the screen's tests.

The current ratio test provides us with some comfort about the state of the balance sheet, though. The ratio compares cash that a company is expected to receive in the next year (current assets) with the amounts it is due to pay (current liabilities).

If this ratio is greater than one, it means the last time a company published its accounts the balance sheet showed more was due to come in than go out in the coming year.

A low current ratio may suggest liquidity problems exist that could result in the dividend being pulled. This test should not be applied to companies from the finance sector, such as banks, due to the nature of their balance sheets.

Adapting the screen

The main adaptation I've needed to make to the High Yield Low Risk screen over the years is simply to allow stocks to fail some of the non-core tests in fallow years in order to create a decent number of positive results.

However, with this screen more than most, it is really important to think about what tests a stock has failed when it comes to doing further research. The kind of quality the screen is looking for is based on consistency through conservative management. If a cyclical business has broken its pay-out record but remained financially strong through a turbulent period, we may still consider it relatively consistent. The cut can be regarded as a commendably conservative move. But if it looks like management was forced into the cut, by high debt levels, for example, then we potentially have a very different story. Where to set the low beta test is also something worth considering. Beta depends on what index a share's volatility is being measured against, so the beta for the same stock can be different depending on what index a data provider is using to calculate it. While I would always recommend keeping the beta test at one or below, play around and see what feels sensible.

CHAPTER 23

FROM QUANTITATIVE TO QUALITATIVE – WHY DIVIDENDS, NOT INCOME?

INVESTORS OFTEN DEVELOP a love for dividend-paying shares that defies common sense. The tangible allure of having a dividend cheque drop on our doormat (or more likely, be electronically transferred into our brokerage account) is so exciting it can override other important considerations.

When it comes to understanding the results from our screen, it's vital to see dividends from the right perspective and avoid falling into dividend traps.

Why dividends matter, and why they don't

We've seen that a company's ability to pay and sustain a dividend can tell us very important things about its business, how it is run, and its financial health. But when it comes to creating shareholder value, the actual direct benefit of being handed cash is negligible.

We risk making poorer investment decisions if our understanding of dividends focuses on the income stream they generate, because this can cause us to lose sight of the bigger picture.

To understand why this is the case, we have to think about how investors make money from owning shares. The total return from a share is made up of the dividends paid out plus the change in the share price. In the grand scheme of things, the relative influence of each component doesn't really matter.

Total return = dividend yields + share price performance

The dream company (the ultimate quality compounder we met when we looked at our High Quality screen) would actually never pay a dividend. That's because it would always be able to recycle all its surplus cash into super-profitable growth.

A company able to do this would be expected to create value that would hugely outweigh the benefit of any dividend payment. For an investor wanting to generate income from such an investment, all that they'd need to do is periodically sell a portion of their shares.

Admittedly, human psychology makes this hard to do, so generating income from dividends could have behavioural advantages in the real world. Intuitively it can feel like selling shares involves a sacrifice whereas receiving a dividend is pure reward. While this is true psychologically, it makes little sense logically.

When investors are paid dividends, something really is being given up. That something is the ability for a company to use the money in other ways to try to create shareholder value. The most basic illustration of this lost opportunity is the fact that share prices fall by the amount of the dividend being paid as soon as investors no longer have the right to receive the payment. From this perspective, it's a zero-sum game.

A share sale can be thought of as an investor's choice to release capital, whereas dividend payments eliminate the element of choice and force capital onto shareholders.

A marketing mistake

To further understand this important point, it is helpful to think of a graph that is often very questionably used to try and demonstrate the importance of dividend income. It is commonly employed as a marketing tool for funds with income strategies.

You may well have come across the graph before. It shows a stock market index without dividends compared with the return of the same index when dividends are taken into account.

You can see an example for the MSCI World Index over the first 20 years of the millennium in Figure 15. In finance jargon this is referred to as an index's capital return (share price without dividends) versus its total return (share price with dividends reinvested).

When we compare the total return including dividend payments (the topmost line) to the change in the share price alone (the line below), the easy conclusion to draw is that dividend income is very important. It looks clear cut.

Figure 15: MSCI World index in first two decades of the 2000s with and without dividends.

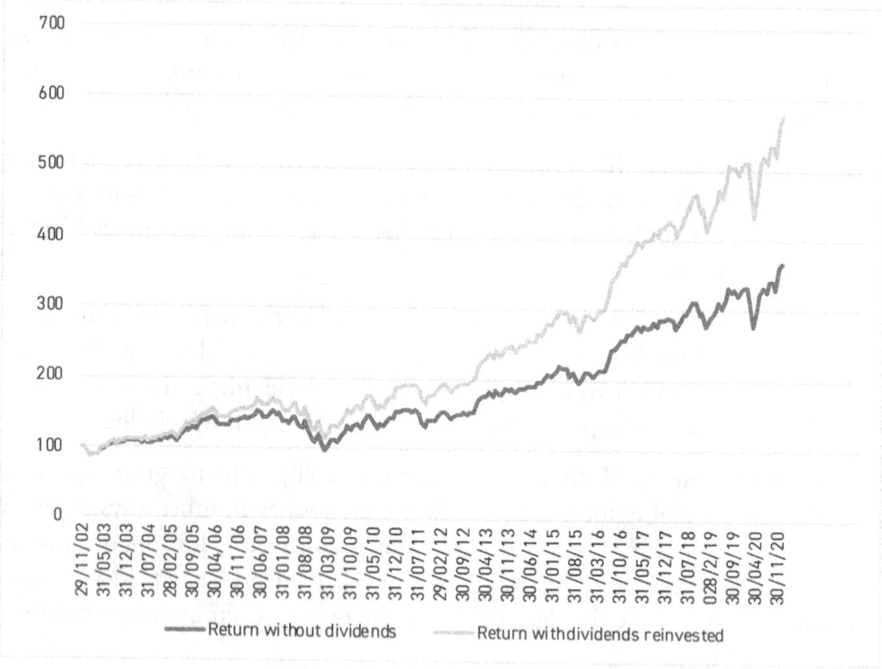

Source: FactSet.

Well yes, but...

If we stop to think about it, this quickly turns out to be absolute nonsense. The simple fact is that if no companies were paying dividends, we'd be left with the question of what they would do with the cash instead?

The line on the graph of the index that ignores dividends essentially assumes companies buried all that money in a pit or incinerated it or something else of that type. Sure, in the parallel universe where no companies paid dividends some of them may have spent the retained funds wastefully. Nevertheless, we should at least assume some value would have been created.

The important point is that a dividend payment should be seen on a par with the other spending decision made by a company. When a dividend is paid, another opportunity to use that cash in a different way is lost. This other opportunity could be investing in the business, making acquisitions, buying back shares or paying down debt.

In fact, one of the biggest traps for income investors is being seduced by the high dividend yield of shares in a mature company, when the company should actually be paying more attention to its balance sheet and less to answering the clamour for income. The clamour for income often comes from professional investors tasked with managing a fund with a myopic mandate based on producing a level of yield that is higher than the index (that really is a rule set for many UK 'income' funds).

Income's bad outcome

The next three graphs show an example of a company stretching too far to feed its shareholders income. They illustrate the experience of UK telecoms giant BT leading up to a dividend cut in 2020.

Figure 16 shows the amounts the company paid out in dividends in each of the five years preceding the cut alongside its borrowings. As we can see, debt climbed while dividends were paid. A proportion of dividends were effectively being paid from debt.

Worse still, the debt pile was substantial to begin with and continued to grow.

Figure 16: BT – dividends paid as borrowings rise

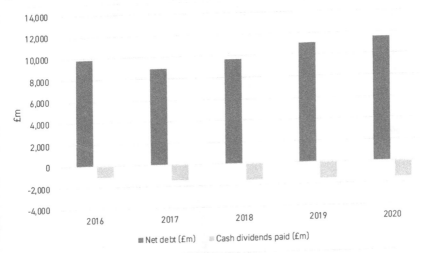

Source: FactSet, ignores impact of IFRS 16 change to lease accounting on 2020 results.

Figure 17 shows that investors became ever more sceptical about the company's unerring commitment to the pay-out. This pushed down BT's valuation based on EV/EBITDA while the dividend yield rose and spiked to levels that expressed utter disbelief that the pay-out could be sustained. The dividend was finally savagely sliced at which point the EV/EBITDA valuation began to improve.

Figure 17: BT's valuation improves after the dividend cut

Source: FactSet.

Finally, Figure 18 shows what would have happened to the company's debt position assuming it had simply funnelled all the money paid as dividends over the five years into debt reduction.

Figure 18: BT – if the dividend cash had been used to reduce debt

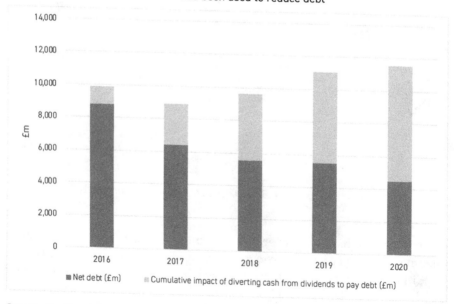

Source: FactSet, ignores impact of IFRS 16 change to lease accounting on 2020 results.

Prioritising debt reduction over dividends may have led to some selling by income funds and other dividend obsessives had it occurred at the start of the five years. That may have meant a short sharp hit to the shares. However, it seems unlikely that the company's valuation would ever have hit the disaster rating it sunk to before BT finally bowed to the inevitable and cut its pay-out, although we can never know what could have been for sure.

Avoid the dividend danger zone

Many investors fetishise dividends and treat them as a thing apart from other capital allocation choices. It is understandable based on our psychology, but it can be dangerous.

As Terry Smith, fund manager and founder of investment firm FundSmith, has commented, "There seems to be something so alluring about dividend income that it often seems to lead investors to abandon common sense or be encouraged to do so by the investment industry."[38]

When screening for dividends we need to avoid succumbing to the siren call of income and instead stay focused on the advantage that rational dividend strategies can provide us with. Namely, that dividend strategies can identify companies that are cash generative and conservatively run. When this is the case, management are likely to know the business well and be managing it for the long term. Indeed, it seems little coincidence that solid dividend-paying companies also often have high levels of family ownership, which tends to foster intergenerational thinking.

A conservative attitude to cash and investment can suggest decisions are more likely to be in the best interest of shareholders, and should the company decide to invest in growth there is a higher likelihood it will be done on the basis that the returns on investment received will be high, and therefore more likely to create shareholder value rather than destroy it.

We'll look at one such case when examining one of the screen's successes in the next chapter. We'll also cast an eye over one of its failures, from which we can learn a lesson or two.

CHAPTER 24

STOCK SELECTION FOR HIGH YIELD LOW RISK

HAVING LOOKED AT why it makes sense to seek out dull-but-reliable companies, we're going to have a look at one stock the High Yield Low Risk screen highlighted in 2013 that was set to become spectacularly more interesting to investors as the decade progressed. However, the reasons to like the stock when it was highlighted were very much to do with the kind of underappreciated winning traits we've been exploring. We'll also look at another stock pick from 2016 that worked out terribly. This was a company that was masquerading as reliable but, with a bit of further research, was revealed to be anything but. Let's start with our success story, though.

The success: sports super star

JD Sports Fashion was something of a UK stock-market star in the 2010s. It is a retailer that sells trainers, sports clothing and accessories. Despite a focus on bricks-and-mortar stores, a sector that has in general suffered due to online competition, JD's business has thrived. Its youthful customers flock to its stores to get their hands on the super-trendy products it sells.

The company has forged lucrative relationships with top sports fashion brands, such as Nike and Adidas. These brands restrict top-end ranges to a select band of high-quality retailers, of which JD is one. The company has also benefited from what is known as the 'athleisure' trend. This is a fashion for people to wear expensive athletics clothes and trainers to look good rather than do sport.

Down at the heel

However, when the High Yield Low Risk screen came across the company the story was very different to the tale just told. At the time, in April 2013, JD was being outgunned by UK rival Sports Direct. It was also struggling to turn around a loss-making camping-goods retailer it had bought on the cheap. The dividend, though, offered a glimmer of hope.

In fact, there was a lot more to recommend JD than just the dividend when the screen selected it. That's because there were already signs that the business might be turning a corner. And, very importantly, the company had previously been far more profitable, suggesting a recovery could turbo charge earnings. What's more, the dividend record helped to demonstrate a degree of reliability despite the tough spot JD found itself in.

Of particular significance was the fact the company was aggressively cutting costs to try to eliminate losses from the camping-goods business, having come up short with its initial turn around attempts. Simply reducing losses from that business had the potential to cause a major uplift in profits. Dealing with this problem also meant there was the prospect that investors' attention would shift back to JD's more successful sports fashion business.

JD also had a sound balance sheet. Strong dividend records often suggest a company's finances are robust. For a company trying to overcome trading difficulties, balance sheet strength is often crucial to success. It provides a safety net should the task ahead be more difficult and more costly than anticipated. It also means a company is more likely to be able to endure more pain before it must cut the dividend, or worse still, make an emergency appeal for fresh money from shareholders.

From dull to divine

Our High Yield Low Risk screen sets out to find dull but reliable stocks. While JD did turn out to be reliable, it has proved far from a dull investment since the screen highlighted its shares. Those who bought the shares when the screen highlighted the stock and held on to March 2021 (the end of the 10-year period our performance review covers) would have enjoyed a 2,750% total return, as shown in Figure 19.

The screen's performance record only reflects a tiny fraction of JD's mighty ascent, though, as the stock only featured as a High Yield Low Risk pick for a single 12-month period. After that it went on to far better things, which saw it appear as a top pick of the momentum screen we'll look at in the final section of the book.

While I have historically monitored screens based on annual reshuffles, there is no reason to be prescriptive about holding periods. Ideally, we're looking for companies so fantastic that their shares should be bought and held forever.

Figure 19: JD Sports Fashion – it was about more than just dividends

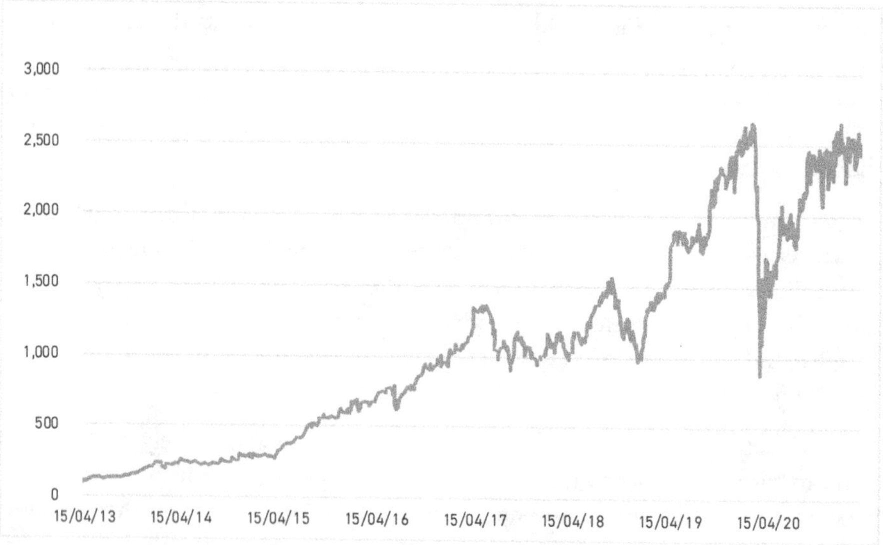

Source: FactSet.

The failure: how the Mitie fall!

Possibly the worst of the 106 stocks highlighted by the High Yield Low Risk screen over 10 years is Mitie. There are shares that have contributed worse performances to the screen's results, but in terms of timing, Mitie was a peach (a rotten one) when it was highlighted in May 2016.

Mitie is a company that takes care of buildings. It provides its clients with services like cleaning, security and catering.

Before the High Yield Low Risk screen came across it, it had been spending a lot of money buying other businesses.

While multiple small acquisitions can be a reliable way to create value for cash generative companies, big and aggressive acquisition strategies tend to be dangerous.

The activities of Mitie's business may be dull and easy enough to understand, but the contracts it entered into with clients were altogether more byzantine, mysterious and difficult for outsiders to fathom. Nevertheless, it was able to pay rising dividends and generate rising profits… or was it?

Contract confusion

Profits for Mitie have not always been what they seemed. The High Yield Low Risk screen looks at underlying profits. These are profits that ignore items that have been deemed as one-off in nature. The purpose of this is to iron out one-off crinkles in individual years. This can be very useful when large items pass through the profit and loss account that genuinely are exceptional and may give an unnecessarily harsh impression about the reliability of a company. Also, as we've seen in previous chapters, certain technicalities around acquisition accounting mean some spending on maintaining certain intangible assets (such as brands and software) can get double-counted by statutory accounting numbers and needs adjusting for.

However, with Mitie, there was one big red flag for investors to heed back in 2016. This was the sheer quantity and magnitude of one-off adjustments this company had been making in the preceding years. We can see this depicted in Figure 20 (the 2016 results were not actually published until after the stock was picked by the screen).

Figure 20: Mitie big adjustments

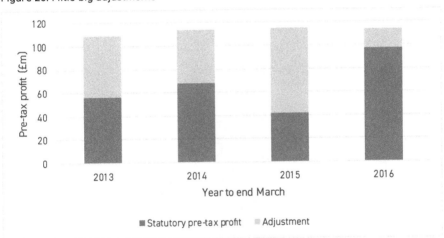

Source: FactSet.

This level of adjustment meant that underlying profits were regularly substantially higher than the official statutory profits. This looked fishy. Often one-off adjustments are reflections of past mistakes. For example, long-term contracts that have been signed on less favourable terms than thought at the time. Or money spent on acquisitions that have not worked out. When such one-offs occur regularly, there is a chance that they are anything but one-off. It can be the sign of a business with deep-rooted problems.

So it proved to be with Mitie. The company issued three profit warnings over four months in late 2016 and early 2017.

This succession of blows came after a new management team took charge. It found revenue had been recorded too soon and that the balance sheet had been used to hide costs. The value of past acquisitions was also massively written down and the accounts for 2015 and 2016 were restated.

The company had been papering over the cracks, and the screen fell for it. Screens just don't do nuance. That's down to diligent investors.

Peak regret!

As it turns out, the High Yield Low Risk screen stumbled upon Mitie near the shares' peak. The stock was a major contributor to the underperformance of the screen in the following 12 months. Mitie delivered a negative 18% total return compared with a positive 21% from the index. While the price made a brief comeback, the longer-term trend was downwards to the end of our 10-year screen-performance period, as can be seen in Figure 21.

Yet for investors prepared to do a bit of legwork, the danger signs were there to spot.

Figure 21: How the Mitie fall

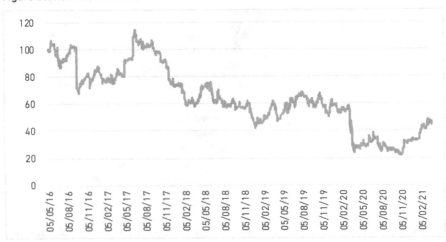

Source: FactSet.

In summary

We've learned why a well-known, sleep-well-at-night investment strategy that tends to outperform the market is routinely overlooked by professional investors. It is simply too dull and fails to shine at the time when potential customers are most likely to be putting money into the market. However, it is possible for investors who are not tied to commercial concerns to exploit this phenomenon. The lack of big money interest also means it is a phenomenon that is more likely to persist over time.

We've also taken a look at a number of the qualitative considerations for researching stocks highlighted by our screen. And if there is one big lesson we've learned, it is not to be greedy about dividend yields. Very high yields are generally a warning sign. Meanwhile dividend payments should not be seen as a thing apart from other capital allocation decisions even if they can signal other attractive company characteristics, such as sound finances and conservative management.

MOMENTUM INVESTING

"Ever wonder why fund managers can't beat the S&P 500? 'Cause they're sheep – and the sheep get slaughtered."

This line was uttered by actor Michael Douglas playing Gordon Gekko in the 1987 Oliver Stone movie Wall Street. But the funny thing is, in investing, sheep often win.

As with most things in life, the reality of so-called 'herding' is nuanced. Sure, investors can take painful losses from following their herd instinct, especially if they are very late to the party. However, there is also the potential to make huge profits from heeding signals from the crowd.

Profiting from momentum is the strategy we're now going to explore. My Great Expectations screen has been very successful at doing this over a decade, although along the way it has also illustrated the pitfalls expressed in the Gekko quote.

The 10-year cumulative total return from the screen since inception of 371%, compared with 109% from the FTSE 350. With that kind of performance, it's perhaps worth taking the rough with the smooth.

The ability to profit from momentum is no secret. In fact, it has been so thoroughly researched and has been found to be so bafflingly pervasive that it has been given the title of 'the premier anomaly'.

We're going to look at some of the curious phenomena that occur when people come together and make collective judgements. These are key forces that make momentum investing work, as too are the behavioural biases that we've looked at in past sections of the book, especially in relation to contrarian investing.

But for those who just want to get down to the workings of the screen, it's time to skip ahead to Chapter 26.

CHAPTER 25

CROWD COMPUTING: WHY MOMENTUM INVESTING WORKS

IN THEORY, A share price represents the collective judgement of all market participants on the future cash flows the share's owner will get. A lot of smart thinking goes into determining the buy and sell decisions that determine a share price.

But there are also a range of not-so-rational motivations at work.

Momentum investing looks to profit from the not-so-rational part of the process. It does this by exploiting a predictable trend that occurs when crowd judgements are made. The trend is simply that shares that have gone up strongly in the past are likely to do the same in the future.

A good place to start trying to understand why this phenomenon exists is at a 19th century country fair.

The curious racist who proved himself wrong

Among the discoveries of Victorian polymath Francis Galton were the statistical phenomena of normal distribution, regression to the mean (see value investing) and standard deviation. He also produced the first weather map, invented fingerprinting, founded the science of psychometrics and devised the questionnaire. He advanced our understanding of the world in many more ways besides. In his books and papers, which numbered more than 340, he even proposed optimum ways to make a cup of tea and slice Christmas cake.

There is no denying he was a man of great accomplishments, but his legacy exists under a very dark shadow. Many of the scientific methods he introduced the world to were created in the pursuit of the pseudo-science of eugenics – a form of so-called scientific racism that has thankfully been discredited due to both outrage at the horrors of the holocaust and by being disproved by discoveries in the field of genetics.

However, Galton's pseudo-scientific pursuits help explain why at the age of 86 he was ambling around the 1906 West of England Fat Stock and Poultry Exhibition near his home in Plymouth. He had an interest in the genetic heritage of animals and what it may tell him about humans. His belief that pockets of genetic superiority also existed in his own species helps explain why he was curious about the increasing popularity of democracy.

At the fair, he stumbled upon a competition that caught his attention. For the price of six pennies, people were given an opportunity to guess the weight of an ox once 'slaughtered and dressed'. The closest estimates would get prizes.

Galton saw the ox-weight judging game as offering valuable insights into the *vox populi* and behaviour at the ballot box.

The stall owner lent Galton all 800 entries to the competition following its conclusion. The stats-mad intellectual then went about tabulating the data. Something remarkable occurred. While no one individual had guessed the weight of the slaughtered-and-dressed ox, the average of all the guesses was bang on.

The result suggested that collectively, the crowd made a far better judgement than one would expect even from someone whose genetics put them at the hereditary pinnacle of ox-weight guessing.

What Galton had discovered is now commonly referred to as the wisdom of crowds. His finding was no one-off.

The observation that the average of many independent judgements is better than even the judgement of the most talented individual has influenced one of the biggest ideas in finance. Equity markets are, after all, mass competitions in judging the value of stocks and shares. The big idea is one we also met when we looked at dividend investing: the Efficient Market Hypothesis.

The EMH assumes all available information must be in the share price at any given time. The wisdom of crowds makes it so. Taken all the way to its logical conclusion, the EMH suggests that risk-adjusted outperformance is only possible through luck.

But then why is momentum so widely and consistently measurable in markets?

A major clue to why markets may be different to ox-weight judging competitions lies in how investors cast their votes. In markets, share prices tell us how the crowd is voting. In the ox competition, judgements were all made independently and with no reference to each other. What's more, knowing the power of the wisdom of crowds provides a big incentive for investors to pay attention to the prevailing price of a share and how it is moving.

This kind of self-referencing feedback loop makes the wisdom of crowds go a bit funny. Sometimes the crowd's wisdom even descends into madness.

Follow the crowd

People are social. That makes markets social. That affects judgements.

An experiment by psychologists into music downloads helps illustrate just how easily our judgements are swayed by social influence when making complex choices.[39]

The experiment recruited 14,341 participants through a teen-interest website. They were able to access 48 songs by unknown bands and were free to download and rate the music they liked after listening to it.

There was a twist.

Some of the participants accessed a version of the site where they were given no idea of what other site users were doing. This was done to tell the researchers what music people downloaded and enjoyed most when selecting it independently. Other participants found themselves on a version of the site where they saw how many downloads each song had got. The researchers displayed the download information in two different ways. One method was designed to put more emphasis on the choices of others and create greater social influence.

The effect of social influence was massive. The researchers measured the difference between the most and least popular songs from the different versions of the website. They found the 'inequality of choice' (the difference between the hits and flops) was about one-and-a-half-times greater on the site that exposed users to the most social influence compared with when people were left to choose songs independently.

Importantly from the perspective of investment decision making, as well as the divergence in popularity being more extreme, the preferences themselves changed.

By splitting the socially influenced participants into eight separate user-groups, the researchers were able to test how predictable outcomes were when social influence was involved. Would the information from the crowd help participants to herd towards the songs that proved most popular among the people who had not been influenced by peers?

The answer was no.

In fact, social influence made it very hard to predict which songs would be winners and which would be losers. While the 'best' songs rarely did poorly and the 'worst' rarely did well, everything else was in play. The researchers found the popularity of the 'intermediate' songs was highly unpredictable in terms of where they ranked.

In the stock market, investors are inundated with information on the investment equivalent of downloads. That's to say, movements in share prices provide a constant commentary on the interaction between buyers and sellers. The price goes up, the stock is a hit. It goes down, it's a flop.

The intelligence of other market participants and our knowledge of the wisdom of crowds means investors would be foolish not to pay attention to this price information. Given it is common knowledge that momentum, or the premier anomaly, is a force at work in markets, there is even more reason to pay attention to price movements. Momentum becomes something of a self-fulfilling prophesy.

Following the signal from share prices while ignoring the substance of the investment case has led to many ridiculous periods of speculation.

The dot-com boom was the most recent example. Many argue the recent popularity of virtual assets, such as cryptocurrency and NFTs, is the latest incarnation of such behaviour. So too the inflated valuation of loss-making tech stocks. Perhaps by the time this book is published, a more concrete judgement will have been made.

Irrational herding (it is only ever truly irrational after the bubble bursts) is something commonly referred to as 'the madness of crowds'. It is easy to get caught up in. Especially for momentum investors.

Crowd confusion

John Maynard Keynes, a great investor as well as a great economist, explained the stock market as being like a beauty contest where judges are rewarded for selecting the face that is most popular with the other judges, rather than the one they personally find most attractive.

This captures a key feature of a pure momentum investing strategy. The key focus is not to buy into excellent businesses, it is simply to second-guess others.

However, second-guessing others is an incredibly hard thing to do without a well-structured process. A well-structured process is what the screen we'll explore in the next chapter attempts to put in place by broadening out the search for momentum beyond share price alone.

Here's a story that demonstrates why the game of second-guessing the second-guesses of other second-guessers is just as confusing as it sounds.

Imagine we're in a room with over 1,000 investment professionals. Everyone is asked to pick a number between zero and 100. The winner of this game will be the person who chooses a number that is two-thirds of the average choice.

This game is one that has been run by James Montier, author of *The Little Book of Behavioural Investing* and an investment strategist at GMO. What he found shows just how hard it is to make good judgements when we are forced to make decisions which reference the actions of a crowd we're part of.

Montier found there were four popular answers in his game. The first was a dumb one. It was 50. In other words, the average if everyone picked a random number between zero and 100.

These people just weren't paying attention. We need two thirds of the average guess. Two thirds of 50 is about 33. That was another one of the four popular answers.

But here's where the mind games come in. If we're picking 33 as two-thirds of an average of 50, then our influence on the overall outcome, and the influence of anyone else as smart as us, means the actual average guess in the room is going to be lower than 50. That means two thirds of the average is going to be lower than 33.

In fact, assuming everyone is as rational as we're being, the only place for our estimate to end up is zero. In a world where everyone is rational, the only answer is zero. It's what game theorists would predict. It was another popular answer when Montier played his game.

But because everyone in the room was human, and not all humans are rational, two-thirds of the average was not zero. The people who said zero were too clever for their own goods.

No, the really smart professionals who understood logic and human behaviour arrived at a number around 22. This is two thirds of 33. So the answer suggests everyone else only got to the answer 33 and did not think any further. That's only giving everyone else in the room a touch more credit than is the case when answering 33. This, the fourth and final popular answer, was the closest to being right. But it was also fairly wide of the mark.

The actual answer is that two-thirds of the average (26) in Montier's game turned out to be 17. Only three of the 1,000 players got this answer.

In the stock market, and in the confusion caused by the real-life second-guessing game that takes place every trading day, momentum prospers. But it also often betrays. Investors jump on hot trends with no real way of knowing when the game will be up and how much froth is already in the price. The crowd's wisdom gets intermingled with its madness.

Eventually, hot stocks and hot themes that lack substance, or that have simply become overvalued, get found out. Changes in sentiment can produce painful whipsaws in performance from share price momentum strategies. High-flying, overhyped trends fall like Icarus.[40]

What can investors do to increase their chances of backing momentum plays that are about more than just hype?

We'll talk tactics in the next chapter. But first we need to look at one other curious trend that our screen is going to exploit.

Profiting from mistakes

The investment industry forks out huge amounts of money to highly qualified and highly intelligent people to forecast the future sales, profits and cash flows of listed companies. The time and effort that goes into this endeavour is immense. But for anyone judging forecasts based on their accuracy, the results are hugely disappointing.

In the 1980s, a star contrarian investor named David Dreman decided to try to measure how accurate brokers really were. He did this with an epic study into the difference between forecast and reported earnings.

His study was later extended to cover the 33 years to 2008 by investment firm Star Capital. Over that entire period, the average error of forecasts made 12 months before actual earnings were reported was a massive 30%. What's more, there was little sign that any major improvements had been made to forecast accuracy over time.

The surprise most of us experience when we first discover quite how wrong analysts' forecasts tend to be is itself a reflection of the fact we suffer from the same affliction as them. We're human.

We humans are overconfident in our ability to predict the future. We overestimate our forecasting abilities, we think we're able to achieve impossible levels of predictive precision, and we think we're better than we really are at forecasting compared with others.[41] What's more, once we've publicly stated a position, we are very adverse to altering it in response to new information, especially if a major revision is required.

One of the basic features of the human condition seems to be our steely resistance to admit the future is very unpredictable. We are far more prepared to believe it is possible to know what the future holds than is justified.

Also aiding our ability to believe financial forecasts despite them normally being wrong is the fact that for companies followed by several analysts, the consensus forecast probably represents a pretty good guess at what future earnings will be based on everything known at the time.

But while we can't predict the future with any real accuracy, the trend in predictions can be predictive. Sometimes broker forecasts keep changing in the same direction. Things keep getting better, or things keep getting worse.

These trends are often driven by forces that analysts do not want to second guess for fear of making fools of themselves. A trend may exist but be hard to quantify with no guarantee of it continuing. It is not worth the risk for analysts to make a laughing stock of themselves by straying from the crowd and trying to base forecasts on something that's inherently unquantifiable. Sticking to hard facts and the herd is safer and less likely to lead to the sack.

Our propensity to put excessive faith in forecasts means when analysts upgrade or downgrade their predictions in response to new information, share prices tend to move in the same direction. This often happens even once upgrades or downgrades have long stopped being a surprise occurrence.

The 10-year graph in Figure 22 offers an example. It charts an equipment-hire company called Ashtead's earnings forecast for the next twelve months, alongside its share price. We'll get much better acquainted with Ashtead in Chapter 27.

The graph uses something called a log scale, which prevents the early portions of the lines being in an illegibly tiny range due to mind-blowing share price gains and earnings growth experienced. Each time there is a jump in the forecast earnings line, it represents upgrades. There are a few downgrades too, especially during the Covid-19 lockdown. However, in the main, upgrades have been staggeringly persistent. Predictable even. Nevertheless, the share price more often than not responds to each new upgrade despite the occurrence seeming anything but surprising.

Upgrades on the up

Many companies may be more capable than ever of delivering bigger upgrades for longer.

Figure 22: Ashtead share price in step with forecasts

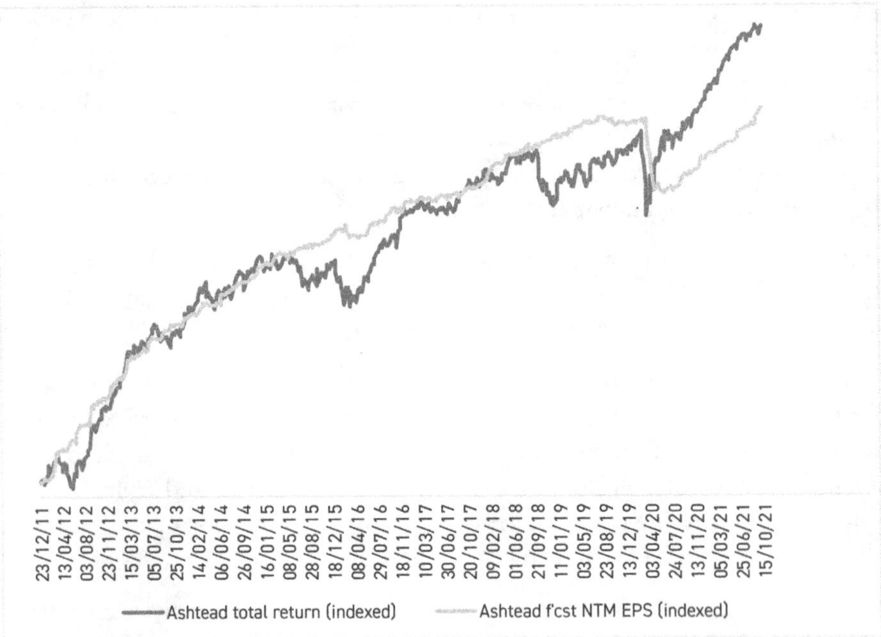

Source: FactSet.

In March 2017, the *Economist* magazine used historical base rates to show that the sales forecasts for online retailer and cloud storage giant Amazon looked ridiculous. Base rates are used to judge how credible our expectations of the future are by comparing them with what has happened in the past. If there is no historical precedent for our predictions, we probably need to double-check our thinking.

When the *Economist* article was written, the level of growth being forecast for Amazon out to 2025 had never been achieved by a company with a market cap of over $100bn. No other company of that size had even come close.[42] That seemed fair grounds on which to question the forecasts.

Amazon did not meet the forecasts. It has done way better. The tech giant looks set to hit the 2025 sales forecast two-and-a-half years earlier than predicted. Analysts were not being overly optimistic. They were not optimistic enough.

The data the *Economist* had based its article on was from a meticulously compiled historical record covering the period between 1950 to 2015 produced by Michael Mauboussin.[43] Mauboussin is a highly influential investment strategist, author and academic. He had a typically thoughtful response to Amazon shattering previous records. He did not jump to the defence of the historical precedent by suggesting this was just a one-off extreme. He considered what may have changed. His answer was 'intangibles'.[44]

Intangible investments, such as intellectual property, brand and software development, have become increasingly important for companies. This is of major significance for investors, as we have already covered in previous chapters. Intangible investment is particularly important for many of the world's most successful companies.

That matters for growth rates because the profits generated from intangible investments are different to those from tangible investments. For one thing, returns from intangibles are less predictable. They are far more hit-and-miss than returns from tangible investments. But when success comes, it can be far more significant.

For example, a software company could develop a new computer programme which fails to gain any significant traction in the market. However, if the product turns out to be a hit, sales can quickly build, and the new software could quickly dislodge an incumbent. In short, success or failure is more likely to be extreme.

Returns from successful intangible investments are also likely to be higher than for tangibles. Going back to the software example, because the major cost of development is upfront, the cost of new sales can be very low but the price-tag remains high. This leads to huge profits if the new software really catches on. The company does not need to invest in new factory capacity or raw materials to sell another software subscription. It just provides a username and password to its new customer.

Because this kind of success is very hard to forecast, upgrades can be substantial. They can also continue for a very long time. That's especially true because many of the companies that have built their success on intangible investments over the last two decades have created natural monopolies; something true of some US big-tech favourites. A natural monopoly can give longevity to growth alongside insane pricing power.

There is a downside to successes built on intangible investments. The fall from grace can be just as extreme as the ascent. In his work, Mauboussin gives the example of Blackberry, an early smartphone innovator.

The company enjoyed fantastic growth for many years, but this was abruptly upended by the launch of the iPhone. After this, Blackberry experienced a 27% average annual revenue decline for a decade.

CHAPTER 26

SCREENING FOR STOCKS WITH GREAT EXPECTATIONS

L ET'S QUICKLY RECAP what we have learned about momentum investing:

- Share price momentum is a dominant market force.

- Share price momentum can be treacherous, especially when it is born from the madness of crowds.

- Broker forecasts are often very wrong, which leads to significant upgrades and downgrades.

- Persistent forecast upgrade trends can develop and drive share prices higher.

- Upgrades may be becoming a more significant force in markets as intangible investment becomes more important for companies.

Momentum squared

One very effective way to build a stock screen is to combine two effective and complementary techniques.[45] Combining price- and earnings-forecast momentum is a case in point, and this is the foundation of the screen we're now going to explore.

As we'll see, this approach cannot altogether overcome momentum investing's biggest flaw, which is whipsaw reversals. However, it may go some way to countering the worst of this while turbo-charging upside during the good times.

The combination of price- and earnings-forecast momentum can also highlight some spectacular long-term growth stories and recovery plays.

Why should these two forms of momentum make such good bedfellows?

The main reason for combining these factors is that they can endorse each other.

Persistent forecast upgrades suggest share price momentum is more than hype. Something positive is happening at the company which is reflected in earnings upgrades. Likewise, strong share price gains suggest investors are judging the upgrades to be something more than a flash in the pan. They may persist. There's also an increased chance that we'll be looking at the kind of earnings growth that creates value (cost of investment below return on investment) rather than the type that destroys it (cost above return).

Track Record

The Great Expectations screen we're about to look at has delivered a total return of 371% over its first 10 years of life. That compares with 109% from the FTSE 350 Index, which the screen picks shares from. Factoring in a 1.5% notional annual charge to reflect dealing costs and the return drops to 305%.

There have been some almighty peak-to-trough falls in that time. In particular, during the March 2020 Covid-19 sell-off, the five stocks then being monitored by the screen plummeted 54% on a total return basis before staging a crazily sharp bounce-back. The FTSE 350 experienced a 35% drawdown in the same period, as shown in Figure 23.

However, the danger of whipsaw moves is perhaps best illustrated by the screen's outing when it was run in January 2021. At the time it highlighted several stocks that had been massive beneficiaries of lockdown.

While it was already clear lockdown was unlikely to continue for the rest of the year, these stocks were nevertheless still riding high. Part of this was due to the expectation that a long-term change to consumer trends had occurred. But with hindsight, it is also clear a lot of what looked attractive at the time was just hype. It was the crowd blindly chasing the latest hot thing, and in some cases, management playing along. It was people being people and momentum being momentum.

One of the stock picks from the start of 2021 fell by more than 70% in value and another by over 50%. The falls reflected some bad luck in the timing of the screen and bad trading at the companies concerned, but it also reflected the pricing of a hype bubble.

Figure 23: Momentum

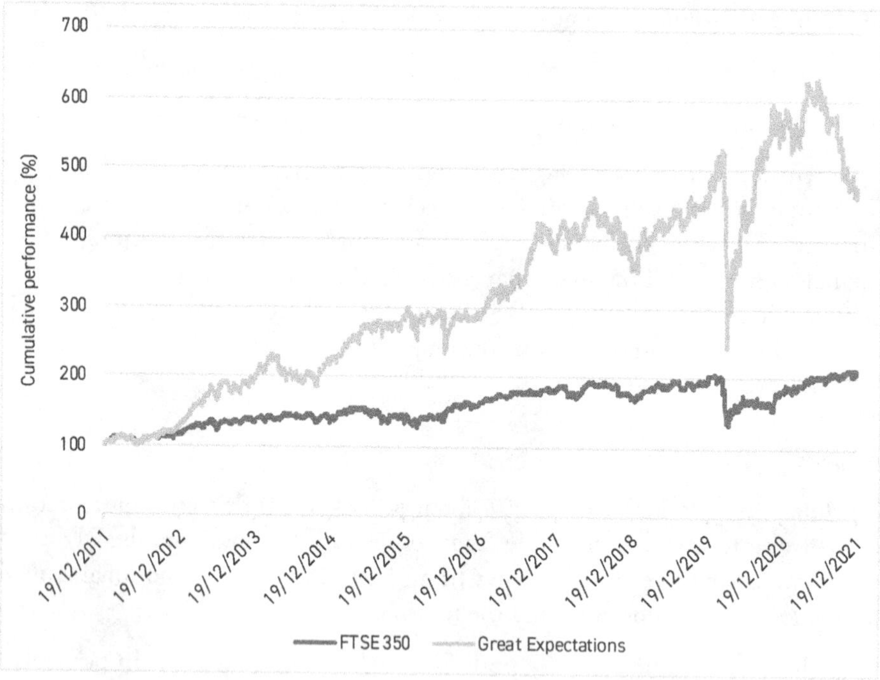

Source: Thomson Datastream.

The important lesson from this experience is that backing super-hot stocks that have already had an eye-popping run can be a case of playing with fire. It is usually best to get in before conditions are truly scorching.

Criteria

It is easy to confuse the idea of momentum investing with growth investing. High-growth companies are often associated with soaring share prices and forecast upgrades. However, momentum investing takes in a far broader range of opportunity.

Unlike the other screens we've looked at, which try to emulate particular investment styles based on company fundamentals, momentum is an anything goes strategy.

If the share price gains and upgrades are due a business turnaround, such as the situations our Contrarian Value screen is designed to identify, then the momentum screen will happily jump aboard. If the shares and earnings are on the up due to a cyclical upswing in end markets, then it's a valid momentum play, too. And if a company is just gunning it on the growth front, welcome aboard the momentum train, so long as the screening criteria are met, of course.

This is our equal opportunities employer out of our four strategies. We will look more closely at the three different types of situation that tend to be most frequently highlighted by the screen a bit later. But first, the criteria:

Share price momentum

- Share price momentum better than the index over three months. **CORE TEST**

- Share price momentum better than the index over one month.

- Share price momentum better than the index over six months.

- Share price momentum at least double that of the index over the past year.

Earnings momentum

- EPS forecasts for next financial year upgraded by at least 10% over the preceding 12 months. **CORE TEST**

- EPS forecasts for the financial year after next upgraded by at least 10% over the preceding 12 months. **CORE TEST**

- EPS growth of 10% or more forecast for the next financial year.

- EPS growth of 10% or more forecast for the financial year after next.

How it works

The screen uses four criteria to test for earnings momentum and four more to test share price momentum. The reason to really go to town on both measures is to try to gain added assurances that we are looking at the real thing.

Relatively short-term share price movements (three months) can be very effective in highlighting really hot stocks. However, the danger is that only looking at the short term will increase the chance of latching on to a very fleeting trend. Essentially, by ignoring longer time frames we could make an already risky strategy riskier.

The criteria of the screen therefore represent a bit of a mix-and-match of time periods. Let's take a closer look.

Share price momentum

The core test

The test: share price momentum better than the index over three months.

Three-month share price momentum (the price rise over the last three months) is a personal favourite of mine. I originally started using this as my main momentum measure after reading an extensive study of momentum across various asset classes by Elroy Dimson, Paul Marsh and Mike Staunton, of London Business School. While there was no recommendation by the authors of the report, their findings did seem to suggest it struck a good balance in capturing recent price movements but also covering a long enough period to be meaningful.

Generally, most fans of momentum seem to gravitate towards tracking price movements based on periods of between three months and one year.

There is an argument that this test could be based on total return rather than share price performance, given that shares drop in proportion to dividends paid when they come due.

The other tests

The tests:

- Share price momentum better than the index over one month.
- Share price momentum better than the index over six months.
- Share price momentum at least double that of the index over the past year.

Two of the three other price momentum tests make sure shares have remained hot over very recent periods, which may reduce the chances that the stock has already peaked. The quite aggressive one-year measure tries to ensure we are looking at stocks which the market is seriously enthusiastic about.

One thing to note is that all of these momentum tests could be passed simply on the basis that a company's share price had been exceptionally strong over the last month of the period being monitored.

The measures are also relative to the index, which is something to watch out for and, if necessary, adapt criteria to take account of. For example, if the market is up 1% over a year and a share is up 2%, this hardly suggests a particularly hot stock. In such a situation, or when momentum has been negative, it can be worth experimenting to see where to sensibly set the screen's bar.

Earnings momentum

The core tests

The tests:

- EPS forecasts for next financial year upgraded by at least 10% over the preceding 12 months.

- EPS forecasts for the financial year after next upgraded by at least 10% over the preceding 12 months.

The earnings momentum tests look at the upgrades made over the preceding 12 months to consensus brokers' forecasts (the average of all broker forecasts for the company). Looking at changes over 12 months seems a good length of time. Looking at upgrades over shorter periods may ignore companies that do not regularly provide triggers for upgrades, such as those with very seasonal trading

The drawback with measuring upgrades over a relatively long period is that we may simply be witnessing the influence of a one-off event. To reduce the chances of this we want to see that upgrades apply to more than just a single financial year.

One danger with this criterion is that the screen could be drawn towards a company that has made a large acquisition, which can often initially cause a big jump in forecasts soon after completion. The problem with large acquisition deals is that they are usually welcomed with a fanfare but often end up destroying value. The fact the earnings tests are coupled with share price momentum tests should help reduce this risk though, as a rising share price suggests the market's approval.

Smaller acquisitions tend to be far better at creating value that big ones.

When companies are covered by very few analysts, consensus forecasts, which represent the average of all broker estimates, can move significantly when a single new analyst with an extreme viewpoint starts to follow the company or one analyst stops making forecasts. The danger is this type of situation can give a false positive result from the screen's core upgrade tests. Focusing this screen on large companies will reduce this risk. Historically, I've conducted the Great Expectations screen on the FTSE 350, which represents the largest 350 London-listed companies.

The focus on large caps is also because they generally represent a safer hunting ground for what is a high-risk strategy. There is no reason we should not apply this screen to smaller companies, but if we do, when assessing the results we need to bear in mind that there can be a lot of hype at this end of the market and sometimes scurrilous behaviour.

The other tests

The tests:

- EPS growth of 10% or more forecast for the next financial year.

- EPS growth of 10% or more forecast for the financial year after next.

The tests for earnings momentum also check that a good rate of earnings growth is being forecast. For upgrades to be meaningful, the forecast growth rate needs to be meaningful too.

One thing this test does not protect against is the screen highlighting companies that are growing EPS from a very low base. Such companies may have had very low forecast profits and now have only slightly improved forecast profits, but the percentage change could all the same look big. Again, share price momentum helps reduce the chance that the earnings levels associated with the growth rates we're testing for are meaninglessly small.

Adapting the screen

The momentum screen is a good time screen. It finds it easier to highlight stocks when trading conditions are strong, which tends to push up broker forecasts, and when the stock market is strong, pushing up share prices. Bear markets, when investors are confronted with heaps of downgrades and falling share prices, can be tricky. Such situations can mean the core price momentum tests are hard to apply.

Generally, torrid conditions require flexibility in dropping non-core tests. However, certain core tests may need to be strengthened at the same time. For example, we should want to see positive share price momentum even if the index performance is deeply in the red.

The great thing about the diversity of the stock market is that there will normally be some companies that stand out from the rest as star performers even when the market is crashing. These are the companies we want this screen to find.

CHAPTER 27

FROM QUANTITATIVE TO QUALITATIVE – WHAT KIND OF STOCKS HAVE GREAT EXPECTATIONS?

A S IT'S STYLE-AGNOSTIC, there is no one type of stock we're looking for with our Great Expectations screen. However, often the companies that this screen highlights broadly fit one of three categories. As we'll see when we look at one of the screen's past successes, sometimes stocks fit all three at once. We'll go through the categories in turn:

1. Structural growth

Some companies find themselves on a more rapid long-term growth trajectory than others. Examples today would include companies in industries such as computer gaming, renewable energy and geonomics.

Often companies in these industries do not even need to be that special to create value through growth. If the expansion of the end market is fast enough, they may be able to grow whilst achieving strong returns on their investments because the sheer scale of the opportunity is enough to mean competition is not a primary concern (temporarily at least).

However, investors in such situations need to be keenly aware that the party will end at some point. It is also important to try and understand the industry dynamics that are powering growth and stay vigilant for any sign of a slowdown.

Naturally, though, it is always preferable if a company that has tapped into a mushrooming market has a major advantage over competitors that will allow it to be highly and sustainably profitable for years and decades to come.

2. Cyclical growth

The subject of cyclicality – companies and industries that are sensitive to the ebbs and flows of economic and business cycles – has come up several times in this book already. Cyclical companies are often evident in the output from the Great Expectations screen.

The problem with investing in any cyclical stock is that the cycle can turn. When it does, expansion turns to contraction and share prices can fall sharply. It is normally very hard to judge exactly when this will happen.

However, one of the most useful ways to think about cyclicality is in terms of supply rather than demand. If a cyclical stock is being considered after a lengthy period of investment in the industry aimed at increasing capacity, the chances are the risks of losing money are substantially higher.

Demand is altogether harder to predict.

3. Turnarounds

Companies being turned around by new management teams are the third frequent feature of the Great Expectations screen. Often such situations start with the appointment of a new chairperson followed by the gradual overhaul of the board. Then a new strategy is usually outlined and implemented.

The really big share price gains with such turnarounds often happen early on, and the Contrarian Value screen we previously looked at is better suited to capturing this type of situation before a big share price jump.

When the Great Expectations screen tends to catch this type of situation is once strategic changes are already underway. This is not a bad thing. At this point in a turnaround there is usually more certainty that management have got a credible plan, and there may already be some tangible results.

What's more, the value companies can unlock through self-help can totally redefine their long-term growth prospects. Our look at Games Workshop in Chapter 16 is a case in point. After being first highlighted by the Quality screen in September 2017, the shares were featured in the Great Expectations screen at the end of 2019 and went on to contribute a 59% total return over the next 12 months.

Other common features and risks

As well as there being some regularity in the type of investment cases the Great Expectations screen latches onto, there are some common characteristics the stocks highlighted tend to have.

High gearing

In Chapter 8 we encountered the concept of operating gearing and financial gearing. When a high proportion of a company's costs are fixed – either costs of goods sold, operating costs or financing costs – a larger proportion of extra sales flows down to the profit line. Essentially, when trading is strong, costs will rise less quickly than revenue.

It is no surprise that companies with high gearing often feature in the results of this screen, given it looks for runaway earnings alongside a share price working hard to keep up.

When gearing is high, earnings growth can be explosive. This can lead to truly spectacular returns for shareholders. But the magnification effect of gearing on profits when sales rise works just as powerfully when sales fall. That makes companies with high gearing much more risky. A seemingly great investment case can evaporate with alarming speed as healthy profits become significant losses.

Aggressive accounting

One way to dazzle analysts into upgrading forecasts is with aggressive accounting techniques.

It's not that surprising that finance directors using sleight of hand go relatively unchallenged by the analysts that follow their companies. For an analyst, the reward for exposing a company's flimsy numbers can be the sack, or at least heavy pressure from the company concerned that they be shown the door.

The pressure is real because broking firms usually produce research on companies with a mind to winning business. Furthermore, much of the broker research available to private investors is actually paid for by the companies that the reports are about. In these cases, questioning the veracity of the accounts is likely to be a sure way of a broker not only losing a client but also getting a veto on the proposed research.

As well as the red flag ratios we met in Chapter 10, we've looked at several stock screen failures and found examples of companies goosing their numbers. In the next chapter we will see one more example of the kind of warning sign we can look out for that may suggest a company is being overly aggressive in its reporting.

The company in question is the now-defunct travel business Thomas Cook. As a stock pick from the Great Expectations screen it was a massive failure and gives us an excellent illustration of where the criteria can go wrong.

Before we look at that failure though, we will look at a success that ticks the boxes for all the positive attributes we've run through: structural growth, cyclical growth and a performance turnaround, all capped off with substantial gearing.

CHAPTER 28

STOCK SELECTION FOR GREAT EXPECTATIONS

CHASING HOT STOCKS is a risky business. But unlike our other high-risk strategy, Contrarian Value, focusing on the positives is an important part of the process of evaluating this screen's output. If we are trying to ride the upside, we want to be confident in the tailwinds.

However, we still cannot afford to neglect potential pitfalls. Thinking about the amount to invest in an exciting stock while understanding the dangers should the good times end is very important. So too is looking for reasons an enticing story may not be as excellent as it first appears.

We'll now look at two examples from the screen's output to help us see both sides of this particular coin.

The success: hire and higher

When the Great Expectations screen highlighted Ashtead in its first ever outing on 19 December 2011, the equipment-hire company was a phoenix rising from the flames. It was first and foremost a turnaround story.

The Great Financial Crisis had been a near-death experience for the cash-hungry company. The pre-credit crunch construction boom had seen Ashtead spend heavily on equipment to rent out to customers. But demand abruptly dried up.

While hire companies can become very cash generative very quickly by halting spending on new rental equipment, this was barely enough to get Ashtead through.

The second-hand market also dried up, meaning the company struggled to raise cash by selling the kit it owned and could not rent out. During these dark days, net debt rose to over £1bn while the company's market capitalisation sunk to just £165m.

Management had to do a lot of work to turn the situation around. But one thing they knew was that if they stayed the course, there were likely to be sunny uplands. That's because Ashtead's end markets are highly cyclical. Market conditions were bad not only for Ashtead but for its competitors too. As it struggled to stay in business, rivals went under. What's more, as rental equipment became obsolete, no one in the industry was rushing to replace the lost capacity.

This is a dream setup for survivors in a cyclical industry. Those shareholders that held on during these dark days ultimately had much to celebrate. Anyone who jumped aboard when the stock was originally highlighted by the Great Expectations screen would have made a return of more than 3,000% over the following 10 years.

Moving up a gear

Ashtead's business model is primed to force brokers to upgrade their forecasts when things are going well. A large amount of its reported costs are linked to its initial outlay for pricey rental equipment. In the profit and loss statement, this is reflected in a hefty depreciation charge each year. The actual cash cost of the kit generally comes upfront.

This all means returns on its investment can vary hugely depending on both how long items spend out on hire and the amount for which they can be rented. Both rise as demand improves and both push up profits. That can turbocharge performance and leave brokers scrambling to keep pace.

When companies require a fair wind from end markets to maintain an upgrade trend, the investment case can be quite unreliable. The economy can turn quickly and unexpectedly. Fortunately for Ashtead and its shareholders, as well as the cyclical growth story that kicked in as the world emerged from the financial crisis, it has also been surfing a 'structural' growth trend over the last decade.

The American dream

Most of Ashtead's sales come from the US. This is a far less developed hire market than the UK, where Ashtead has its roots. A long-term structural move by the US construction industry away from ownership and toward rental has been a massive boost.

Ashtead has further capitalised on this trend by making many small acquisitions of rivals. This has helped the company grow its market share at the same time as the market itself has expanded.

It also doesn't do any harm that the company is a very slick operator. In particular, it has benefited from a strategy of clustering its branches in order to improve the use of equipment and availability across local networks.

The company's cash flows are a bit weird, which may explain why investors have sometimes seemed a bit reticent about jumping on such a pronounced trend of forecast upgrades.

Poor conversion of profits into cash is often a sign of weakness. But there is no 'one rule fits all'. In the case of Ashtead, poor cash conversion can actually be a sign of optimism. It is an indicator that the company sees the potential for growth and is spending heavily on equipment in anticipation of lucrative rental opportunities in the future.

Ashtead's shares were one of the UK stock market's most tremendous success stories of the 2010s. The stock has been highlighted no less than five out of 10 possible times by the screen over that period, as Figure 24 shows. It is precisely the kind of momentum stock that we can sift from the Great Expectations screen's results, and that makes the approach so valuable.

Figure 24: Ashtead's stunning 10 year run

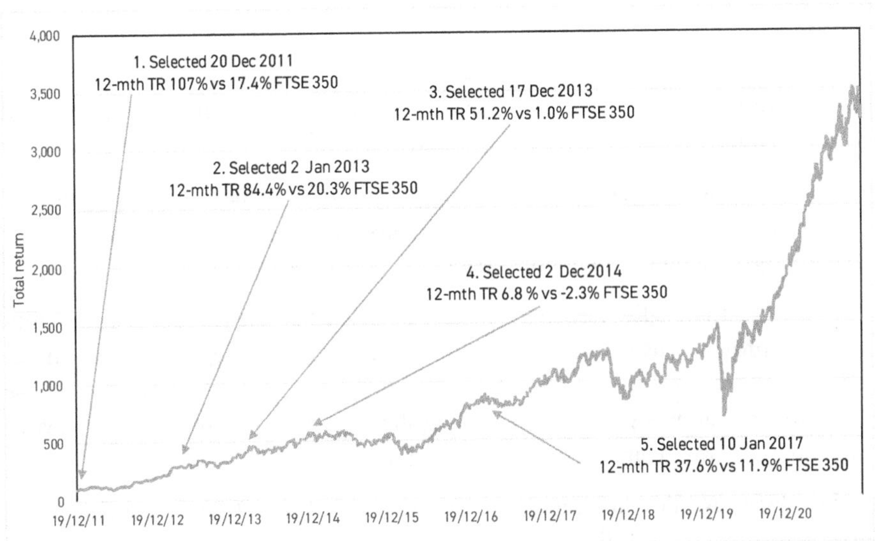

Source: FactSet.

The Failure: crash landing!

The Great Expectations screen highlighted tour operator Thomas Cook on 16 December 2013. This was soon after it had published its report and accounts for the 12 months ending 30 September. Brokers had bumped up forecasts over the year, and reading the first page of the company's freshly minted results left one with little doubt as to why.

The results' strapline declared "Transformation, the first 365 days: this is just the start." This was a much more upbeat message from the company than the previous year's could-do-better mantra of "Energise, Focus, Rebuild."

And the numbers emblazoned on page one of the report looked wonderful. The highlights included:

- an underlying operating profit up from £86m to £263m (take off!);

- cost savings of £194m (thrusters on!);

- net debt down from £788m to £421m (turbocharge!).

View from the ground

But if we needed to be convinced of why it's worth heeding the advice from Chapter 11 to never start reading a company's annual report at the beginning, Thomas Cook's 2013 results make a compelling case.

Thomas Cook was (it went into compulsory liquidation in 2019 when lenders refused to give it any more rope with which to hang itself) far better at reporting so-called underlying profits than it was at reporting statutory profits or generating cash. Statutory numbers are the official ones that accord with accounting rules, whereas underlying numbers are the ones management wants investors to look at.

If we dig beneath the 2013 results-day fanfare, it quickly becomes apparent that the progress being made was – to be generous – at an earlier stage than we may have thought based on the report's page-one razzmatazz.

For investors that realise cash generation is usually a key indicator of profit quality (Ashtead provided us with a special case to the contrary), the reported fall in net debt would seem a major positive. However, this is less of an achievement because the company raised £414m cash by selling shares in a rights issue during the year. That amount was greater than the reported drop in net borrowings.

In fact, free cash flow for the year was a negative £51m. This continued a long history of negative cash flows, as can be seen in Table 10.

That said, this FCF number is based on my calculation. Thomas Cook managed to calculate its own 2013 FCF at a positive £53m. It's always worth keeping in mind that FCF is one of many commonly used financial metrics for which there is no one accepted definition. We're always best off using a calculation method we're comfortable with while also trying to understand the methods finance directors and data providers push upon us.

Table 10: Thomas Cook – cash flows

Year to end Sept	2009	2010	2011	2012	2013
Net cash from operations	178	289	287	152	341
CAPEX*	−205	−272	−178	−102	−222
Finance costs**	−277	−268	−133	−93	−170
FCF	−304	−251	−24	−43	−51

* excludes cashflows associated with acquisitions and disposals
** interest paid and lease finance obligations
Source: Company.

Exceptionalism

But investors didn't even need to delve into the cash flow statements to realise everything was not quite as rosy as it seemed on page one.

Even if we started looking through the company's financial statements with the P&L statement, we would have struggled to miss the gargantuan numbers reported in a column labelled 'separately disclosed items'.

These separately disclosed items were deemed by Thomas Cook not to be part of the underlying profit number. In the company's words they were costs "which management believes are not the result of normal operating activity and performance."

The only trouble is, for Thomas Cook, large separately disclosed items were *normal*. They occurred pretty much every year. It was also very normal for these items to be huge relative to statutory profits, or more often statutory losses.

The red flag hoisted by Thomas Cook's underlying profit adjustments makes the red flag we looked at in Chapter 24 in relation to Mitie look like a red post-it note stuck to a lollipop stick.

Figure 25 shows Thomas Cook's underlying profits versus the statutory equivalents for the five years to 2013. Horrid!

Many investors are prepared to overlook non-underlying costs because they are often non-cash items. This includes things like the write-down to the value of assets on the balance sheet. However, just because the money has already been spent on these assets does not mean such costs should be ignored.

Figure 25: Thomas Cook's profits: what lies beneath

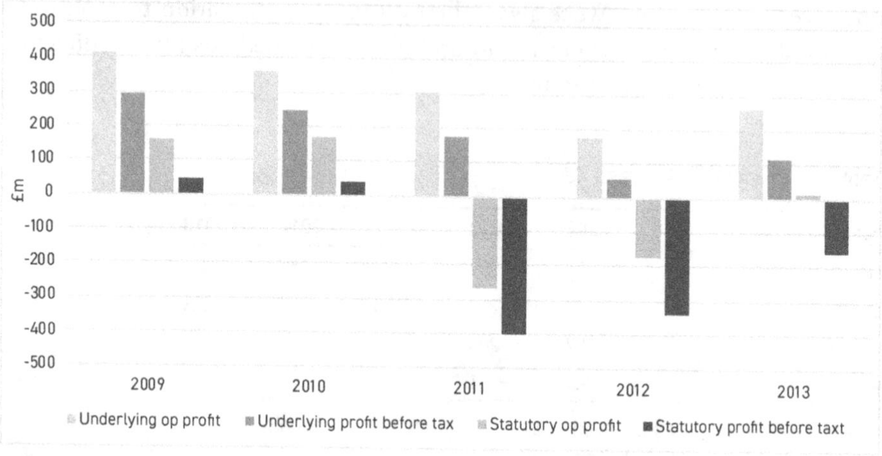

Source: Company.

Write-downs and impairments tell shareholders that their money has been spent badly in the past. Even when a company's management has changed, capital allocation problems can be endemic and reflect structural problems at the company or in its industry. What's more, the falling value of a company's asset often points to negative long-term trends in its end markets.

Debt, the grim reaper

There was another slightly quizzical aspect to the numbers Thomas Cook chose to shove in investors' faces on page one of its 2013 annual report. Why operating profits?

Operating profits are stated before interest payments. Cash-guzzling Thomas Cook had to make absolutely gigantic interest payments each year. This made operating profits of much less value to investors researching the shares than would have been the case with a less indebted company.

In all, in 2013 Thomas Cook told a good story, but there were clear reasons for investors to ask how much was fact and how much was fiction.

Management was indeed trying to turn the business around. However, there were many signs that the company still had a mountain to climb. In fact, the company looked like it still needed to pull itself out of a pit before the ascent could even begin. It never really managed to.

R.I.P. Thomas Cook 1841–2019.

In summary

We've explored how contradictory forces, the wisdom and madness of crowds, give rise to powerful momentum trends. It is possible for investors to use these trends to great advantage, but there is also the risk of savage reversals. Our screen attempts to limit the damage of reversals while also improving the upside by tapping into share price rises that are backed by strong brokers' upgrades.

We've also looked behind the numbers to understand the factors that drive momentum and make us better able to identify momentum stocks with real promise and filter out those that are overhyped and headed for a fall.

CONCLUSION

WE'VE COVERED A lot of ground, and I really hope this book has been both an enjoyable and worthwhile read. Most of what we've been through represents what for me is knowledge that has been hard-won over decades. It's the stuff I wish someone had sat down and explained to me early on, as I grappled to build an understanding of markets, stocks and investing. But it is also based on what I could only have found out through the experience of tracking screening strategies.

As we've run through our four strategies, I hope it has become abundantly clear that investing is not a one-size-fits-all game. There are plenty of approaches that work. However, the consistency of an approach tends to be very important. Investors are always best advised to concentrate on a style of investing that suits their personality and appetite for risk.

Assessing risk appetite is something most of us only really truly understand when losing money, but thinking about it as more of an emotional than intellectual question is a good place to start.

Most of all, my hope is that our journey through ideas and practical tips will have armed readers with both an enthusiasm and realism about investing.

There's absolutely nothing wrong with putting money to work in index funds; it is an excellent way to build wealth with fewer emotional demands than building a portfolio of individual shares. But for those with an appropriate respect for the risks involved, building and managing a portfolio of shares can be fascinating and highly lucrative.

APPENDIX 1

HIGH QUALITY LARGE CAP STOCKS

Stocks identified by the High Quality Large Cap screen over the 10 years since August 2011

Started 11 Aug 2011	2011		2012		2013		2014		2015	
	STOCKS SELECTED	TOTAL RETURN	STOCKS SELECTED	TOTAL RETURN	STOCKS SELECTED	TOTAL RETURN	STOCKS SELECTED	TOTAL RETURN	STOCKS SELECTED	TOTAL RETURN
	ROTORK	51.6	PAYPOINT	74.0	ABERDEEN ASSET MAN.	19.3	MICRO FOCUS INTL.	48.5	UNILEVER (UK)	43.8
	EXPERIAN	42.2	NEXT	40.1	MICRO FOCUS INTL.	14.1	TELECITY GROUP	47.1	ASHTEAD GROUP	31.8
	JAMES HALSTEAD	38.1	SHIRE	21.0	BRITISH AMERICAN TOBACCO	8.6	BERKELEY GROUP HDG. (THE)	45.6	PHOTO-ME INTL.	11.3
	JARDINE LLOYD THOMPSON	37.3	JARDINE LLOYD THOMPSON	20.8	INTERNATIONAL PSNL.FIN.	-11.0	BT GROUP	12.3	ITV	-11.0
	SPIRAX-SARCO ENGR.	24.4	-	-	-	-	NEXT	12.1	CREST NICHOLSON HOLDINGS	-17.2
	HALMA	17.1	-	-	-	-	DUNELM GROUP	11.1	EASYJET	-32.5
	-	-	-	-	-	-	ASHTEAD GROUP	-5.2	-	-
	-	-	-	-	-	-	-	-	-	-
	-	-	-	-	-	-	-	-	-	-
	-	-	-	-	-	-	-	-	-	-
	-	-	-	-	-	-	-	-	-	-
	-	-	-	-	-	-	-	-	-	-
	FTSE ALL SHARE	17.3	FTSE ALL SHARE	19.9	FTSE ALL SHARE	7.7	FTSE ALL SHARE	-5.1	FTSE ALL SHARE	15.0
	QUALITY LARGE CAPS	35.1	QUALITY LARGE CAPS	38.9	QUALITY LARGE CAPS	7.8	QUALITY LARGE CAPS	24.5	QUALITY LARGE CAPS	4.4
CUM. FTSE ALL SHARE	£100,000		£117,256	-	£140,539	-	£151,316	-	£143,590	-	£165,186
CUM. QUAL LRG CAP	£100,000		£135,135	-	£187,768	-	£202,331	-	£251,923	-	£262,882
CUM. QUAL LRG CAP WITH 1.5% CHG	£100,000		£133,108	-	£182,177	-	£193,362	-	£237,144	-	£243,749

Source: Thomson Datastream.

Start date: 11 Aug 2011. Reshuffle dates: 10 Aug 2012, 13 Aug 2013, 01 Sep 2014, 01 Sep 2015, 09 Aug 2016, 25 Sep 2017, 17 Sep 2018, 02 Sep 2019, 08 Sep 2020. End date: 11 Aug 2021

APPENDIX 1: HIGH QUALITY LARGE CAP STOCKS

2016		2017		2018		2019		2020	
STOCKS SELECTED	TOTAL RETURN	STOCKS SELECTED	TOTAL RETURN	STOCKS SELECTED	TOTAL RETURN	STOCKS SELECTED	TOTAL RETURN	STOCKS SELECTED	TOTAL RETURN
BELLWAY	51.3	GAMES WORKSHOP	101.5	DIAGEO	38.7	GAMES WORKSHOP	97.8	SPIRAX-SARCO ENGR.	53.5
ASHTEAD GROUP	51.0	REDROW	7.8	RELX	31.1	SPIRAX-SARCO ENGR.	30.7	CRODA INTERNATIONAL	50.0
MONDI	31.5	SMITHS GROUP	5.4	UNILEVER (UK)	27.9	HIKMA PHARMACEUTICALS	29.8	MEDICA GROUP	43.0
TAYLOR WIMPEY	29.8	PERSIMMON	4.4	RECKITT BENCKISER GROUP	-1.8	SAFESTORE HOLDINGS	18.2	GAMES WORKSHOP	38.9
BERENDSEN	5.0	TAYLOR WIMPEY	-2.3	-	-	RECKITT BENCKISER GROUP	16.3	PERSIMMON	28.8
HOWDEN JOINERY GP.	0.0	MONEYSUPERMARKET COM GP.	-8.4	-	-	HALMA	12.2	RELX	25.6
-	-	MERLIN ENTERTAINMENTS	-10.8	-	-	BIG YELLOW GROUP	5.2	FDM GROUP	19.8
-	-	CREST NICHOLSON HOLDINGS	-23.8	-	-	MARSHALLS	-2.0	RIGHTMOVE	14.0
-	-	PHOTO-ME INTL.	-24.7	-	-	GLAXOSMITHKLINE	-9.8	EXPERIAN	7.6
-	-	-	-	-	-	RELX	-10.0	UNILEVER (UK)	-6.2
-	-	-	-	-	-	DIAGEO	-25.7	MONEYSUPERMARKET COM GP.	-10.6
-	-	-	-	-	-			POLYMETAL INTERNATIONAL	-21.8
FTSE ALL SHARE	12.4	FTSE ALL SHARE	4.6	FTSE ALL SHARE	3.0	FTSE ALL SHARE	-13.9	FTSE ALL SHARE	27.9
QUALITY LARGE CAPS	28.1	QUALITY LARGE CAPS	5.5	QUALITY LARGE CAPS	24.0	QUALITY LARGE CAPS	14.8	QUALITY LARGE CAPS	20.2
-		£185,684	-	£194,286	-	£200,054	-	£172,208	-	£220,295	120%
-		£336,804	-	£355,174	-	£440,324	-	£505,429	-	£607,641	508%
-		£307,606	-	£319,518	-	£390,177	-	£441,150	-	£522,407	422%

219

APPENDIX 2

CONTRARIAN VALUE STOCKS

Stocks identified by the Contrarian Value screen over the 10 years since July 2011

Started 27 Jul 2011	2011		2012		2013		2014		2015	
	STOCKS SELECTED	TOTAL RETURN	STOCKS SELECTED	TOTAL RETURN	STOCKS SELECTED	TOTAL RETURN	STOCKS SELECTED	TOTAL RETURN	STOCKS SELECTED	TOTAL RETURN
	888 HOLDINGS	129.5	GVC HOLDINGS	122.6	ACM SHIPPING GROUP	53.7	HILL & SMITH	39.0	SDL	0.3
	GVC HOLDINGS	51.7	CSR	107.0	MDM ENGINEERING GP	32.4	SDL	22.1	SCHRODERS	-13.0
	M&C SAATCHI	15.5	CLARKSON	47.7	DRAX GROUP	11.3	CHARLES TAYLOR	20.2	SENIOR	-23.8
	CSR	4.6	MURGITROYD GROUP	39.4	SDL	8.1	STAGECOACH GROUP	11.1	LSL PROPERTY SERVICES	-33.6
	PV CRYSTALOX SOLAR	-59.8	YOUGOV	5.9	M&C SAATCHI	-2.8	MURGITROYD GROUP	-0.1	ANGLO-EASTERN PLTNS	-33.8
	FTSE ALL SHARE	-2.8	FTSE ALL SHARE	27.3	FTSE ALL SHARE	6.9	FTSE ALL SHARE	2.1	FTSE ALL SHARE	5.0
	CONTRARIAN VALUE	28.3	CONTRARIAN VALUE	64.5	CONTRARIAN VALUE	20.5	CONTRARIAN VALUE	18.5	CONTRARIAN VALUE	-20.8
CUM. FTSE ALL SHARE	£100,000	£97,240	-	£123,767	-	£132,275	-	£135,076	-	£141,841
CUM. CONTR. VAL.	£100,000	£128,297	-	£211,067	-	£254,356	-	£301,291	-	£238,709
CUM. CONTR. VAL. WITH 1.5% CHG.	£100,000	£126,372	-	£204,783	-	£243,081	-	£283,616	-	£221,335

Source: Thomson Datastream.

Start date: 27 Jul 2011. Reshuffle dates: 24 Jul 2012, 22 Jul 2013, 29 Jul 2014, 28 Jul 2015, 18 Jul 2016, 25 Jul 2017, 23 Jul 2018, 23 Jul 2019, 18 Aug 2020. End date: 27 Jul 2021

2016 STOCKS SELECTED	TOTAL RETURN	2017 STOCKS SELECTED	TOTAL RETURN	2018 STOCKS SELECTED	TOTAL RETURN	2019 STOCKS SELECTED	TOTAL RETURN	2020 STOCKS SELECTED	TOTAL RETURN	
DIALIGHT	86.1	SENIOR	26.8	PETS AT HOME	78.4	PETS AT HOME GROUP	47.9	TEN ENTM GROUP	101.2	
SENIOR	23.6	DRAX GROUP	15.7	GCP INFRASTRUCTURE INVS	10.7	BELLWAY	-11.7	CREST NICHOLSON HOLDINGS	101.2	
RESTAURANT GROUP	14.8	REDROW	-7.9	BLOOMSBURY PBL	6.1	REDROW	-13.4	MCCARTHY AND STONE	69.9	
LSL PROPERTY SERVICES	2.7	PETS AT HOME GROUP	-19.9	DRAX GROUP	-16.7	TAYLOR WIMPEY	-25.4	TAYLOR WIMPEY	38.6	
CHARLES TAYLOR	1.6	CREST NICHOLSON HOLDINGS	-25.5	DIALIGHT	-34.1	TED BAKER	-85.9	PLAYTECH	7.0	
FTSE ALL SHARE	16.5	FTSE ALL SHARE	7.4	FTSE ALL SHARE	2.1	FTSE ALL SHARE	-14.5	FTSE ALL SHARE	21.5	
CONTRARIAN VALUE	25.7	CONTRARIAN VALUE	-2.2	CONTRARIAN VALUE	8.9	CONTRARIAN VALUE	-17.7	CONTRARIAN VALUE	63.6	
-	£165,245	-	£177,498	-	£181,209	-	£154,936	-	£188,279	88%
-	£300,153	-	£293,611	-	£319,621	-	£263,048	-	£430,271	330%
-	£274,133	-	£264,135	-	£283,221	-	£229,594	-	£369,917	270%

APPENDIX 3

HIGH YIELD LOW RISK STOCKS

FOUR WAYS TO BEAT THE MARKET

Stocks identified by the High Yield Low Risk screen over the 10 years since March 2011

Started 28 Mar 2011		2012		2013		2014		2015	
STOCKS SELECTED	TOTAL RETURN	STOCKS SELECTED	TOTAL RETURN	STOCKS SELECTED	TOTAL RETURN	STOCKS SELECTED	TOTAL RETURN	STOCKS SELECTED	TOTAL RETURN
TELECOM PLUS	54.7	BROWN (N) GROUP	95.3	JD SPORTS FASHION	130.5	DEVRO	31.8	ADMIRAL GROUP	31.0
NEXT	52.4	UNILEVER (UK)	44.1	S & U	77.4	UNITED UTILITIES GROUP	28.7	CHARLES TAYLOR	19.9
MITIE GROUP	48.6	GO-AHEAD GROUP	41.5	XP POWER	34.6	WILLIAM HILL	22.3	NATIONAL GRID	18.9
NORTHUMBRIAN WATER GP	46.9	NATIONAL GRID	31.6	PROVIDENT FINANCIAL	23.4	SEVERN TRENT	21.7	XP POWER	13.4
BRITISH AMERICAN TOBACCO	36.7	CLARKSON	27.2	COBHAM	22.6	TARSUS GROUP	13.4	ELECTROCOMP	10.4
GLAXOSMITHKLINE	27.1	ASTRAZENECA	26.3	ASTRAZENECA	16.7	NATIONAL GRID	10.9	FIDESSA GROUP	8.7
PENNON GROUP	19.5	STAGECOACH GROUP	24.4	BRITISH AMERICAN TOBACCO	-0.2	CHESNARA	7.2	WIRELESS GROUP	7.3
ALBEMARLE & BOND HDG	8.0	TESCO	23.8	-	-	GLAXOSMITHKLINE	2.3	TATE & LYLE	5.6
CLARKSON	7.9	GLAXOSMITHKLINE	20.9	-	-	KIER GROUP	-0.3	PAYPOINT	4.7
ASTRAZENECA	3.8	XP POWER	18.7	-	-	XP POWER	-1.4	LEGAL & GENERAL	-10.5
CENTRAL AFRICAN GOLD	2.4	MENZIES (JOHN)	18.6	-	-	ITE GROUP	-6.8	ASHLEY(LAURA) HOLDINGS	-11.0
HILL & SMITH	1.5	MARKS & SPENCER GROUP	11.2	-	-	MAJESTIC WINE	-11.1	NEXT	-23.3
RM	-50.5	DE LA RUE	8.2	-	-	-	-	BHP BILLITON	-41.7
-	-	MORRISON(WM)SPMKTS.	0.2	-	-	-	-	-	-
-	-	IMPERIAL TOBACCO GP.	-3.9	-	-	-	-	-	-
-	-	MORGAN SINDALL GROUP	-11.3	-	-	-	-	-	-
-	-	ALBEMARLE & BOND HDG	-34.8	-	-	-	-	-	-
-	-	-	-	-	-	-	-	-	-
FTSE ALL SHARE	0.5	FTSE ALL SHARE	16.7	FTSE ALL SHARE	8.5	FTSE ALL SHARE	10.8	FTSE ALL SHARE	-6.9
HIGH YIELD LOW RISK	19.9	HIGH YIELD LOW RISK	20.1	HIGH YIELD LOW RISK	43.6	HIGH YIELD LOW RISK	9.9	HIGH YIELD LOW RISK	2.6
CUM. FTSE ALL SHARE	£100,000	£100,473	-	£117,228	-	£127,193	-	£140,941	-	£131,225
CUM. DIVI	£100,000	£119,900	-	£144,003	-	£206,734	-	£227,170	-	£233,016
CUM. DIVI WITH 1.5% CHG	£100,000	£118,101	-	£139,715	-	£197,570	-	£213,844	-	£216,056

Source: Thomson Datastream.

Start date: 28 Mar 2011. Reshuffle dates: 12 Apr 2012, 15 Apr 2013, 15 Apr 2014, 05 May 2015, 05 May 2016, 18 Apr 2017, 04 Apr 2018, 08 Apr 2019, 31 Mar 2020. End date: 29 Mar 2021

APPENDIX 3: HIGH YIELD LOW RISK STOCKS

	2016		2017		2018		2019		2020	
STOCKS SELECTED / TOTAL RETURN	STOCKS SELECTED	TOTAL RETURN	STOCKS SELECTED	TOTAL RETURN	STOCKS SELECTED	TOTAL RETURN	STOCKS SELECTED	TOTAL RETURN	STOCKS SELECTED	TOTAL RETURN
	XP POWER	58.5	BERENDSEN	67.5	TELECOM PLUS	29.3	PENNON GROUP	57.4	JOHNSON MATTHEY	73.9
	HEADLAM GROUP	40.5	FIDESSA GROUP	62.7	GO-AHEAD GROUP	18.3	NATIONAL GRID	20.4	INCHCAPE	72.1
	JARDINE LLOYD THOMPSON	36.0	NEXT	22.1	HEADLAM GROUP	7.9	ADMIRAL GROUP	6.7	MORGAN ADVANCED MRA	67.9
	CHESNARA	29.3	CHARLES TAYLOR	16.5	CHESNARA	1.6	LONDONMETRIC PROPERTY	-6.9	STHREE	65.1
	HISCOX	24.4	S & U	14.8	SSE	-1.6	STHREE	-15.9	S & U	46.3
	GLAXOSMITHKLINE	15.1	DUNELM GROUP	-8.2	PAGEGROUP	-3.0	STD.LF.PRIV.EQ.TST.	-25.9	BUNZL	44.0
	S & U	-0.8	HEADLAM GROUP	-28.6	S & U	-14.0	HEADLAM GROUP	-26.1	ADMIRAL GROUP	41.7
	STHREE	-5.2	-	-	PLAYTECH	-36.7	MEARS GROUP	-40.9	VP	35.4
	MITIE GROUP	-18.4	-	-	-	-	-	-	PAGEGROUP	28.4
	GO-AHEAD GROUP	-30.1	-	-	-	-	-	-	BARR (AG)	8.1
	-	-	-	-	-	-	-	-	MONEYSUPERMARKET COM GP	-9.8
	-	-	-	-	-	-	-	-	-	
	-	-	-	-	-	-	-	-	-	
	-	-	-	-	-	-	-	-	-	
	-	-	-	-	-	-	-	-	-	
	-	-	-	-	-	-	-	-	-	
	-	-	-	-	-	-	-	-	-	
	FTSE ALL SHARE	20.9	FTSE ALL SHARE	2.3	FTSE ALL SHARE	9.4	FTSE ALL SHARE	-20.4	FTSE ALL SHARE	27.0
	HIGH YIELD LOW RISK	14.9	HIGH YIELD LOW RISK	21.0	HIGH YIELD LOW RISK	0.2	HIGH YIELD LOW RISK	-3.9	HIGH YIELD LOW RISK	43.0
	-	£158,602	-	£162,210	-	£177,514	-	£141,320	-	£179,417 79%
	-	£267,831	-	£324,013	-	£324,746	-	£312,110	-	£446,306 346%
	-	£244,612	-	£291,485	-	£287,762	-	£272,417	-	£383,703 284%

APPENDIX 4

GREAT EXPECTATIONS STOCKS

Stocks identified by the Great Expectations screen over the 10 years since December 2011

Started 19 Dec 2011	2011		2012		2013		2014		2015	
	STOCKS SELECTED	TOTAL RETURN	STOCKS SELECTED	TOTAL RETURN	STOCKS SELECTED	TOTAL RETURN	STOCKS SELECTED	TOTAL RETURN	STOCKS SELECTED	TOTAL RETURN
	ASHTEAD GROUP	102.5	EASYJET	101.1	BARRATT DEVELOPMENTS	43.5	TAYLOR WIMPEY	56.3	JD SPORTS FASHION	62.2
	OXFORD INSTRUMENTS	50.2	CSR	81.9	ASHTEAD GROUP	37.9	BELLWAY	55.5	DCC	18.4
	ROTORK	44.2	SPORTS DIRECT INTL.	81.8	BELLWAY	31.4	CARNIVAL	48.3	DOMINO'S PIZZA GROUP	15.2
	BERKELEY GROUP HDG. (THE)	38.5	ASHTEAD GROUP	79.2	TAYLOR WIMPEY	29.5	UNITE GROUP	41.3	CARNIVAL	11.6
	BOVIS HOMES GROUP	37.4	SMITH (DS)	64.4	DIXONS RETAIL	29.4	BARRATT DEVELOPMENTS	38.0	GREGGS	-3.3
	TELECOM PLUS	23.8	TAYLOR WIMPEY	61.6	CARPHONE WAREHOUSE	25.4	PERSIMMON	37.8	BELLWAY	-3.8
	BTG	10.6	BARRATT DEVELOPMENTS	59.7	PACE	25.3	BIG YELLOW GROUP	35.6	BETFAIR GROUP	-6.6
	FENNER	4.3	GALLIFORD TRY	53.9	HOWDEN JOINERY GP	21.2	HOWDEN JOINERY GP	31.7	MARSHALLS	-10.0
	WEIR GROUP	-0.1	PERSIMMON	53.2	INTL.CONS.AIRL. GP (CDI)	20.7	INTL.CONS.AIRL. GP (CDI)	30.2	MONEYSUPERMARKET COM GP	-17.5
	SHIRE	-11.8	ESSENTRA PLC	50.6	BERKELEY GROUP HDG (THE)	7.1	GRAFTON GROUP UTS	14.1	INTL.CONS.AIRL.GP (CDI)	-19.7
	-	-	BERKELEY GROUP HDG. (THE)	49.8	TED BAKER	1.1	DIXONS CARPHONE	13.3	-	-
	-	-	BELLWAY	42.7	REDROW	-0.8	GO-AHEAD GROUP	3.0	-	-
	-	-	BOVIS HOMES GROUP	32.1	BREWIN DOLPHIN	-3.3	ASHTEAD GROUP	1.5	-	-
	-	-	MONEYSUPERMARKET COM GP	28.3	BRITVIC	-3.5	-	-	-	-
	-	-	ABERDEEN ASSET MAN.	27.7	SPORTS DIRECT INTL.	-4.5	-	-	-	-
	-	-	ANITE	-32.3	HARGREAVES LANSDOWN	-23.8	-	-	-	-
	-	-	-	-	THOMAS COOK GROUP	-26.0	-	-	-	-
	-	-	-	-	-	-	-	-	-	-
	FTSE 350	16.3	FTSE 350	16.4	FTSE 350	5.5	FTSE 350	-4.9	FTSE 350	24.5
	GREAT EXP	29.9	GREAT EXP	52.2	GREAT EXP	11.6	GREAT EXP	31.3	GREAT EXP	4.6
CUM. FTSE 350	£100,000	£116,292	-	£135,380	-	£142,829	-	£135,865	-	£169,199
CUM. QUAL LRG CAP	£100,000	£129,942	-	£197,814	-	£220,711	-	£289,760	-	£303,216
CUM. QUAL LRG CAP WITH 1.5% CHG	£100,000	£127,993	-	£191,924	-	£210,927	-	£272,762	-	£281,147

Source: Thomson Datastream.

Start date: 19 Dec 2011. Reshuffle dates: 02 Jan 2013, 16 Dec 2013, 01 Dec 2014, 12 Jan 2016, 09 Jan 2017, 15 Jan 2018, 14 Jan 2019, 14 Jan 2020, 12 Jan 2021. End date: 20 Dec 2021

APPENDIX 4: GREAT EXPECTATIONS STOCKS

2016		2017		2018		2019		2020	
STOCKS SELECTED	TOTAL RETURN	STOCKS SELECTED	TOTAL RETURN	STOCKS SELECTED	TOTAL RETURN	STOCKS SELECTED	TOTAL RETURN	STOCKS SELECTED	TOTAL RETURN
FERREXPO	144.9	EVRAZ	52.8	JD SPORTS FASHION	103.3	GAMES WORKSHOP	59.1	ROYAL MAIL	49.1
GLENCORE	39.4	SPIRAX-SARCO ENGR	13.0	SPIRENT COMMUNICATIONS	90.9	KAINOS GROUP	40.4	888 HOLDINGS	-4.1
ASHTEAD GROUP	35.5	ANGLO AMERICAN	4.7	ANGLO AMERICAN	28.0	FUTURE	26.9	RIO TINTO	-12.7
ELECTROCOMP	30.5	PERSIMMON	-7.1	3I INFRASTRUCTURE	15.4	AVEVA GROUP	-10.3	FRESNILLO	-19.4
JD SPORTS FASHION	11.6	VESUVIUS	-8.4	SSP GROUP	2.2	RANK GROUP	-44.7	CMC MARKETS	-38.7
RPC GROUP	-13.9	VICTREX	-8.7	EVRAZ	-9.2	-	-	AO WORLD	-75.7
-	-	ICTL.HTLS.GP.	-8.8	PLUS500	-29.9	-	-	-	-
-	-	REDROW	-10.0	-	-	-	-	-	-
-	-	IBSTOCK	-10.5	-	-	-	-	-	-
-	-	INTERMEDIATE CAPITAL GP	-10.6	-	-	-	-	-	-
-	-	COMPUTACENTER	-11.0	-	-	-	-	-	-
-	-	BELLWAY	-16.1	-	-	-	-	-	-
-	-	ANTOFAGASTA	-18.6	-	-	-	-	-	-
-	-	RENISHAW	-21.4	-	-	-	-	-	-
-	-	B&M EUROPEAN VAL.RET	-24.1	-	-	-	-	-	-
-	-	GLENCORE	-25.6	-	-	-	-	-	-
-	-	FERREXPO	-27.7	-	-	-	-	-	-
-	-	KAZ MINERALS	-43.9	-	-	-	-	-	-
FTSE 350	12.5	FTSE 350	-8.2	FTSE 350	17.3	FTSE 350	-7.5	FTSE 350	10.5
GREAT EXP	41.3	GREAT EXP	-10.1	GREAT EXP	28.7	GREAT EXP	14.3	GREAT EXP	-16.9
-		£190,267	-	£174,729	-	£204,906	-	£189,440	-	£209,244	109%
-		£428,499	-	£385,157	-	£495,561	-	£566,379	-	£470,591	371%
-		£391,352	-	£346,490	-	£439,124	-	£494,349	-	£404,581	305%

ACKNOWLEDGEMENTS

I have been influenced by many of the great investors and financial thinkers whose work I have read and who I've had the pleasure of interviewing over the years in my work as a journalist. Those whom this book owes a particular debt to have already been mentioned in its pages, and their details are also to be found in the accompanying Further Reading and Notes sections.

I've also been delighted while working with Harriman House, the publisher of this book. Craig Pearce has been a stunningly insightful editor and has taught me a lot as a writer. My special thanks, too, to Nick Fletcher and Chris Parker at Harriman House.

I'm hugely indebted to some very wise people who were kind enough to agree to read this book before publication and offer their suggestions: Rosie Carr, Steve Clapham, Peter Higgins, and Lawrence Lever.

A special mention should also be given to Jonathan Eley, who originally commissioned the stock screening column much of the data used in this book is drawn from while he was editor of the *Investors' Chronicle* magazine in 2010. Originally, I was one of several writers who was asked to contribute screens. However, after a year it became clear that I was chomping at the bit to write more on the subject, while my colleagues were more than happy to offload their duties to me.

I would also like to mention some of the other wonderful people I've been lucky enough to work with over the years who have taught me so much, made me think and challenged my ideas: Patrick Sherwen, Graeme Davies, Simon Thompson, Philip Ryland, Phil Oakley, John Hughman, Oliver Ralph, Claer Barrett, Julian Hoffman, Theron Mohamed and Oliver Telling.

And naturally, I also want to thank my wife Emily and children Madeleine, Gilbert and Arrietty, who are a wonderful support in everything I do and make everything feel so much more worthwhile.

FURTHER READING

Chapter 2

Paul Meehl, in G. Lindzey (Ed.), *A History of Psychology in Autobiography* (Vol. 8, pp. 337–389). Stanford: Stanford University Press, 1989.

Michael Lewis, *The Undoing Project: A Friendship that Changed the World*. Penguin Books, 2016.

Cass Sunstein, Daniel Kahneman, and Olivier Sibony, *Noise: A Flaw in Human Judgement*. Little, Brown, 2021.

William Hart, Dolores Albarracı, Alice Eagly, Inge Brechan, Matthew J. Lindberg, Lisa Merrill, 'Feeling Validated Versus Being Correct: A Meta-Analysis of Selective Exposure to Information', *Psychological Bulletin*, Vol. 135, No. 4, 555–588, 2009.

Michael Mauboussin, *The Success Equation: Untangling Skill and Luck in Business, Sports, and Investing*. Harvard Business Review Press, 2012.

Kai Wu, 'Intangible Value' Sparkline Capital, 2021.

Jennifer Bender, Remy Briand, Dimitris Melas, Raman Aylur Subramanian, 'Foundations of Factor Investing', MSCI, 2013.

Guanhao Feng, Stefano Giglio, Dacheng Xiu, 'Taming the Factor Zoo: A Test of New Factors', *The Journal of Finance*, Vol. 75, No. 3, 1327–1370, 2020.

Carmen Reinhart, Kenneth Rogoff, *This Time is Different: Eight Centuries of Financial Folly*. Princeton University Press, 2011.

Elroy Dimson, Paul Marsh and Mike Staunton, 'ABN Amro Year Book', ABN Amro, London Business School, 2008.

Chapter 3

Geoffrey Holmes, Alan Sugden, *Interpreting Company Reports & Accounts: Seventh Edition*. Prentice Hall, 1999.

Chapter 5

Jesse Livermore (pseudonym), 'The Earnings Mirage: Why Corporate Profits are Overstated and What It Means for Investors', O'Shaughnessy Asset Management, 2019.

Chapter 8

Phil Oakley, *How to Pick Quality Shares: A Three-Step Process for Selecting Profitable Stocks*. Harriman House, 2017.

Chapter 16

Eugene Fama, Kenneth French, 'The Cross-Section of Expected Stock Returns', *The Journal of Finance*, Vol. 47, no. 2: 427–65, 1992.

Rob Arnott, Campbell Harvey, Vitali Kalesnik, 'Reports of Value's Death May Be Greatly Exaggerated', Research Affiliates, 2021.

Chapter 24

Jamie Catherwood, *The Factor Archives: Shareholder Yield*, O'Shaughnessy Asset Management, November 2019, osam.com/Commentary/the-factor-archives-shareholder-yield

Chapter 25

The Meb Faber Podcast no. 107, 2018.

David Dreman, *Contrarian Investment Strategies: The Next Generation*. Simon & Schuster, 1998.

Rob Brotherton, *Suspicious Minds: Why We Believe Conspiracy Theories*. Bloomsbury, 2015.

Adam Grant, *Think Again: The Power of Knowing What You Don't Know*. WH Allen, 2021.

Chapter 27

Karsten Müller, Simon Schmickler, 'Interacting Anomalies', NUS Business School, Princeton University, 2020.

NOTES

1 Robert Novy-Marx, 'The Other Side of Value: Good Growth and the Gross Profitability Premium', National Bureau of Economic Research, 2010.

2 Eugene Fama, Kenneth French, 'The Cross-Section of Expected Stock Returns', *The Journal of Finance*, Vol. 47, no. 2: 427–65, 1992.

3 Rob Arnott, Campbell Harvey, Vitali Kalesnik, 'Reports of Value's Death May Be Greatly Exaggerated', Research Affiliates, 2021.

4 Elroy Dimson, Paul Marsh and Mike Staunton, 'ABN Amro Year Book', ABN Amro, London Business School, 2008.

5 Paul Meehl, *Clinical Versus Statistical Prediction: A Theoretical Analysis and a Review of the Evidence*. University of Minnesota Press, 1954.

6 William Grove, 'Clinical Versus Mechanical Prediction: A Meta-Analysis', *Psychological Assessment*, Vol. 12, no. 1: 19–30, 2000.

7 Daniel Kahneman, *Thinking, Fast and Slow*. Farrar, Straus and Giroux, 2011.

8 Paul Slovic, 'Behavioral Problems of Adhering to a Decision Policy', Oregon Research Institute, 1973.

9 Ap Dijksterhuis, Maarten Bos, Loran Nordgren, Rick Van Baaren, 'On Making the Right Choice: The Deliberation-Without-Attention Effect', *Science*, 2007.

10 Robyn Dawes, 'The Robust Beauty of Improper Linear Models in Decision Making', University of Oregon, 1979.

11 Robert Arnott, Campbell Harvey, Vitali Kalesnik, Juhani Linnainmaa, 'Alice's Adventures in Factorland: Three Blunders That Plague Factor Investing', Research Affiliates, 2019.

12 Jesse Livermore (pseudonym), 'The Earnings Mirage: Why Corporate Profits are Overstated and What It Means for Investors', O'Shaughnessy Asset Management, 2019.

13 Phil Oakley, *How to Pick Quality Shares: A Three-Step Process for Selecting Profitable Stocks.* Harriman House, 2017.

14 Jim Slater, *The Zulu Principle.* Orion, 1992.

15 O'Shaughnessy Asset Management research team, 'Stocks You Shouldn't Own' 2016.

16 Michael Aked, 'Factor Returns' Relationship with the Economy? It's Complicated', Research Affiliates, November 2020.

17 Hans Rosling, with Ola Rosling and Anna Rosling Ronnlund, *Factfulness: Ten Reasons We're Wrong About The World – And Why Things Are Better Than You Think.* Flatiron Books, 2018.

18 Lawrence Beesley, *The Loss of the RMS Titanic: Its Story and Its Lessons.* Originally published 1912, republished by Amberley Publishing, 2011.

19 Daniel Kahneman, *Thinking, Fast and Slow.* Farrar, Straus and Giroux, 2011.

20 Daniel Kahneman and Amos Tversky, 'Prospect Theory: An Analysis of Decision under Risk', *Econometrica*, Vol. 47, No. 2, March 1979, www.jstor.org/stable/1914185?seq=1.

21 Daniel Kahneman, Jack Knetsch, Richard Thaler, 'Experimental Tests of the Endowment Effect and the Coase Theorem', *Journal of Political Economy*, Vol. 98, No. 6: 1325–1348, 1990.

22 Samuel Hartzmark, Samuel Hirshman and Alex Imas, 'Ownership, Learning, and Beliefs', University of Chicago, 2020.

23 Christoph Merkle, Michael Ungeheuer, 'Beliefs about Beta: Upside Participation and Downside Protection' Aarhus University, 2021.

24 Klakow Akepanidtaworn, Rick Di Mascio, Alex Imas, Lawrence Schmidt, 'Selling Fast and Buying Slow: Heuristics and Trading Performance of Institutional Investors', University of Chicago, 2019.

25 Rob Arnott, Campbell Harvey, Vitali Kalesnik, 'Reports of Value's Death May Be Greatly Exaggerated', Research Affiliates, 2021.

26 Baruch Lev, Anup Srivastava, 'Explaining the Recent Failure of Value Investing', NYU Stern School of Business, 2019.

27 Brian Chingono, Daniel Rasmussen, 'Leveraged Small Value Equities', University of Chicago, Verdad Fund Advisers, 2015.

28 Edward Chancellor (Editor), *Capital Returns: Investing Through the Capital Cycle: A Money Manager's Reports 2002–15.* Palgrave Macmillan, 2015.

29 Clayton M. Christensen, *The Innovators Dilemma: When New Technologies Cause Great Firms to Fail.* Harvard Business School Publishing, 1997.

30 Michael Lewis, *Moneyball.* W. W. Norton & Company, July 2004.

31 Robert Haugen and James Heines, 'On the Evidence Supporting the Existence of Risk Premiums in the Capital Market', 1972, papers.ssrn.com/sol3/papers.cfm?abstract_id=1783797.

32 Erik Snowberg and Justin Wolfers, 'Explaining the Favorite–Long Shot Bias: Is it Risk-Love or Misperceptions?', *Journal of Political Economy*, Vol. 118, No. 4, August 2010, www.jstor.org/stable/10.1086/655844?seq=1.

33 Nicholas Barberis and Ming Huang, 'Stocks as Lotteries: The Implications of Probability Weighting for Security Prices', *The American Economic Review*, Vol. 98, No. 5, December 2008, www.jstor.org/stable/29730162?seq=1.

34 Eugene F. Fama and Kenneth R. French, 'Dissecting Anomalies with a Five-Factor Model', *Review of Financial Studies*, Vol. 29, No. 1, January 2016, www.researchgate.net/publication/287122523_Dissecting_Anomalies_with_a_Five-Factor_Model.

35 Pim Van Vliet and Jan De Koning, *High Returns from Low Risk.* Wiley, Dec 2016,

36 Christoph Merkle and Michael Ungeheuer, 'Beliefs About Beta: Upside Participation and Downside Protection', 1 Mar 2021, papers.ssrn.com/sol3/papers.cfm?abstract_id=3794224.

37 Michael Aked, 'Factor Returns' Relationship with the Economy? It's Complicated', Research Affiliates, November 2020, www.researchaffiliates.com/en_us/publications/articles/factor-returns-relationship-with-the-economy.html.

38 Terry Smith, 'Busting the myths of investment: who needs income?' *Financial Times*, Wednesday 3 October 2018, www.fundsmith.co.uk/global/sef/news/article/2018/10/03/financial-times---busting-the-myths-of-investment-who-needs-income.

39 Matthew Salganik, Peter Dodds, Duncan Watts, 'Experimental Study of Inequality and Unpredictability in an Artificial Cultural Market', *Science*, 2006.

40 Jesse Livermore (pseudonym) 'Trend Following In Financial Markets: A Comprehensive Backtest', Philosophical Economics blog, 2016.

41 Don Moore, Paul Healy, 'The Trouble With Overconfidence', Ohio State University, 2007.

42 'Are investors too optimistic about Amazon?', *Economist*, 2017.

43 Michael Mauboussin, Dan Callahan, Darius Majd, 'The Base Rate Book', Credit Suisse, 2016.

44 Michael Mauboussin, Dan Callahan, 'The Impact of Intangibles on Base Rates', Morgan Stanley, 2021.

45 Karsten Müller, Simon Schmickler, 'Interacting Anomalies', NUS Business School, Princeton University, 2020.

ABOUT THE AUTHOR

Algy Hall is an award-winning financial journalist and an investment editor at Citywire Elite Companies.

He began his career in 1998 as a researcher for a small investment fund and writer for *The Investment Trust Newsletter*. He assisted in the founding of Citywire in 1999 where he worked for several years tracking the activities of fund managers and shrewd investors and reporting on the shares they bought and sold.

Algy joined *Investors' Chronicle* in 2007 and began writing his stock screening column for the magazine in 2011. He used the column to try to mimic the investment styles he had seen used by successful investors as well as to apply ideas from the literature on finance and quantitative investing.

In 2022, Algy re-joined Citywire to help establish the Elite Companies project, which rates companies by their popularity with the world's best fund managers.

Algy has won CFA awards for his writing on ESG and on Value and Transparency and was named the CFA UK's 2021 Financial Journalist of the Year.